TWELVE MILLENNIA

Laurie:
Thanks for your
participation in our
2004 NEH Institute.

James J. Theler

A BUR OAK BOOK

Twelve Millennia

Archaeology of the Upper
Mississippi River Valley

James L. Theler and Robert F. Boszhardt

University of Iowa Press Iowa City

University of Iowa Press, Iowa City 52242

Printed in the United States of America

Design by April Leidig-Higgins

http://www.uiowa.edu/uiowapress

The publication of this book was generously
supported by the University of Iowa Foundation.

Printed on acid-free paper

Library of Congress Cataloging-in-Publication Data
Theler, James L., 1946–
Twelve millennia: archaeology of the upper
Mississippi River Valley / by James L. Theler and
Robert F. Boszhardt.
p.   cm.
Includes bibliographical references (p.   ).
ISBN 0-87745-847-2 (pbk.)
1. Indians of North America—Mississippi River
Valley—Antiquities. 2. Mound-builders—
Mississippi River Valley. 3. Excavations
(Archaeology)—Mississippi River Valley.
4. Mississippi River Valley—Antiquities.
I. Title: 12 millennia. II. Boszhardt, Robert F.
III. Title.
E78.M75 T44 2003
977'.01—dc21   2002073296

*For the people of the
Upper Mississippi Valley,
past and present*

CONTENTS

The story of pre-European people living in the Upper Mississippi River Valley, as told in the archaeological record, spans at least 12,000 years. To put that in perspective, envision a foot-long ruler with each inch representing a millennium. On that scale, Columbus would have reached the New World half an inch ago, the United States declared independence less than a quarter of an inch ago, the automobile was invented a tenth of an inch ago, and the age of computers occupies only the last one-thirtieth of an inch. The more than 11 inches before these events represent the time the region was occupied by pre-European Native American cultures. It is a time before written records in much of North America and is therefore technically prehistory. This prehistoric story survives only in oral traditions of Native people and as material remains or archaeological artifacts.

The story presented here is one based on archaeology in the Upper Mississippi River Valley region. It is a story of cultural and natural continuity and change. Sometimes the changes were minor and gradual, but at several critical points change was dramatic, revolutionizing cultural adaptations to the environment and between societies. Some changes were instigated by climatic shifts, such as the end of the last Ice Age, while others were mirrored in technological innovations, such as the development of pottery, the introduction of the bow and arrow, and the adaptation of corn agriculture.

This book presents the story of past peoples of the Upper Mississippi River Valley from the first inhabitants through the era of European contact. The story is preceded by an introduction to archaeology, providing the reader a context for archaeological interpretation. The topography and resources available to Native people of the Upper Mississippi Valley are then described. The Mississippi River drains a vast portion of North America, connecting a diverse range of natural and cultural regions. We focus only on that portion of the Upper Mississippi River that cuts through the rugged Driftless Area, an area from Lake Pepin, below Red Wing, Minnesota, to Dubuque, Iowa. The people of this region interacted with and were influenced by cultures occupying adjacent areas, but the Driftless Area presents a distinct environmental zone that allows us to comprehend cultural change through time.

Peoples who inhabited the Upper Mississippi basin were influenced by a sequence of environmental changes. Shifts in lifestyles, as reflected by their artifacts, often correspond with shifts in climatic regimes. Archaeologists base many of their interpretations about the past on the artifactual remains and the contexts of those remains. This reliance on artifacts is especially critical in the Upper Mississippi Valley because there was no written record until the French first explored the region after about A.D. 1650 and began describing the Native peoples they encountered. By that time, dramatic changes had occurred in the material culture of the Native Americans and in the locations of various groups. Preceding direct contact, European influences that included brass kettles, iron tools, and new diseases had spread well into the North American heartland through established networks. Not only did these changes result in dramatic population reductions and widespread tribal movement, but survivors almost immediately stopped making ceramic vessels and stone tools. These disruptions make it difficult or impossible to connect specific historic tribes directly with pre-European archaeological cultures.

Because of the dramatic break in the archaeological record between the historic and pre-European (prehistoric) periods, Upper Mississippi River Valley cultures identified by distinctive artifact styles before A.D. 1650 are not referred to by tribal names. Instead, archaeologists refer to the prehistoric cultures by names that have little if any relationship to named historic tribes. For example, Paleoindian and Archaic refer to the early cultures, while Woodland refers to the builders of burial mounds that were widespread in the woodlands of the eastern United States.

Although the archaeological labels rarely refer to identifiable tribal groups of the historic period, they do signify a sequence of human groups identifiable by patterned traditions in artifact styles that changed over time and space. The sequence of archaeologically defined cultures in the Upper Mississippi Valley shows a continuum of human adaptation over a period of nearly 12,000 years. The accompanying chart summarizes this culture sequence, placing these cultures in time and with corresponding climatic regimes. The following chapters describe in some detail each of these cultures as represented by artifactual remains and selected sites along the Upper Mississippi River. Unless otherwise specified, all city and county names in the book refer to Wisconsin localities.

MILLENNIA BEFORE PRESENT (B.P.)

12	11	10	9	8	7	6	5	4	3	2	1	0
	P	R	E	H	I	S	T	O	R	Y		HISTORY
COLD	WARM / DRY								MOIST		WARM / DRY	COLD
PALEOINDIAN	ARCHAIC									WOODLAND	ONEOTA	TRIBES

On any given day our phones ring or people from all walks of life stop in our offices to show us things they have found. Sometimes these collections consist of a few broken stone tools; other times we are presented with hundreds of artifacts. People come to ask us to identify their artifacts, and we share our knowledge of age, use, material, and other aspects that come to mind. More often than not, however, it is we, the archaeologists, who learn during these sessions. Each piece that is brought in is part of an enormous puzzle, and, over time, parts of the picture come into focus. Occasionally, viewing a collection precipitates a flash of understanding that sends us scurrying to libraries to pull out piles of reference books to verify other occurrences. Sometimes these realizations are prompted by the simplest of inquiries, and we kick ourselves for not having asked that question sooner. Interspersed between too many meetings and mountains of paperwork, these moments of discovery make archaeology a career to envy.

This book is dedicated to the hundreds of individuals who have contributed over the past two decades to share their knowledge of and their artifacts from the Upper Mississippi Valley with us. We are privileged to be able to compile this information and experience the sensation of discovery. We hope that this synthesis gives back at least some of our thanks.

While those who have shared in the curiosity and study of the past are far too numerous to mention individually, several stand out for their cooperation in reporting multiple sites. These include Chad Burows, Loren Cade, Dave Jackson, Milan Quall, John Swennes, Otto Swennes, Gary Steele, Betty Steele, Steve Raith, Alfred Reed, Todd Richert, Steve Allen, and Paul Wiste.

On a professional level, we are indebted to all who have encouraged and challenged our research efforts in this region, particularly our colleagues at the University of Wisconsin–La Crosse and the Mississippi Valley Archaeology Center. We would like to thank the College of Liberal Studies at the University of Wisconsin–La Crosse for a grant to support graphics for this book. Illustrations were prepared with the assistance of Jody Bruce, Jean Dowiasch, Jiro Manabe, Laura Jankowski, Megan Rivers, and Liz Schultz. We are grateful for the detailed constructive and insightful comments provided by William Green and James Stoltman on an early draft of this manuscript. We appreciate the quality and detail of the work done by Robert Burchfield, our copyeditor.

Finally, our thanks to family and friends who have tolerated the four years of on-and-off-again spells in which we indulged in preparing this book.

TWELVE MILLENNIA

CHAPTER ONE

Introduction to Archaeology

Archaeologists study past human societies. Archaeologists do not study dinosaurs or fossils that date to geologic periods before our human ancestors. Paleontologists study ancient life forms before people and culture. Most of the materials made and used by past cultures have been lost to time. With rare exceptions, wood, hide, and flesh disintegrate rapidly. Because the remaining pieces are often fragile, archaeologists work with extreme care to expose, document, and recover the remains. Archaeology is often compared to detective work. The clues that archaeologists find and use to reconstruct the human past are the patterns of tools and other debris that have survived the ravages of time.

Archaeologists apply methods of recovery, analysis, and interpretation that follow principles of the scientific method. Archaeological use of the scientific method requires the collection of facts or data in as unbiased a manner as possible. Initial collection and analysis often lead to perceived patterns that may reflect past human behavior. For example, artifacts from one site may include side-notched spear tips but no pottery fragments. These observations may lead to a hypothesis, such as that side-notched spear tips were made during a different time period than pottery. Hypotheses are then tested by collecting more data. In this example, excavation of a series of deeply buried sites may show that side-notched spear tips were repeatedly found in layers beneath pottery fragments and are therefore older. Hypotheses are never proved absolutely, but accumulated data can strengthen arguments that a particular idea is probably correct or lead to revisions in the hypothesis that require additional data gathering.

Archaeology is a subfield of anthropology, defined broadly as the study of all humankind in both the past and present. Anthropology is usually broken down into four subfields: archaeology (the study of the human past); biological anthropology (the study of human physical variation); cultural anthropology (the study of traditional and modern societies); and linguistic anthropology (the study of language in its cultural context).

Why We Study the Past

People are unique among living things in having a conscious interest in the past and future. No other animals are concerned with questions such as where they came from, how they got here, and what the future may hold. People, on the other hand, routinely ask these types of questions. A portion of humanity's past can be learned from history, which is technically the period when written records exist. However, more than 99 percent of the human past occurred before written records, or in prehistory. The origins of human beings, domestication of plants and animals, beginnings of metallurgy, and rise of cities are a few of the more significant events in humanity's past that occurred before written records. In general, writing was adopted when the number of people and the information load became too great to track necessary information in one's mind. The first uses of writing were usually for commerce and governmental tracking of people for purposes of taxation and conscription. The first preserved written records are clay tablets documenting commercial transactions of the Sumarian civilization about 4,900 years ago in what is now Iraq. While this was the beginning of the historic era in the Middle East, the rest of the world remained in prehistory until writing was adopted. This occurred at various times, with some isolated places adopting writing only in the twentieth century. In the Upper Mississippi Valley, history began with French exploration in the seventeenth century, providing the first written record of the region and its inhabitants.

All societies use oral histories to maintain traditions, and oral history is generally more important to societies that do not have writing. When handed down through generations, oral histories, often in the form of stories, may contain information from the distant past. But oral history is flexible and adaptable, changing when advantageous, particularly during times of profound stress. Furthermore, over the past three centuries, as the world has shifted from predominantly prehistoric societies lacking writing to near total historic cultures, many oral histories have been lost. Indeed, most indigenous languages have vanished, lost as populations were decimated by diseases, war, movement, and mixing during the colonial period of exploration and conquest. Only in the late nineteenth century did anthropologists begin systematically to record oral histories of vanishing cultures. Consequently, while oral history may provide important insight into past traditions, in order to understand basic questions about such things as human origins, technological developments, ancient trade patterns, the rise and fall of cultures, and population increases and migrations, archaeology is an essential discipline.

Navajo 82% in the last 5 yrs

How the Past Is Studied

Archaeologists study things that were made or modified and left behind by people in the past. These remains comprise the archaeological record. Things that are unquestionably shaped or modified by humans are called artifacts. Artifacts are either portable or nonportable. Portable artifacts include objects that were easily transported, such as a stone arrow point. Nonportable artifacts include such things as mounds, fire hearths, house basins, storage pits, ridged agricultural fields, and deposits of garbage, called middens. Archaeologists commonly call nonportable artifacts features (figs. 1.1, 1.2). Organic remains that are the by-products of food harvest and processing, such as animal bones and plant remains, are sometimes called ecofacts. Ecofacts allow archaeologists to reconstruct the diet and seasonal activities of the people who left the remains at a site. Naturally occurring materials, such as climate-sensitive snails, plant pollen, and insect remains that become mixed into site sediments during the human occupation, can be extremely useful in reconstructing the site's natural setting.

Archaeological sites are distinct clusters of artifacts and sometimes ecofacts. Sites may be historic or prehistoric in age and are often classified by the principal activity that is believed to have taken place. Habitation sites may include everything from an overnight camp represented by a fire hearth (a feature) and a few pottery sherds (artifacts) to a city with several square miles of structural remains. Burial sites include cemeteries, mounds, and isolated graves. Kill sites are locations where larger animals such as mammoths, bison,

1.1. An Oneota baking pit lined with rock; west half excavated.

1.2. A 3-foot-wide exploration trench clarifying the size of an abandoned Oneota house basin filled with refuse. Note the artifacts concentrated within the darker, organically enriched house feature.

1.3. Pedestrian survey of plowed fields in the spring. Archaeologists walk a field adjacent to a series of mounds remaining in the tree line outside of Prairie du Chien.

or deer were killed and butchered. Quarry sites are locations where stone material or metal was mined. There are many other types of sites, and often we find more than one type of site together. For example, it is common to find camps near quarry sites and burials at habitation sites.

Locating sites can involve a variety of methods. One of the most productive ways is to contact knowledgeable individuals in the region being studied. These people may include farmers, hunters, and others who spend time outdoors. Archaeologists also conduct systematic site surveys on foot (pedestrian survey) over exposed ground surfaces, such as newly cultivated fields or along eroded stream banks, to locate sites. Identifying site locations and areas where there are no sites provides valuable research data and assists land managers in planning for future development. When assisted by volunteers or professional crews, many acres of land can be covered by pedestrian survey in a single day (fig. 1.3). Sites are located by looking for the tell-tale signs of ancient human occupation. In the Upper Mississippi Valley, these signs are often small artifacts, such as flakes from chipping stone tools or ceramic sherds from broken pots.

Locating sites in vegetated areas such as forests, pastures, or urban parks and lawns is more difficult. The standard method for these settings is to excavate small shovel tests at regular intervals (usually 50 feet) and screen the soil to search for artifacts. A number of geophysical survey and remote-sensing techniques have been developed to search for patterns of subsurface disturbance, such as burial or storage pits. Technologies, including ground-penetrating radar, soil resistivity, and electromagnetic survey, hold promise for detecting subsurface anomalies, but detected anomalies must be "ground truthed" through excavation to determine what they are. Aerial photography, sometimes with special film, has been used successfully to locate some major archaeological sites. One such example in the Driftless Area was the discovery of the ghost eagle bird mound with a wingspan of nearly a quarter mile along the Lower Wisconsin River. Although this mound has been completely plowed down, the shape is clearly revealed in an aerial photograph of the field.

Dating the Past

Ordering the past by time is an essential job of the archaeologist. Without knowing the age of sites and artifacts, it is not possible to understand which artifacts and cultures came before or after others. Dating the past is critical for learning about change in human societies through time with any degree of accuracy. There are many methods for estimating the age of archaeological remains. Stratigraphy, radiocarbon dating, and the seriation of artifacts by style are used with regularity in the Upper Mississippi River Valley.

Stratigraphy involves interpreting the vertical placement of artifacts within individual layers, or strata, in the soil at sites. This method is based on the geologic "law of superposition," which holds that the layer on the bottom of a sequence of layers will be the oldest, while those on the top are the most recently deposited and therefore the youngest (fig. 1.4). Natural and cultural factors such as animal burrows and plowing can alter the ideal layer-cake pattern of sediment and artifact deposition. Still, stratigraphic position remains a practical indicator of relative age at most archaeological sites. Because the stratigraphic method offers a relative date, indicating the general sequence in which artifacts were deposited, it cannot provide actual age estimates or calendar dates.

Radiocarbon measurement is the most widely used absolute dating method in the world. This method, while based on statistical probability, provides actual time estimates or absolute dates within a margin of error. The radiocarbon, or C14, method was developed by chemist Willard F. Libby in 1949. Libby found that cosmic radiation causes nitrogen in the atmosphere to add a neutron, becoming the unstable carbon isotope C14. Libby also knew that plants absorb C14 atoms during the process of photosynthesis. Animals that eat

1.4. Stratigraphic layers at the Sand Lake site near Onalaska.

green plants or animals that prey on herbivores also absorb radioactive C14 at the same rate at which it occurs in the atmosphere.

Nearly all living things, then, accumulate C14 during their lifetimes. When organisms die, they stop absorbing C14, and the process of radioactive decay begins, in which C14 atoms break down into stable C12 at a regular rate. Because C14 has a known half-life (the time it takes for half of the accumulated C14 atoms to have changed back to C12 atoms) of about 5,700 years, it is possible to estimate the age of ancient plant and animal remains by measuring the amount of remaining C14. For example, if a piece of wood has half the amount of C14 as fresh material, the tree probably died about 5,700 years ago. If it has 75 percent of the C14 remaining, it would date to about 2,850 years ago. Radiocarbon laboratories have sophisticated equipment to measure the amount of remaining C14 in ancient organic ecofacts. Conventional C14 dates require 4 or 5 ounces of datable material. Recent advances in radiocarbon dating have led to the widespread use of Accelerator Mass Spectrometry (AMS) dating. This technique allows dating of samples as small as .001 ounce by counting actual C14 ions. For instance, AMS was used to date individual thread fragments from the Shroud of Turin at three separate radiocarbon labs, causing minimal damage to the fabric.

Radiocarbon dating is often done on carbonized plant remains such as wood charcoal. But virtually all organic remains, including animal bones, plant parts, and shells, can be radiocarbon dated, as long as they are not contaminated by modern organic compounds. Nonorganic artifacts such as pottery and stone tools cannot be directly dated by C14. Instead, age estimates for such artifacts are based on finding the artifacts in undisturbed contexts directly associated with organic materials that can be dated. For example, a refuse pit might contain broken pottery, stone arrow tips, and charcoal. Because the materials in the pit feature were probably discarded at about the same time, a C14 date for the charcoal can establish the age of the associated pottery and arrow tips. A potential problem with conventional C14 dating is that the charcoal may be from a several-hundred-year-old tree that was burned by the site occupants. It is nearly impossible to identify these old wood dates, but some C14 dates are obviously older than the actual site occupation. This possibility can be avoided by dating short-growth materials such as charred twigs or nutshell. AMS dates also can be obtained from charred residue on ceramic sherds that probably represents burned food, providing unquestionable association of the carbon and the pottery vessel. However, even these dates are not infallible.

One problem with the radiocarbon method is that the amount of cosmic radiation coming into the earth's atmosphere has varied over time. Consequently, plants and animals from some periods absorbed more or less C14 than organisms from other periods, and this affects the half-life decay ratios. To correct for these variations, dates were obtained from ancient bristle-cone pine trees in the White Mountains on the California-Nevada border. Climatologists and tree-ring specialists have established a continuous sequence of annual growth-ring patterns from these living and dead pine trees that extend back more than 8,000 years. These trees provide samples of wood from long ago for which the exact age is known. Radiocarbon measurements from these control samples have allowed scientists to detect fluctuations in past cosmic radiation and to develop a calibration to correct radiocarbon dates. In this book, we use uncalibrated ages in radiocarbon years, but calibration of individual dates is easily accomplished through several computer programs (for example, Calib or OxCal) that are available on the Internet.

Culture

The concept of culture comes from the field of anthropology and is key for archaeologists to frame an understanding of past human societies based on material remains. Human culture is structured and patterned behavior that people learn as members of their societies. Culture is not genetic. Instead, individuals acquire cultural guidance from parents and other group members on what is useful and acceptable in their particular society. One obvious example of learned and patterned cultural behavior is language. Nearly all infants are capable of learning any language, but as children they speak the tongue of their parents or guardians. Since it is learned and patterned, human culture, especially in traditional societies, is regionally distinct. In mountainous regions or on island archipelagos, language dialects are often discernible to individual valleys or islands. Even in our modern global society, the distinctive dialects of people raised in various parts of the United States are easily recognized. Similarly, other forms of culture, from art and architecture to clothes and tools, often vary across different regions.

At the same time, culture is also dynamic. All societies have the ability to adjust to changes in their social and natural environments. Culture, put simply, is the package of learned guidelines for human behavior, and past cultures are detectable in regional artifact styles manufactured by patterned human behavior. When archaeologists refer to an ancient culture, they mean a recognized pattern of artifacts from restricted areas that date to a specific period of time. When patterns persist over an extended period of time, this is referred to as a tradition.

The time and space relationship of artifacts at a site is the all-important context (for example, the association of pottery, arrow tips, and charcoal in a refuse pit). Without context, it is rarely possible to determine the age and association of artifacts and therefore is impossible to reconstruct past human behavior. The more detailed the contextual information, the more one can learn from artifacts and sites, which is one reason why archaeologists so painstakingly detail the exposing, mapping, photographing, and recovering of artifacts. Another reason is that archaeologists destroy the context of sites when they excavate them, so recording the precise three-dimensional location of all finds allows reconstruction of context in the laboratory.

In summary, archaeologists can learn about the human past since much of this past is knowable because human cultural behavior is structured and patterned in both time and space and is observable through the presence of artifacts. Even disturbances to the record of the past by natural or cultural means are structured and therefore knowable.

Burial of the Dead

Throughout the world, there is an amazing variety of ways that people have buried deceased members of their societies. Perhaps more than any other as-

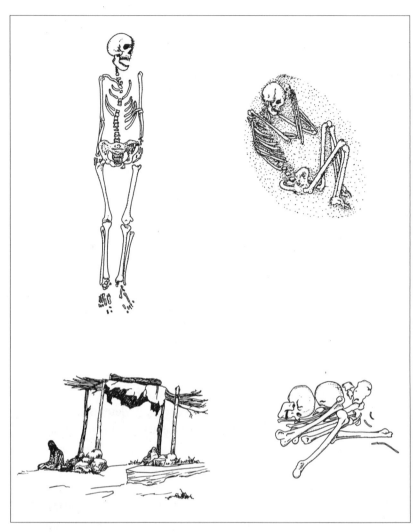

1.5. Variation in burial types found in the Upper Mississippi River Valley. Clockwise from top left: extended, flexed, bundle, and scaffold. Drawings by Laura Jankowski.

pect of culture, burial practices are culturally patterned and strictly adhered to. Archaeologists use a set of standard terms to describe common burial methods of ancient societies (fig. 1.5). A primary burial is an individual buried in the flesh and not subsequently moved. Primary burials may be in the extended position, with the arms, legs, and torso in a straight line, or in the flexed (fetal) position, with the knees folded toward the chest and the hands often brought up near the head. Sometimes the dead were moved from seasonal encampments to other locations for final burial. In these cases, bones were gathered from temporary resting places (such as a scaffold) and wrapped in a bundle for transportation to the final burial location. These secondary, or bundle, burials usually do not contain all of the bones of the skeleton. Typically, the skull and major long bones were bundled and reburied, with smaller bones frequently missing. Another relatively common means of treating the dead is cremation, and archaeologists have found deposits of burned bones in some mortuary settings.

Social Organization

All human groups develop a social and political structure to serve the needs of their society. At its most basic level, social organization is adapted to the survival of any group. Seasonally nomadic people surviving on the harvest of wild plants and animals have very different organizational patterns than do agricultural people or those who live in cities. Anthropologists often classify human social organization into basic divisions based on organized complexity.

The band level of sociopolitical organization is the least complex and is made up of a small number of cooperating families. Most bands are hunters and gatherers of wild resources who move on an annual round or cycle that allows optimal harvest of those resources. For most of the year, bands have three to six families, and they often number about 25 people, including adults and children. The bands are egalitarian, meaning that members have equal rights within the society, although all individuals have well-defined roles based on their age and whether they are female or male. Bands do not have institutionalized leaders, but typically the experience of senior members is acknowledged, and they lead by example. Individuals have relatively few material possessions since they move several times a year. Bands do not own land but occupy defended territories where they regularly hunt and gather. They spend most of the year in small, family groups, sometimes called microbands, but also participate in annual gatherings when larger numbers of related people assemble.

The small size of microbands creates problems, not the least of which is finding a suitable marriage partner. Eligible adults are almost certainly too closely related to all other unmarried members of their microband to find a partner. All societies around the world have incest taboos and related rules that specify who one may marry, thus limiting possible mates. In addition, conflicts that develop within microbands must be dealt with in nonviolent ways. Yet a certain number of cooperating adults is necessary to allow a microband to function safely and successfully.

Band societies have dealt with these issues by assembling several microbands together into macrobands at regular, predetermined gatherings. A macroband may involve 15 or 20 microbands. Anthropologists have calculated that it takes a mating network with a minimum of 200 people to have the necessary potential mates for everyone to find a suitable partner. Macrobands provide mating networks. In some cases, it is evident that two or more macrobands would congregate. In addition to arranging marriages at macroband assemblies, the structure of cooperating families would reorganize. In historic times, most microbands reorganized each year, in part to relieve internal stresses.

Macroband assemblies occurred during the season when food resources were most abundant. Along the Upper Mississippi Valley, that would have been in the summer, when fish, mussels, waterfowl, and many other riverine foods were readily available. For most of prehistory, people of the Upper Mississippi probably came together annually at geographically distinctive locations, such as the landmark Trempealeau Mountain or at Prairie du Chien, where the Wisconsin River empties into the Mississippi. As microbands congregated into a macroband during the summer, courtships and marriages took place, microbands reorganized, and friendships were renewed. During these warm-season gatherings, with all members of extended families and friends assembled, ceremonies that served to bind the macroband together could be held. The most important of these would have been burial of the dead. In some periods, the bodies or bones of persons who died during the winter were brought to the macroband assembly, where all could be involved in the burial. Participation in funerals is a classic means of paying respect to the dead and maintaining group solidarity among the living.

Tribes have a greater sociopolitical complexity than bands. Many tribal societies are characterized by a subsistence base founded on agriculture and/or domestic animal herding. Tribal-level people who farm often live in year-round villages that usually contain about 100 people. Tribal villages seldom grow any larger because they have a relatively weak political organization. When frictions between member families become too great, the group often splits, with dissidents forming a new village. The concept of "tribe" as we are using it here is different than modern sovereign tribal nations such as the Ho-Chunk and Menominee of Wisconsin.

Because good-quality, tillable farmland is frequently a limited resource, it is often considered to be owned by the tribe or by the family or individual who has it under cultivation. Unlike bands, tribes have nominal leaders who act and serve at the pleasure of the tribal members. Sedentary agricultural groups typically invest in facilities such as storage pits and more permanent houses. Tribal societies, like bands, are egalitarian with weak political structures and are held together by hereditary clans or fraternal organizations called sodalities. Clans are groupings of lineages that claim descent from a common ancestor. Upper Mississippi Valley tribes often established clan structures around mythical animal spirits such as bear, buffalo, deer, thunderbird, or water-panther, each of which was delegated specific functions. For example, the Ho-Chunk bear clan has traditionally served in the role of tribal police, enforcing rules. Many regional tribes also structured village residence plans according to clan affiliations and often grouped clans into earth and sky moieties, with each group occupying one side of the settlement. Moieties also clarified reciprocal relationships in ceremonial and ritual activities. For instance, one moiety may have been responsible for burying the dead from the other. Sodalities are age- and -sex-specific organizations that link members from different villages into a web of tribalwide relationships. A widespread type of sodality on the Great Plains, for example, involved warrior societies.

Chiefdoms are larger and more complex than tribes and are fundamentally different. At their core, chiefdoms are distinguished by hereditary inequality. An individual is given status at birth; one is either born into the socially distinct chiefly class or one is born as a commoner. No amount of prestigious work during a lifetime can elevate a commoner to the chiefly rank. Therefore, chiefdoms are ranked or stratified societies. The chief and his or her high-status relatives are often called divine, being messengers from and to a supreme spirit world. The chief, his or her family, and assistants live in a central town where religious and administrative duties are conducted. Towns have religious architectural focal points, usually constructed by the commoners, that serve to reinforce the divine status of the chief and the chief's connection to the spirit world. Chiefdoms are nearly always based on agriculture, and towns are linked to satellite farming villages. These outlying villages support the chief and the chiefdom as an insurance policy against attack by enemies, food shortages, and natural disaster. In return, the chief ensures that the satellite villages are maintained and protected.

Complex societies like chiefdoms appear to arise out of necessity under external threat. Villages may join together under a prophetlike leader whom it is believed will deliver followers from harm. In the process, the leader may become deified through divine direction from supreme powers. Once groups

Social Complexity	Settlement Type	Numbers of People	Annual Movement	Subsistence Base	Social Organization	Leadership	Historic Examples
Bands	Camps	10's	Mobile	Harvest wild plants and animals	Egalitarian— related through kinship	Informal leadership	Inuit (Eskimo) Australian Aborigines Apache, Shoshoni
Tribes	Villages	100's	Mobile to sedentary	Wild resources and/or domestic plants and animals	Egalitarian— linked through kinship and pantribal organizations	Nominal leader	Pueblo Indians of south-western U.S. (Zuni, Hopi) 19th-century Plains bison hunters (Cheyenne, Mandan, Crow)
Chiefdoms	Towns and villages 2-Tier	1,000's	Sedentary	Primary domestic plants and animals	Hereditary inequality— two or more social classes— linked by kinship within classes	Hereditary, divine leader	17th–18th century Hawaii, Tahiti, Pacific Northwest Coast
States	Cities, towns, and villages 3-Tier	10,000's	Sedentary	Domestic plants and animals	Central bureaucracy– class based, codified laws, tribute, and taxation	Emperor or king	Aztec, Maya

UNRANKED SOCIETIES (Bands, Tribes)

RANKED SOCIETIES (Chiefdoms, States)

1.6. Levels of social complexity.

in an area nucleate into a chiefdom, others in surrounding regions have few choices except to join the chiefdom, leave the region, or nucleate with others to form a rival chiefdom.

States are stratified societies that are larger than chiefdoms. States are headed by a religious and political elite who are quartered at an administrative center or city. Cities are surrounded by towns that have minor administrators who interact on behalf of the elites with the neighboring villages and small hamlets. Taxes and products flow into the city from the villages, and information and protection flow out from the center. Writing first developed in states as a means to track larger populations for taxes and conscription to public work or military service. Because the number of people is too great for kin to apply sanctions for socially unacceptable behavior, written laws are enacted that prescribe specific punishment for crimes. Crimes are now against the state rather than against an individual, and only the state has the authority to punish violators.

In summary, bands and tribes are unranked societies, and the size of their individual settlements are similar. These are sometimes referred to as one-tier settlements. Chiefdoms are ranked or stratified societies that characteristically have a two-tier settlement pattern, with a town that houses the elite and religious headquarters surrounded by smaller, simple agricultural villages. States are stratified societies and often have a three-tier settlement, with a city as the central religious-political-administrative center, outlying towns with lesser administrative-religious functions, and most abundantly agricultural villages (fig. 1.6).

Prehistoric Food

Archaeologists are able to identify many of the foods eaten in prehistoric times from remains recovered during excavations. These subsistence remains include the bones of vertebrate animals or shells from invertebrates such as freshwater mussels, collectively called faunal remains (fig. 1.7; see Appendix A). Plant remains, typically burned, also can be found during excavation. Corn kernels, pieces of nutshells, and seeds that were burned and became carbonized are the most common type of floral remains at Upper Mississippi River Valley sites. Faunal remains are studied by specialists called zooarchaeologists and the floral remains by paleoethnobotanists.

Faunal and floral specialists often can identify the species of animals and plants represented based on their unique sizes and shapes. Identification requires comparative specimens of modern animal skeletons and plant parts.

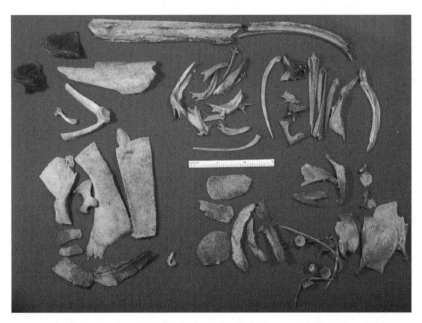

1.7. An assortment of archaeological faunal remains, including mammal, turtle, and fish bones. The scale is 3 inches long.

Size, weight, and estimated caloric values can frequently be gleaned from floral and faunal evidence, providing insights on diet and nutrition. Additionally, the age and season of death for some animals can be determined by growth patterns of teeth or annual growth lines that develop on fish scales and certain bones. For example, wildlife managers routinely determine the age of modern deer kills by looking at tooth eruption and wear patterns, a technique that is valid because all deer are born in late spring. The time of availability for certain plants and animals can also provide evidence for the season of harvest. For instance, nutshells indicate a late summer–early fall collection, while eggshell fragments reveal a springtime activity. The combined plant and animal remains provide evidence for seasonal patterns of hunting-and-gathering activities.

We have learned from the careful study of animal and plant remains that most prehistoric people of the Upper Mississippi River Valley moved two or more times each year in annual or seasonal rounds. The annual round is scheduled to position people in the best location to harvest the most abundant foods at each season. For this reason, most prehistoric habitation sites in the Upper Mississippi Valley are seasonal camps rather than year-round settlements. Archaeologists are therefore keenly interested in the plant and animal remains that can be used as seasonal indicators at each site. During every major cultural stage in the prehistory of the Upper Mississippi Valley, subsistence remains indicate what economic activities were being pursued during each part of the seasonal round.

CHAPTER TWO

Environment of the Upper Mississippi River Valley

The portion of the Upper Mississippi River that cuts through the unglaciated Driftless Area (fig. 2.1) is a unique setting of rich and diverse natural habitats. The Driftless Area is an island of rugged ridges and valleys surrounded by more gently rolling terrain. While the Driftless Area was not plowed over by glacial ice lobes, the surrounding regions were, and they are typically covered with a mixture of churned-up clay, sand, and boulders of various rock materials. In the Driftless Area, virtually all exposed rock is Cambrian-aged sandstone or Ordovician limestone. These represent a series of seabeds formed between about 500 million and 350 million years ago. Due largely to a bulge in the earth's crust that is centered in northern Wisconsin (where 1- to 2-billion-year-old Precambrian granite, rhyolite, and quartz are exposed), younger rock formations dip to the south, forming a series of concentric bedrock rings that become more recent farther from the bulge. These formations are well exposed in the unglaciated Driftless Area and, from north to south, are Cambrian sandstone, Ordovician limestone, and Silurian limestone. The Cambrian sandstone is the dominant surface rock north of La Crosse, dipping

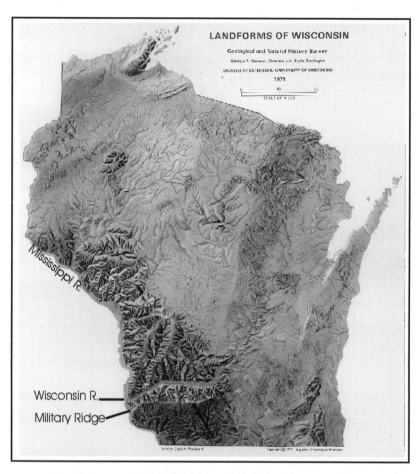

2.1. Relief map of Wisconsin with Driftless Area in southwest corner. Courtesy of the Wisconsin Geological and Natural History Survey.

below the surface about 20 miles south of La Crosse, where it is replaced by massive layers of Ordovician limestone. The upper levels of the Ordovician limestone are broken by a relatively thin layer of sandstone called the St. Peter Formation. This in turn dips below the surface south of the Wisconsin River, where it is capped by the Galena Formation, a dolomitic limestone that is best known for containing deposits of nearly pure lead.

The bedrock formations of the Driftless Area are exposed along the steep sides of thousands of deep, narrow valleys and are particularly prominent along the Mississippi River trench (fig. 2.2). The exposures offer two important resources for people living off the land. First, erosion has created hundreds of small caves or overhangs, offering protected rockshelters that be-

2.2. View of the Upper Mississippi River Valley showing deep glacial outwash incising of the trench. Note the flat blufftops on the far horizon.

came particularly important locations during the cold, harsh winter months. Second, the sandstone and limestone both contain irregular deposits of flint-like material that can be flaked or flint-knapped in a controlled fashion to produce tools such as arrow and spear tips, knives, hide scrapers, and drills. These lithic (stone) resources were critical for survival to people whose lives depended largely on hunting and gathering. Once located, sources of high-quality stone became the equivalent of a modern hardware store and were returned to on a regular basis for retooling. Sites focused on the manufacture of stone tools and littered with knapping debris are referred to as workshops.

Sand is composed primarily of silica (used to produce glass). Through the eons, groundwater dissolved some silica in the sandstone and then reconstituted it in the rock layers where it cemented, forming very hard and brittle silicified sandstone. A number of silicified sandstone deposits have been discovered in the northern portion of the Driftless Area, and these vary widely in color and quality. Many natural exposures were used by prehistoric flint-knappers, with two major sources known. The most famous is Silver Mound at the northeast edge of the Driftless Area in Jackson County.* The other major source was in the central portion of the Driftless Area. There, silicified sandstone occurs over a 30-square-mile area as weathered slabs that are buried

*Unless otherwise specified, all city and county names in this book refer to Wisconsin localities.

2.3. Outcrop of Hixton silicified sandstone at the Dwyer Rockshelter on Silver Mound in Jackson County.

within eroded sand. Quarry pits and workshop sites occur throughout this locality and suggest as much intensity as seen at Silver Mound but spread over a larger area. Smaller silicified sandstone quarries and workshops have been found in Trempealeau County, near Arcadia.

Silver Mound is an outlier sandstone hill encompassing nearly 200 acres on the northeastern margin of the Driftless Area in Jackson County. The mound contains a massive deposit of orthoquartzite commonly referred to as Hixton silicified sandstone or simply sugar quartz (fig. 2.3). The flanks of Silver Mound are pocked with hundreds of quarry pits. Early white settlers saw these pits and assumed there were valuable mineral deposits—the glint of the rock suggested silver. Geologists had determined by the 1860s that there is no silver at Silver Mound, but prospectors continued to seek their fortunes there through the late 1800s, to no avail. Yet the quarry pits do reflect valuable mineral deposits to the cultures who excavated them: it was the silicified sandstone needed by pre-European knappers to produce spear tips, knives, hide scrapers, awls, drills, and other tools.

Because the Upper Mississippi River Valley has relatively poor quality flinty

2.4 Large biface preform made of Hixton silicified sandstone. Blanks like this were made at quarry sites to test the quality of the material and lighten the weight for transport to other locations, where they could be used as stock to manufacture a variety of tools as needed. This preform is approximately 10 inches long.

rock, major sources of high-quality stone such as at Silver Mound became critical resource locations that were visited regularly over the prehistoric millennia to replenish tool kits. The hundreds of quarry pits at Silver Mound were all dug by hand with tools such as stone mauls and digging sticks. Some of the pits there are 30 feet across and 10 feet deep, giving an indication of the labor invested and the value of Hixton silicified sandstone.

Silver Mound is also littered with millions of waste flakes and other artifacts. Concentrations of the waste flakes reflect places where prehistoric flint-knappers tested the quarried silicified sandstone, selecting the best quality and reducing the weight for transport to other seasonal camp sites or for trade. In doing so, the knappers created preforms, or blanks (fig. 2.4), which served as stock for a variety of tools that would be needed later, when the group was away from Silver Mound. Sometimes the preforms would break in manufacture, and so workshop sites often have broken blanks and hammerstones in addition to large flakes created in removing the weathered outer surface of silicified sandstone slabs. Along streams that surround Silver Mound, camp sites tend to have smaller flakes from thinning the preforms and finishing tools. Often worn-out tools made from other materials were discarded at these camps.

Silver Mound was discovered by archaeologists in the 1920s but was only thoroughly surveyed in the 1970s and 1990s. Investigations documented quarry pit complexes, rockshelters, rock art paintings (pictographs), and carvings (petroglyphs). The mound is privately owned and has been listed on the National Register of Historic Places. Most of Silver Mound remains in pristine condition, although some damage from farming and development has occurred on the lower margins. Recent logging and all-terrain vehicle

(ATV) activity have encroached into remote wooded areas. In order to ensure long-term preservation of portions of this significant site, the Archaeological Conservancy has acquired several parcels.

Ordovician-aged Prairie du Chien limestone contains siliceous deposits of fine-grained material called chert. Throughout the region north of the Wisconsin River, the Prairie du Chien limestone contains two chert-bearing strata, the Shakopee and Oneota Formations. Chert is very common in both of these but is generally of poor quality. Chipped-stone artifacts made of Prairie du Chien chert are found throughout the area. Many are grayish red with a lustrous surface, indicating that the material was heat-treated to improve the flaking quality. Heat-treating involves baking the stone to temperatures between 400 and 800 degrees Fahrenheit, when the chemical composition and crystalline character are altered. Because this material is found nearly everywhere in the central Driftless Area, small workshops abound. To date, only one major workshop locality has been identified, located in Monroe County. There, massive nodules of relatively high quality Prairie du Chien chert are exposed in ravines and dry washes, and workshop sites cover the ridgetops and adjacent valleys.

The lead-bearing Galena Formation is exposed on the main ridgetop above Prairie du Chien and more commonly south of the Wisconsin River. It harbors chert that is generally superior to the Prairie du Chien Formation. The Bass site is a major Galena chert workshop situated on the main upland divide south of the Wisconsin River, called the Military Ridge (fig. 2.1). Other workshops are clustered on the ridgetop divide north of Prairie du Chien between the headwaters of two small valleys, called Mill Coulee and Gran Grae.

Another flint source occurring along the Upper Mississippi River Valley is called Cochrane chert. This material is found sporadically on ridgetops in western Wisconsin. It is not found in bedrock but in upland clays of the Reedstown member, an ancient weathered surface within the Ordovician sequence. Cochrane chert is highly variable, ranging from chocolate brown to tan and white and from a glossy, jasperlike texture to coarse, banded slabs that resemble petrified wood. Only one workshop is known: the Chocolate site in Trempealeau County.

A similar-looking chert, called Root River jasper, is found in southeastern Minnesota. This chert also occurs in residual upland clay deposits but is Devonian in age (420–350 millions of years old), perhaps associated with the Cedar Valley Formation. The Challey-Turbensen workshop site in Fillmore County, Minnesota, is one example of prehistoric exploitation of this source.

Prior to the Ice Age, or Pleistocene as it is called by scientists, the Mississippi River flowed atop a relatively flat bedrock base, well above its current level. Over millions of years, the exposed Driftless Area slowly eroded, forming valleys that branched in treelike patterns, leaving ridges between them. It was not until the cycles of the Pleistocene that the Upper Mississippi Valley was carved into a deep gorge and Driftless Area valleys became deep and narrow. Although the Upper Mississippi River flows through an unglaciated region, the trench itself is a direct by-product of glaciation. During the past 2 million years, as glaciers advanced and retreated all around the Driftless Area, there were numerous times when glacial meltwater became dammed behind sediment or moraines, forming huge glacial lakes. Lake Superior rose to levels hundreds of feet higher than today, as did Glacial Lake Agassiz (now indicated only by Lake of the Woods in Canada). When these natural dams were breached, the glacial lakes drained rapidly in catastrophic floods that swept down the Mississippi Valley. During these floods, the river flowed from bluff to bluff, with water spilling back into tributary valleys. The water scoured and eroded the Mississippi trench, picking up sedimentary outwash debris along the way. The trench was carved hundreds of feet deep, and bluffs were undercut and collapsed, forming sheer cliffs. Where the floodwaters cut through softer sandstone, the trench was carved wider than in places where more resistant dolomite abuts the river. Thus at La Crosse, the trench is nearly 10 miles across, while downstream at Prairie du Chien it is only 2 miles from bluff to bluff. At its peak, the river created a gorge that was nearly 1,000 feet deep. Then, as the current subsided, sand and gravel dropped out of the flowing water, refilling the bottom half of the gorge.

When the river returned to normal, receding waters left vast expanses of barren land. From this plain, fine particles were raised by the wind and dropped in a mantle of loess, which tapers from 30 feet thick along the Wisconsin bluff line to only a few inches thick 50 miles to the east. The loess was unstable. Massive erosional gullies soon formed, and some hillsides slumped before finally stabilizing as vegetation eventually took hold on the landscape.

After the last glacial meltwater flood nearly 9,500 years ago, the Mississippi began to carve new channels in the fresh sediments, leaving a series of terraces. Virtually every major town along the Upper Mississippi River—from Red Wing and Winona, Minnesota, to La Crosse and Prairie du Chien and down to Dubuque, Iowa—is situated on the glacial outwash sand-and-gravel terrace that had been the bed of the river during glacial meltwater floods (fig. 2.5). The terrace gravels contain a mix of rounded cobbles from farther north, including agates, basalt, granite, quartz, quartzite, and small pieces of fine-grained chert. When reexposed through erosion or excavation,

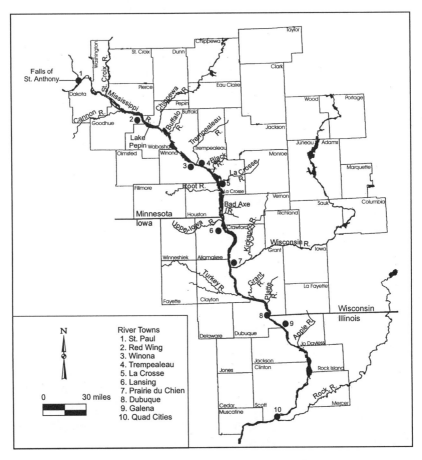

2.5. River towns, each correlating to a major Pleistocene outwash terrace along the Upper Mississippi River.

these cobbles (particularly basalt) provided material for tools such as hammerstones, grinding stones, and axes. Although these materials were readily available along the Mississippi River, basalt hammerstones and axes had to be carried to interior Driftless Area locations, where the only naturally available rock is limestone with chert and sandstone, some of which is silicified. On occasion, outwash agates and water-worn chert pebbles were chipped into small tools such as scrapers, and red cobbles were sometimes used as a substitute for nonlocal pipestone and carved into ornamental and ritual objects.

The Upper Mississippi changes dramatically as it courses through the Driftless Area (fig. 2.6). Below the Falls of St. Anthony at St. Paul, the river cuts southeastward to be joined by the St. Croix, forming the boundary between Minnesota and Wisconsin. Here it begins cutting through a region that was

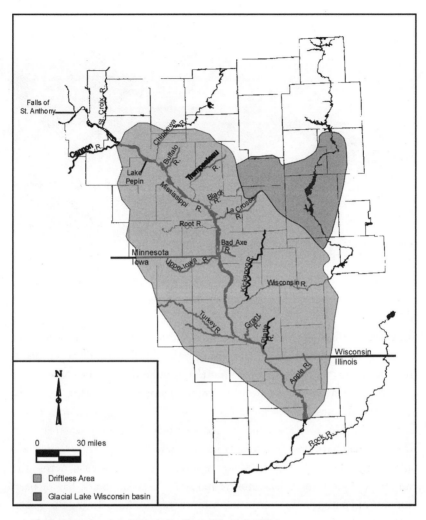

2.6. The Driftless Area in relation to the Upper Mississippi River.

glaciated early in the Pleistocene. Near Red Wing, the river is marked by the joint delta of the Cannon and Vermillion Rivers. There, a series of stepped terraces overlook the braided floodplain. Below this delta, the river has been blocked by massive quantities of sand from the Chippewa River, which drains the heart of central Wisconsin's Cambrian sandstone region. The delta of the Chippewa has forced the Mississippi River channel to the Minnesota side; the current is not strong enough to flush the sand away. Consequently, the Mississippi is backed up above the mouth of the Chippewa, forming Lake Pepin, a unique 30-mile-long natural impoundment. Below Lake Pepin, a major outwash terrace system occurs at the mouth of the Zumbro River, where

2.7. Trempealeau Mountain, an outlier bedrock hill in Perrot State Park, covered with a modern forest.

Wabesha and Kellogg, Minnesota, stand. Another major terrace system exists near the mouth of the Buffalo River on the Wisconsin side and is occupied by the towns of Nelson, Cochrane, and Buffalo City. Throughout this relatively narrow upper section, the trench margins are marked by steep, 400-foot-tall limestone bluffs.

Beginning at Winona, which developed on the next major downstream terrace, the trench widens considerably, having carved through softer Cambrian-aged sandstone, and the river makes a notable turn to the east. Across the way, the unique Trempealeau bluffs stand as a natural landmark, having been cut off from both the Wisconsin and Minnesota bluff lines during the glacial meltwater floods. The westernmost of these bluffs, called Trempealeau Mountain, is an island that is entirely surrounded by water, and it is from this unique landform that the locality received its French name, "La Montagne qui trempe a l'eau" (the hill that soaks in the water) (fig. 2.7). The largest terrace system along the Upper Mississippi exists from Trempealeau to La Crosse. These massive outwash deposits reflect the exceptionally wide section of the gorge here but also correspond to the confluences of the substantial Black and La Crosse Rivers on the Wisconsin side. The terraces overlook an equally broad floodplain, with the Black River delta in particular forming a major marsh system. The main Mississippi channel bends around this delta, meeting the La Crosse terrace at the mouth of the smaller La Crosse River, thereby preventing the formation of a similar delta there. On the opposite side, the comparable-sized Root River enters a marshy delta just below La Crescent, Minnesota. From here, the Mississippi meanders first west, then east to the modern riverfront towns of Brownsville, Minnesota, and then to Genoa, 20 miles below La Crosse.

At Genoa, the Cambrian sandstone dips beneath the surface, and the valley constricts to a sharply narrower trench cut through harder dolomite. Across from Genoa, the Upper Iowa River has formed a delta that has pushed the main channel of the Mississippi back to the Wisconsin side, where it removes sediment from the weaker Bad Axe River. Below the Bad Axe, the Mississippi again switches back to the west, where it touches the Iowa mainland at Lansing. The constriction continues in a great bend past the small towns of Ferryville and Lynxville and past Harpers Ferry, Iowa, to Prairie du Chien. In this narrower section of the gorge, the current increases proportionally, creating extremely fertile bedding conditions for certain species of freshwater mussels. At Prairie du Chien, the Wisconsin River joins the Mississippi, having traversed its entire name state. The Wisconsin, like the Chippewa, carries massive quantities of sand, but the stronger current of the Mississippi in the constricted trench at Prairie du Chien carries the sand away rather than creating a pool as at Lake Pepin.

From here the river continues on its way to the Illinois border, where the bedrock bluffs begin to decrease from 500 to about 200 feet. Between here and the mouth of the Rock River at Rock Island, Illinois, the river flows as a gentle braided stream, passing the Turkey River on the Iowa side and the Galena and Apple Rivers on the Illinois side. At Rock Island, the river met a resistant bedrock layer, creating a massive rapids that offered a firm bed with well-oxygenated riffles, an ideal habitat for many kinds of freshwater mussels.

The Upper Mississippi Valley includes a mosaic of landforms and biotic communities. The biomes can be grouped into those associated with the bedrock uplands, steep-sided interior valleys, outwash terraces, and floodplains of both the Mississippi River and the interior streams. Each of these settings supported various types of plants and animals, many of which provided food for prehistoric people, and these areas are therefore considered economic resource zones.

Traveling through the Upper Mississippi Valley today gives a false impression of past conditions. For example, most of the bluffs today are forested, with small patches of prairies remaining on south- and west-facing slopes. Yet only 150 years ago most of the upland ridgetops were covered in prairie grass. The prairie was maintained through periodic fires, such as that described by J. C. Beltrami as the steamboat *Virginia* passed the Upper Iowa

2.8. Battle Bluff in Vernon County showing more typical natural hill or "goat prairie."

2.9. Lock and Dam 9 at Lynxville showing natural forested island floodplain below the dam to the left and inundated/eroded bottomland above the dam to the right.

River on a summer evening in 1823: "The flames towering above the tops of the hills and mountains, where the wind rages with most violence, gave them the appearance of volcanoes, at the moment of their most terrific eruptions; and the fire winding in its decent [sic] through places covered with grass, exhibited an exact resemblance of the undulating lava of Vesuvius. . . . This fire accompanied us with some variations for fifteen miles."

2.10. Rick Nascak with ancient elk antlers he recovered in the Mississippi River near Winona, Minnesota. The antlers are coated with modern zebra mussels.

Since 1850, fire has been substantially reduced as a consequence of breaks created by plowing and because modern fire departments routinely put out unintentional fires. Currently, a few small, isolated "goat prairies" remain on warm/dry southwest-facing bluff points (fig. 2.8), and prairie preserves are artificially maintained through periodic controlled burns. Virtually all of the outwash terraces supported lush prairie savannas with scattered bur oaks. Many of the original town settlements were named after their historic prairie designations, such as Prairie du Chien and Prairie la Crosse. Today the city of La Crosse boasts of its designation as a tree city, and its taxpayers support a forestry management program.

The floodplains have suffered even more dramatic change in the past century and a half. In 1846 Charles Lanman described the water of the Upper Mississippi River as perfectly translucent. Today it is a silt-laden river carrying massive amounts of runoff from farms and paved urban centers. Original floodplain surfaces are sometimes covered by many feet of alluvium caused by the pre-1930's farming practices. The most notable changes in the floodplain are the 26 artificial locks and dams placed every 15 to 30 miles between the Twin Cities and Alton, Illinois (fig. 2.9). Constructed in the 1930s, this navigation system inundated approximately half of the natural floodplain in a series of artificial pools. Subsequent wave erosion removed thousands of islands, so that river managers currently are constructing artificial islands made of quarried blufftop rock and dredged sediment to reestablish some natural habitat.

The pre-European environment provided habitat for varied game animals and edible flora, often in abundance. While ridgetops and south- and west-facing slopes supported prairies, cooler and damper north- and east-facing slopes harbored stands of deciduous trees, including oak, hickory, maple, basswood, ash, and birch. This mosaic ecotone of prairie and deciduous forest was an ideal habitat for deer and elk as well as smaller game (fig. 2.10). In some regions where sandstone outcrops are common, relict stands of white and red pine remain. Poorly drained interior floodplains, developed upon backwater ponds created during the glacial meltwater floods, supported marsh grasses and stands of tamarack.

As noted, the sand-and-gravel outwash terraces supported prairie and oak savanna. This econiche offered relatively few food resources but provided ideal settings for habitation sites overlooking the floodplains. These prairies were occasionally visited by buffalo, as recorded by early French explorers. The Buffalo River is named for bison that French missionary Father Louis Hennepin observed there in 1680. The nearest herds of buffalo, however, were located on the much more extensive Little Prairies of southern Minnesota and adjacent portions of Iowa.

In contrast to the high terraces, the Mississippi River floodplain offered a tremendous wealth of food resources for Native peoples during the warm-weather season. These included innumerable quantities of fish, waterfowl, mussels, beaver, muskrat, and even crawfish. Edible plants included the roots and shoots of cattail, tubers of the arrowleaf plant (duck potato), and wild rice. Of course, the Upper Mississippi freezes over each winter, during which time it provides almost no plant foods and little opportunity for collecting animal food resources. While ice fishing is popular today, there is little evidence for this in the archaeological record of the Upper Mississippi River.

CHAPTER THREE

Past Climate of the Upper Mississippi River Valley

The Pleistocene is a term given to that period of time between about 2 million and 11,000 years ago when the earth's atmosphere cooled, permitting the development of huge amounts of glacial ice. During this Ice Age, portions of the earth's Northern Hemisphere experienced several episodes of expansion and contraction of continental glaciation, particularly in areas of northern North America and western Europe. In North America, much of what is today Canada and the Midwest as far south as Missouri and Ohio were covered by a succession of glacial advances during at least four major periods. The ice advances were fed by compacting snow, forming glaciers that remained cool enough during the warm season that loss from melting and evaporation was less than the net annual gain. The main glaciers grew to several miles thick, deformed under their own weight, and spread out from their margins. The glacial margins acted as a combination plow and conveyer belt that incorporated sediment into the glacial ice. As they grew in size, glaciers shaped the land in a variety of ways, creating natural features such as the Great Lakes, the Upper Mississippi Valley, and the poorly drained lake districts of the northern Midwest.

The expansion of continental glaciers in North America during the Pleistocene caused shifts in vegetation communities over vast areas. Drainage systems were redirected and forever changed. The tremendous weight of the ice sheets compressed the earth's surface over which they spread. Even though glacial ice has been gone for thousands of years, in some portions of Canada the land continues to rebound about half an inch per year. Because the glaciers contained so much of the world's freshwater, the sea levels of the world's oceans were as much as 400 feet lower than today. The lower sea levels exposed large areas of the continental shelf, including the region between northeast Asia and Alaska now covered by the Bering Sea.

The land connection between northeast Asia and Alaska that was exposed during the last glacial maximum is called Beringia (formerly the Bering Land Bridge). Beringia was a flat, grassy plain nearly 1,000 miles wide that was exposed for thousands of years. Neither northeast Asia nor western Alaska was covered by glacial ice, permitting the two-way passage of plants and animals. At the last peak of glaciation, about 18,000 years ago, the continental ice sheet spreading out from Hudson Bay merged with alpine glaciers extending out of the Rocky Mountains to block any overland passage between Beringia and the heart of North America. After about 14,000 years ago, these glacial masses separated as climate warmed, opening an ice-free corridor on the eastern slope of the Canadian Rockies.

The best-known Pleistocene animals of North America are the extinct large land mammals, including the mammoth and the mastodon, relatives of the modern elephant. Other extinct animals include types of horses, camels, giant ground sloth, dire wolf, short-faced bear, and giant beaver, the latter of which reached weights of 400 pounds. These large Ice Age mammals are collectively called Pleistocene megafauna (fig. 3.1). The remains of the mammoths and mastodons are relatively abundant east of the Rocky Mountains, with thousands of specimens recovered from stream valleys, eroded areas, and construction sites. The finding of several unquestionable kill sites shows that human hunters encountered and pursued these animals at the end of the Pleistocene in many parts of North America. Nearly 20 finds of mammoths and mastodons are recorded in the Driftless Area (fig. 3.2), and one of these, the Boaz mastodon, appears to have been a kill.

Our record of Pleistocene vegetation communities comes largely from the recovery of microscopic pollen grains from ancient deposits. Pollen grains collected from a stratigraphic sequence and extracted by special sampling

3.1. Megafauna. Top: mastodon; left: long-horned *Bison occidentalis*; right: mammoth. Drawings by Laura Jankowski.

3.2. Example of megafauna find in the Driftless Area. Otto Swennes (left) and John Swennes (right) holding the upper end of the front leg bone of a mastodon found after a flash flood in Long Coulee, near Holmen.

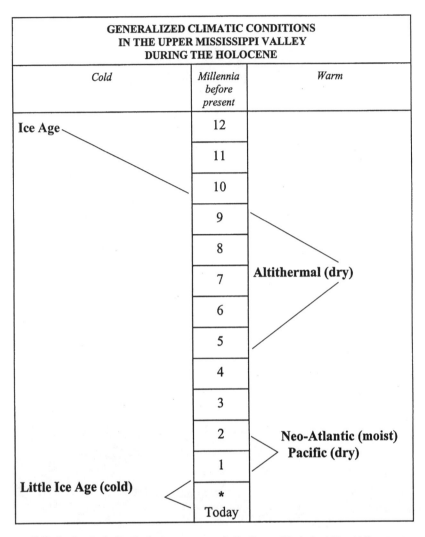

GENERALIZED CLIMATIC CONDITIONS IN THE UPPER MISSISSIPPI VALLEY DURING THE HOLOCENE		
Cold	*Millennia before present*	*Warm*
Ice Age	12	
	11	
	10	
	9	
	8	
	7	**Altithermal (dry)**
	6	
	5	
	4	
	3	
	2	**Neo-Atlantic (moist)**
	1	**Pacific (dry)**
Little Ice Age (cold)	* Today	

3.3. Shifts in climate during the last 12,000 years in the Upper Mississippi River Valley.

procedures are identified and counted to build a pollen profile that may be read as a signature of ancient vegetation communities through time. These pollen profiles show that the vegetation south of the glaciers in the upper Midwest graded from tundra to spruce-fir forest to deciduous forest.

Understanding of the sequence of cultures whose remains are found in the Upper Mississippi Valley requires knowledge of the region's climatic (fig. 3.3) and environmental history. The first record of human existence along the Upper Mississippi and much of North America coincides with the transition from the Pleistocene to the post-Pleistocene period covering the last 11,000 years. The period since the last Ice Age is referred to as the Holocene. The Pleistocene ended with major climate shifts, which resulted in the northward retreat of the melting continental glacial ice. This retreat was interrupted one last time by a sudden glacial advance called the Younger Dryas. The Younger Dryas has been dated to about 12,000 B.P. (before the present), coinciding with the first human presence in the New World, and thus is critical for understanding the probable means of colonization. As the glaciers melted, vast quantities of water were released through the Mississippi River, Great Lakes, and St. Lawrence River systems, producing torrents of seasonal floodwaters that shaped many stream valleys of the Midwest, including that of the Upper Mississippi River.

By about 10,000 years ago the climate had begun to dry and warm in response to a climate pattern dominated by westerly winds. This warm and dry period persisted for several thousand years and is known as the Altithermal. Peaking about 7,000 years ago in many regions, the Altithermal produced expansion of prairie vegetation and associated animal life, including buffalo well to the east of their modern range. At the same time, this prolonged drought undoubtedly affected the Mississippi River itself, perhaps greatly reducing its flow and lowering the water levels.

After 7,000 years ago, moist conditions gradually returned, so that by about 4,000 years ago the climate was similar to that of today. Over at least the past four millennia the Upper Mississippi floodplain has been a rich resource corridor similar to that documented in the first written descriptions of European explorers more than 300 years ago. Throughout this late Holocene period, the river offered a wealth of natural resources during the warm season and supported human populations, including the region's first agriculturalists nearly 1,000 years ago. These farming cultures were particularly sensitive to less drastic climatic shifts such as the warm and moist Neo-Atlantic from A.D. 1000 to 1250, a warm and dry Pacific climatic episode lasting until about A.D. 1450, a short reoccurrence of the warm and moist conditions, and a much cooler and moister period from A.D. 1550 to 1850 called the Neo-Boreal or Little Ice Age.

CHAPTER FOUR

A Brief History of Upper Mississippi River Valley Archaeology

To understand how we know what we know about past cultures, it is useful to outline the history of archaeological research that has taken place in the Upper Mississippi Valley. Throughout this summary, the theme of salvaging remains in the face of site destruction is apparent, a situation that is even more prevalent today. All current and future research stands on the foundation laid by prior efforts and what is preserved of the archaeological record.

In 1838 Richard Taylor published the first detailed report of prehistoric remains in western Wisconsin. Taylor described a number of animal-shaped effigy mounds lying along the prairie-covered Military Ridge, the drainage divide that served as a transportation corridor between Fort Winnebago at Portage and Second Fort Crawford at Prairie du Chien (fig. 2.1). Fourteen years after Taylor's paper, Wisconsin's pioneer scientist Increase A. Lapham mapped mound groups between Genoa and Stoddard and on the dividing ridge between the Mississippi and Kickapoo Rivers near Eastman. Lapham's work, *The Antiquities of Wisconsin as Surveyed and Described,* was first published in 1855 and has recently been reissued (fig. 4.1).

Along the margin of the "Dog Prairie" [Prairie du Chien] we could dis-
cover traces of ancient works, apparently similar to those on the ridge, but
from cultivation + other causes now very obscure. A number of very large
mounds exist along the island between the slough and the river; + what is
very remarkable these are on such low ground that their bases are often
washed by the high water of the Mississippi. In 1826 the highest flood
known, being 8 feet higher than the flood of 1832, the mounds were all that
could be seen of the island above water. Advantage is taken of these great
embankments for the site of the better class of residences; so that they are
always safe from the flood. This is probably the only instance where the
results of ancient labor has [sic] been appropriated for the rises of civilized
life; for in general the mounds are in our way + have to be removed to fit
the ground for our purposes.

Some traces of a ditch etc evidently intended as a military work; proved
on inquiry to be [sic] from long residents here to be the remains of the first
American fort established here, + which was taken by the British in the
War of 1812, and not aboriginal workmanship. The destruction of the works
here is much to be regretted, for it was doubtless an important point with
the mound builders as it has always been with the Indian and French population and now too people in general. (Field Journal, Increase A. Lapham,
June 13, 1852)

In the 1880s Twin Cities' magnate Alfred J. Hill sponsored the Northwestern Archaeological Survey, employing Theodore H. Lewis to map more than
10,000 mounds in the Upper Mississippi Valley. This survey emphasized pristine mounds, and consequently the majority of the recorded effigy mounds
were in southern Wisconsin, eastern Iowa, and southeastern Minnesota.
Lewis also documented conical mounds and fortifications, and he made rub-
bings of rock art carvings. He often wrote to Hill, lamenting the destruction
of the earthworks: "I did not survey 2 groups because they were to [sic] mu-
tulated [sic]. . . . It's a pitty [sic] that I could not have explored this valley
3 or 5 years ago. . . . The best groups that I have surveyed so far would have
been under cultivation in another year, some being already grubbed out"
(Bell Centre, June 22, 1885).

Lewis's careful surveys are the only existing record of thousands of mounds
subsequently obliterated by farming and development. Records of the Northwestern Archaeological Survey for Minnesota were compiled by N. H. Winchell and published in his 1911 classic, *Antiquities of Minnesota*. Only recently

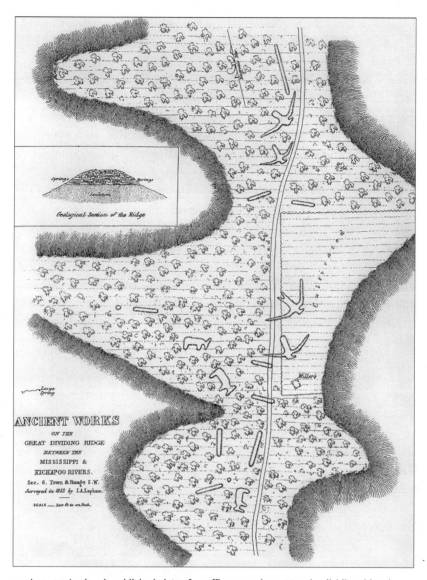

Inside the image:
Geological Section of the Ridge

Large
Spring

ANCIENT WORKS
ON THE
GREAT DIVIDING RIDGE
BETWEEN THE
MISSISSIPPI &
KICKAPOO RIVERS.
Sec. 6. Town 8.Range 5.W.
Surveyed in 1852 by I.A.Lapham.
SCALE — 200 ft to an Inch.

4.1. Increase Lapham's published plate of an effigy mound group on the dividing ridge that separates the Mississippi and Kickapoo Rivers in Crawford County.

have archaeologists reexamined the wealth of information in Lewis's and Hill's unpublished notes and correspondence for Wisconsin.

The first substantial archaeological surveys and excavations along the Upper Mississippi Valley were overseen by Cyrus Thomas in the 1880s under the auspices of the Smithsonian Institution. Thomas was charged by John

Wesley Powell, director of the newly formed Bureau of American Ethnology, with exploring mounds in eastern North America to determine if they were constructed by a vanished race of Mound Builders or by the ancestors of modern American Indians. This debate had raged for decades, coinciding with the main period of U.S.-Indian wars and the removal of American Indians to reservations. The Mound Builders were suggested to be everything from the lost tribes of Israel to the population from the lost continent of Atlantis—anybody but the barbaric, savage Indians believed by many Euro-Americans to be too uncivilized and lazy to have built the mounds.

For more than ten years, Thomas's field agents methodically mapped and excavated mounds throughout the eastern and midwestern United States, including a number of groups in the Upper Mississippi Valley from northwestern Illinois to just below La Crosse. They excavated mounds near Albany and East Dubuque in northern Illinois and a series of Middle Woodland mounds on the Prairie du Chien terrace and farther north, including the Polander and Bad Axe groups in Wisconsin. They also excavated several mounds at Stoddard. In Iowa, they excavated mounds on the Hartley Terrace in the Upper Iowa River Valley, and they mapped a few bird-shaped effigy mounds near Hokah in the Root River Valley of southeastern Minnesota.

Thomas reported his findings in 1894 in the massive, 700-page *Report on Mound Explorations of the Bureau of American Ethnology*. In this report, he detailed the exploration of some 2,000 mounds, including the previously mentioned mounds in the Upper Mississippi Valley. His conclusions left no doubt that the North American mounds were affiliated with the ancestors of the American Indians, and the idea of a separate race of Mound Builders was relegated to the status of myth.

At the turn of the twentieth century, Ellison Orr began a long and productive career documenting the archaeology of northeastern Iowa. Orr was from the small town of Waukon Junction, Iowa, and most of his early work was conducted in Allamakee and Clayton Counties as an avocational archaeologist. During this period, Orr published a brief article on the High Banks site that was eroding from an island in the Mississippi River. This was the first formal record of a prehistoric habitation site in the Upper Mississippi River floodplain.

In the summer of 1924, the writer found along the Wisconsin shore of the Mississippi River, during a period of low water . . . many small fragments of prehistoric Indian pottery, flint chips and a couple of arrowheads. . . . Future opportunities to collect will undoubtedly yield more material the study of which may enable some definite conclusion to be reached as to culture and age. (Ellison Orr, March 20, 1927)

Very much to our regret we must write "finis" to our account of finds at the "High Bank." What we have written is probably the complete history of this old camping place of the Indians so far as it will ever be revealed to the student of this or any other age.

This is for the reason that during the winter of 1926–27, and the early summer of 1927, the Government, in order to protect the down-stream high bank . . . first, with a powerful steam shovel cut this bank to a uniform slope of about forty-five degrees, then covered it from below water mark to the top . . . with eighteen inches or more of rock rip-rap. Thus effectively burying this very interesting hunting ground out of sight for all time.

And now when the great dams across the Mississippi, built to create a nine foot navigable channel, are completed, as they will be in a couple of years hence, the water imponded [sic] above them . . . will raise . . . to a permanent water at five feet above the present low water mark, which even if rip-rap were not there, cover the relic bearing stratum at the "High Bank." (Ellison Orr, December 8, 1936)

While in his seventies, Orr was enticed by Charles Keyes, head of the Iowa Archaeological Survey, to come out of retirement and direct Works Progress Administration (WPA) surveys and excavations for the state of Iowa during the Great Depression. Orr mapped and excavated mounds, camps, villages, and rockshelters in this region, in addition to documenting rock art sites. His extensive and detailed records are housed at Effigy Mounds National Monument in northeastern Iowa. This national monument and the state preserve at the Fish Farm Mound Group near New Albin, Iowa, are lasting testaments to Orr's preservation efforts. The research of Orr and Keyes in the Upper Iowa River Valley also led to recognition of the ceramic distinction between the Woodland and Oneota traditions, and the early historic Oneota complexes in that region are called the Orr phase in honor of Orr's critical role.

In the summers of 1928 through 1930 Will C. McKern (fig. 4.2) of the Milwaukee Public Museum excavated several mounds and habitation sites along the Mississippi River in Crawford, Vernon, La Crosse, and Trempealeau Counties. McKern's efforts were directed toward understanding the variation in prehistoric cultures in an east-to-west transect across the southern part of Wisconsin. In 1929 he excavated at White Camp near Stoddard and at the Midway Village site between La Crosse and Trempealeau. At White Camp,

4.2. Will C. McKern examining artifacts excavated at Trempealeau in 1928.

McKern found Oneota artifacts stratigraphically above Woodland artifacts and first recognized that the Woodland tradition occurred before Oneota. Midway was an important Oneota habitation and burial site.

McKern and the Milwaukee Public Museum crew worked in 1928 and 1930 at Middle Woodland mounds near Trempealeau and at the nearby Shrake-Gillies Oneota village. Excavation of the mounds, including the relatively large Nicholls Mound, provided the basis for the identification of a variant of the Hopewell Culture in western Wisconsin.

> The people whose remains lie in these tumuli had a pronounced appreciation for beautiful materials, a taste which is illustrated in the jasper, yellow chert, chalcedony, obsidian and other attractive mediums from which they shaped their chipped-stone implements. Either they or their neighbors must have been astute, diligent traders, possibly daring travelers, since they had possessed themselves of copper and silver from Lake Superior, pipestone from Ohio, fine quartzites, jaspers, chalcedony and colorful cherts from foreign sources, obsidian from fabulously distant western mountains, if not from still more remote, southern lands. And who shall say what tales of strange adventure, and cultural innovations, of which no

record remains, accompanied these materials? Such conjectures are not the products of imagination out of control, but are reflections of truth as real and as scientifically important as the materials themselves. A majority of these materials probably came to the local possessors through the agency of sluggishly progressive trade, but even so, they did not travel unaccompanied by an excess baggage of social as well as material cultural elements. For where people trade material objects they also trade ideas. (Will C. McKern, 1931)

Although McKern was promoted to administrative duties at the Milwaukee Public Museum soon thereafter, his field investigations enabled him to write the first modern summary of Wisconsin prehistory in 1942. He also published a definitive work on the Oneota cultures of Wisconsin in 1945. He recognized that these were related to Mississippian cultures to the south and named the Wisconsin variants Upper Mississippian. In addition, McKern devised a classification method to help standardize how sites and prehistoric cultures could be organized using comparable trait markers and geographic relationships. His method, called the Midwest Taxonomic System, was adopted by archaeologists throughout America for several decades. The Midwest Taxonomic System was weakened by the lack of time control, and once C14 dating became available in the late 1950s, a modified system was developed.

In 1945 Robert Ritzenthaler of the Milwaukee Public Museum excavated the Osceola site, an Old Copper Archaic cemetery along the Mississippi River in Grant County. In the 1950s Wilfred Logan of the National Park Service conducted a brief excavation at the Stonefield village site in Grant County, as did the University of Wisconsin's David A. Baerreis. In 1956 Chandler Rowe published his doctoral dissertation on the Effigy Mound Culture, and he included an analysis of the Raisbeck Mound Group in Grant County, a site excavated by McKern in 1932.

Also in the 1950s, Warren Wittry from the University of Wisconsin excavated portions of five Driftless Area rockshelters in Sauk and Iowa Counties, including the important and well-stratified Raddatz and Durst sites. The results of his work, published in two 1959 issues of the *Wisconsin Archeologist*, provided the first well-defined chronological sequence for the Middle and Late Archaic cultures in western Wisconsin. These included the first radiocarbon dates for Wisconsin's Driftless Area. Wittry's research initiated the now-standard practice of analyzing and describing faunal remains recovered from excavated sites. The faunal material from Raddatz and Durst was reported by Paul Parmalee of the Illinois State Museum (see Appendix A).

Following the 1949 establishment of Effigy Mounds National Monument along the Mississippi River in northeastern Iowa, some archaeological research was undertaken on the monument grounds. This included excavation of a set of mounds near the visitors center and others on nearby blufftops and at the Sny-Magill Mound Group to the south. A companion study examined soil development in various mound types in an attempt to establish relative age through rates of soil development. Some of this work was published in various articles by Paul Beaubien, but the most comprehensive work to date is that of Wilfred Logan, who synthesized the earlier work of Orr and others in the region into the 1976 book *Woodland Complexes in Northeastern Iowa*. Logan describes excavations and recovered artifacts from mounds, rockshelters, and camps, and he establishes the chronological framework for the Woodland cultures in this region.

From 1947 to 1955, Lloyd Wilford of the University of Minnesota conducted excavations at a series of mound and village sites at Red Wing, Minnesota, including the Bartron, Bryan, and Silvernale sites. Wilford recognized that the complexes at Red Wing were related to the Upper Mississippian cultures defined by McKern. Within the Midwest Taxonomic System, Wilford referred to these as Silvernale focus.

During the 1950s, Wilford also undertook a series of surveys and small-scale excavations along the Upper Mississippi River in southeastern Minnesota. These included attempts to relocate and assess the condition of mounds first mapped by Theodore Lewis in the 1880s and excavation at a series of sites being destroyed by expansion of Highway 61. The latter included a rockshelter near the small town of La Moille, located across the Mississippi River from Trempealeau Bluffs. In addition, Wilford conducted brief excavations at the interior Oneota complex along the South Fork of the Root River, in which he documented early historic French artifacts in direct association with Oneota pottery, and he tested several other rockshelters in the region. Some of Wilford's research was published, but the majority resides in notes and records at the University of Minnesota and the Minnesota Historical Society.

In the 1960s and early 1970s Marshall McKusick, state archaeologist of Iowa, conducted several investigations in northeastern Iowa. These included brief excavations at Hartley Fort in the Upper Iowa River Valley, where he found both Late Woodland and Middle Mississippian artifacts within the remains of a hilltop palisade. He subsequently conducted salvage excavations at Grant Village, on a terrace below Hartley Fort, and discovered Oneota longhouse structures that date to about A.D. 1300. During this period, McKusick undertook a rock art survey, relocating and assessing the condition of many of the sites previously recorded by Orr. He also excavated at the Turkey River Mound Group and at historic Fort Atkinson in northeast Iowa.

Archaeological survey and excavation intensified in western Wisconsin during the 1960s and 1970s. In 1969 Joan E. Freeman of the State Historical Society of Wisconsin reported on her 1962 salvage excavations at the important late Middle Woodland Millville site in Grant County. Freeman also excavated the Price sites in Richland County, including the remarkable Archaic cemetery at the Price Site III. In 1966 she led State Historical Society crews in the excavation of two mounds within the Schwert group at Trempealeau and tested a number of nearby camp sites. During the 1960s, Harris A. Palmer of the University of Wisconsin–Platteville excavated portions of the Preston Rockshelter, which contained a stratified sequence of Archaic and Woodland components, and Robert Nelson, a high school teacher in Platteville, excavated the multicomponent Brogley Rockshelter in Grant County. In 1968 Peter Storck of the University of Wisconsin–Madison excavated the Late Woodland occupation zone at Mayland Cave in Iowa County. William Hurley of the State Historical Society of Wisconsin conducted survey in Buffalo County and tested the Armstrong Oneota site in the early 1970s. While at Platteville in the early 1970s, Clarence Geier excavated one mound group and the multicomponent Hog Hollow site, both in Grant County. He also conducted archaeological survey along the Mississippi and Platte Rivers in Grant County, which located more than 200 sites. During that decade, John Halsey of the State Historical Society of Wisconsin recorded mound and habitation sites in Crawford County.

A proposed flood control project in the Middle and Upper Kickapoo River Valley of Vernon County resulted in a large-scale archaeological survey and limited site excavations. Most of the work was undertaken in the 1960s and 1970s by the State Historical Society of Wisconsin, and this remains the most intensively studied locality in the Driftless Area. Early surveys were directed by William Hurley and Peter Storck, who together recorded more than 300 sites, many of which are attributable to the Archaic tradition. Subsequent excavations were directed by John Halsey at the Markee site, the multicomponent Gillen 9 site, and the stratified Bard Lawrence (or Boy Scout) Rockshelter. Phillip Salkin test-excavated the Rose II Rockshelter as well as Earll Mound I. Barbara Mead and others continued surveys and test excavations in the mid-1970s, and Mead later conducted salvage excavations at a portion of the Rehbein I Mound Group, just below the Kickapoo Reservoir project, due to highway construction needs.

In 1976 James Stoltman (fig. 4.3) of the University of Wisconsin–Madison

4.3. James Stoltman at one of the many field schools he taught near Prairie du Chien in the 1980s and 1990s.

directed excavations at the Bass site, an Early Archaic quarry and workshop in Grant County. In 1978 Stoltman undertook survey and limited excavations at several sites in Crawford County. Survey activities were undertaken in 1979 and 1980 by graduate students James Theler, Constance Arzigian, Robert Boszhardt, and Jeffery Behm at Mill Coulee and Gran Grae, two adjacent interior streams near Prairie du Chien. During the 1980s and early 1990s, Stoltman directed a series of excavations in Grant and Crawford Counties. Aided by avocational archaeologist Alfred Reed (fig. 4.4) of Prairie du Chien, Stoltman oversaw the first productive modern floodplain surveys in the Upper Mississippi Valley as well as excavations at a series of Woodland tradition shell middens that included Mill Pond and related sites. Much of the 1980s' work was carried out by University of Wisconsin graduate students, one of whom (James Theler) prepared a 1987 book, *Woodland Tradition Economic Strategies*. Stoltman and Arzigian later teamed up with graduate student Fred Finney to excavate the Woodland/Mississippian Fred Edwards site along the Grant River. Most recently, Stoltman wrapped up his field career with excavations at the Tillmont site on a floodplain island near Prairie du Chien.

The University of Wisconsin–Madison discoveries of rich, stratified, and well-preserved archaeological sites on islands near Prairie du Chien inspired the two leading government agencies that now manage the Upper Mississippi floodplain to take note. Like all federal agencies, the U.S. Army Corps

4.4. Alfred Reed of Prairie du Chien holding a ground-stone ax.

of Engineers and U.S. Fish and Wildlife Service are required by law to inventory archaeological sites on lands they own and manage and assess whether their actions damage these sites. In the 1980s and 1990s the Corps of Engineers sponsored nearly annual surveys of the Upper Mississippi floodplain, locating many sites that are eroding from shorelines and undertaking the first detailed geomorphological mapping of the floodplain to evaluate where buried sites may exist. In a few instances, such as Red Oak Ridge in Lake Onalaska, the Kipes Island site in the Trempealeau National Wildlife Refuge, and the FTD site below Effigy Mounds National Monument, severely eroding sites have been excavated or were protected by rip-rapping.

In the 1970s R. Clark Mallam of Luther College in Decorah, Iowa, conducted research in northeastern Iowa counties along the Upper Mississippi River. Mallam sought to relocate rock art sites (see Appendix B) that had been originally recorded by Lewis and Orr, and he also focused research on the effigy mounds, the latter work resulting in his 1976 book, *The Iowa Effigy Mound Manifestation*. Mallam directed the mapping and aerial photography of all known mound groups in northeastern Iowa, and he initiated an effigy mound survey of southern Wisconsin that his field supervisor, Robert Petersen, conducted on a shoestring budget. Mallam's premature death cut short a promising career, but Luther College continues his rock art study through Lori Stanley's ongoing work in this region.

4.5. James Gallagher, founder of the Mississippi Valley Archaeology Center at the University of Wisconsin–La Crosse, giving a tour of the Midway Village site excavations in 1988. Alton Fisher, a member of the Milwaukee Public Museum crew that excavated at Midway in 1929, is in the white hat. Note the gravel pit edge in the background that has destroyed much of the site.

In 1977 James Gallagher (fig. 4.5) arrived at the University of Wisconsin–La Crosse in the midst of an era of accelerated urban sprawl. Within a year, he had initiated salvage excavations with students and volunteers at the Valley View Mall, where an Oneota village had been exposed during construction. The site had been known to collectors for years (in fact, it had been mapped by Theodore Lewis in 1889), but at that time only two Oneota sites were recorded in the La Crosse area. Excavations continued at Valley View in 1979 with the assistance of a grant from the Dayton-Hudson Corporation. The crew included Katherine Stevenson, who went on to write her doctoral dissertation and publish several articles on this unique site. By 1980 Gallagher, Stevenson, and Roland Rodell had initiated surveys of areas threatened with unregulated sprawl, and they soon came to realize that La Crosse was home to a major cluster of Oneota villages. In 1982 the Mississippi Valley Archaeology Center (MVAC) was founded at La Crosse as an organization devoted to research, preservation, and public education in the Upper Mississippi Valley. The formation of the MVAC allowed the controlled excavation of a series of Oneota sites, including Midway Village, Sand Lake, State Road Coulee, and Pammel Creek, as well as at various localities within the Sanford Archaeological District, all of which have since been substantially damaged by development. Other MVAC research efforts, many within the realm of the Region 6 Archaeology Program, an adjunct of the State Historical Society of Wisconsin, have included surveys and excavations at a variety of sites along the Mississippi River and at interior valley locations. These include projects at Trempealeau and in the Bad Axe, Coon, La Crosse, and Root River Valleys; surveys for chert and orthoquartzite quarries and workshops; and rock art studies. Survey of Coon Valley was complemented by Robert Sasso's dissertation through Northwestern University, and the Root River survey followed an earlier study by Thomas Trow for the Minnesota Historical Society.

In sum, the history of archaeology in the Upper Mississippi Valley mirrors that of much of North America. Early surveys focused on mounds, with the burning research question: Who built them? The dawn of the twentieth century coincided with the recognition of distinct cultures such as Hopewell and Oneota, based on both mounds and artifacts from village sites. In addition, chronological order was initiated through stratigraphy. The middle of the century included a flurry of rockshelter studies, which further clarified stratigraphic ordering and provided information about Archaic cultures. At the same time, C14 dating began to provide the first actual age estimates for past cultures. Since the 1960s, the majority of archaeology has been driven by federal regulations, and the quantity of work and resulting information have increased geometrically. During this period, the existence of incredibly preserved sites on Mississippi River islands was recognized. For as much work as has been done and the information that has been gained, we have lost vast amounts of irreplaceable knowledge through the thousands of sites that have been destroyed in this region with no archaeological study.

CHAPTER FIVE

The First People

The initial peopling of the Americas persists as the most publicized and controversial issue in all of American archaeology. Two facts seem clear: first, humans did not evolve in either North or South America but arrived in the Western Hemisphere as physically modern *Homo sapiens sapiens*. Second, humans did not arrive in the New World until the later portion of the Pleistocene, probably after 25,000 years ago. Northeast Asia has long been suggested as the place of origin for the first people in North America. There is little doubt that hunters and gatherers moved in small bands across Beringia (fig. 5.1) into the Alaskan Peninsula by about 15,000 years ago. Recently, some archaeologists have suggested that early venturers may have boated down the western coast of Alaska and the British Rockies during this period. However, it was not until after 14,000 years ago that glacial retreat opened an inland corridor from Alaska to the Great Plains, and we find successful colonization in the heart of North America about 12,000 years ago.

The late 1990s' accidental discovery of a 9,000-year-old human skeleton near Kennewick, Washington, created a theoretical and political controversy, largely because initial reports suggested that the skull had caucasoid features. Biological anthropologists have identified a series of cranial characteristics

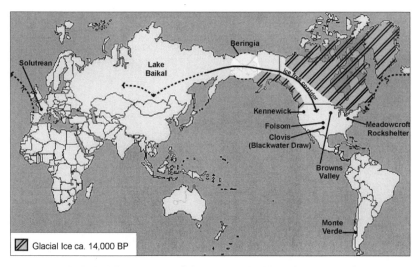

Glacial Ice ca. 14,000 BP

5.1. Key sites in the initial colonization of the New World, with modern political boundaries.

that tend to differ between the broad human races. Using these characteristics, anthropologists see differences between modern Native Americans and Kennewick Man and the few other American skulls dating to nearly 10,000 years ago. The mention of caucasoid features with Kennewick Man suggested to some that the first Americans were of European ancestry and reinvigorated alternate ideas of the peopling of the New World. One suggested route for early European entry to North America would have been by way of boat travel from Spain via the Faeroe Islands to Iceland, then on to Greenland, and finally to the North American continent. Others have pointed out similarities between well-crafted chipped-stone tools of the Solutrean Culture (fig. 5.1) of France and Spain with those of the first documented culture in North America, called Clovis. However, the possibility of circum-Atlantic navigation during a peak period of the Ice Age seems remote, and there is a 5,000-year gap between the end of Solutrean and Clovis. While an imaginative alternative, racial identification of individual skeletal specimens is extremely problematic due to the normal range of variation within any single population. In essence, evidence for European origin of late Pleistocene/early Holocene immigrants is undemonstrated and much less likely than what has been called the Beringia-Walk model.

The earliest undisputed evidence for people in North America consists of finely crafted stone spear tips found with the skeletal remains of extinct Pleistocene mammals. In the 1920s Colorado Museum of Natural History paleontologist Jesse Figgins was directing the excavation of skeletons from an

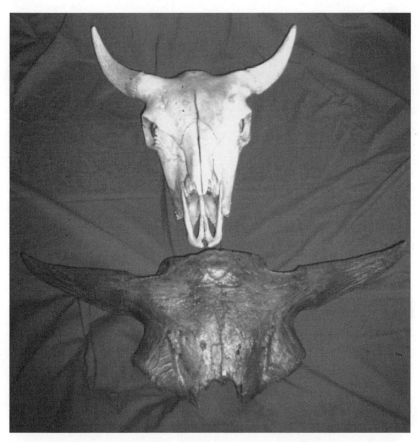

5.2. Modern (*Bison bison*) buffalo skull (top) and the Rud bison skull (*Bison occidentalis*), which was the same size and contemporaneous with *B. antiquus*. Note the much straighter horns of the extinct form.

extinct species of bison known as *Bison antiquus* in northeastern New Mexico near the town of Folsom. *B. antiquus* was a late Pleistocene species some 25 percent larger than its modern descendant, the American buffalo (*Bison bison*) (fig. 5.2). To Figgins's surprise, his workers found delicately fashioned stone weapon tips among the bones, including some in a position indicating that the animals had been speared. The stone spear tips had a distinctive groove, or flute, running up each side of the bifacially chipped points. These uniquely shaped fluted points are a variety often referred to as Folsom after the name of the nearby town.

This first scientifically accepted occurrence of humanly produced artifacts and Pleistocene mammals was followed by two important finds in the 1930s. In 1932 near Dent, Colorado, an excavation of several mammoth skeletons re-

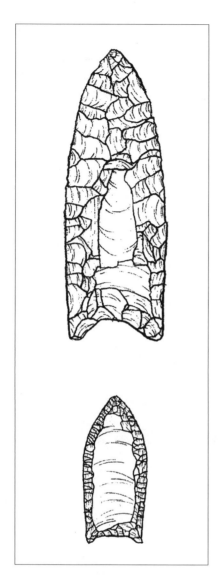

5.3. Clovis (top) and Folsom (bottom) points. The Clovis point is approximately 4 inches long. Drawings by Jiro Manabe.

covered two fluted points, one found in direct association with articulated bones. The points found with the Dent mammoth were somewhat larger than the specimens found at Folsom, with distinctly larger blades and shorter flutes on each side (fig. 5.3). That year also saw the beginning of a series of discoveries at Blackwater Draw Locality #1, a gravel quarry between the towns of Portales and Clovis in eastern New Mexico. Excavations there also found large points with relatively short flutes in direct association with extinct Pleistocene-age mammoths. These larger fluted spear points are called Clovis points after the name of the nearby town.

Blackwater Draw is located at the edge of a flat plateau known as the Llano Estacado, or Staked Plains. For this reason, artifact assemblages containing Clovis points are sometimes referred to as the Llano complex or culture. The specialized bifacial flaking seen in Clovis is comparable to tools found at late Pleistocene sites in northeast Asia. However, fluting is not known in Asia, and this specialized technology may have developed in the now-submerged Beringia or in North America. As noted, some researchers have suggested similarities to finely flaked tools of the Solutrean Culture in western Europe. But fluting is not present there, and the Solutrean dates from about 25,000 to 17,000 B.P., ending at least 5,000 years before Clovis.

The tools associated with fluted points at megafauna kill sites are restricted to relatively few items, including end scrapers, knives, and flakes with spurs, called gravers, which apparently were used for engraving or scoring bone. More rarely, bone projectile points and bone and ivory rods that may be portions of spear foreshafts have been found. A distinctive ivory tool from an Arizona mammoth kill site called Murray Springs is a shaft wrench. This artifact looks like a large eye-bolt, with a short handle and an enlarged hole at one end. This tool is interpreted as having been used to straighten wooden spear shafts. A warped wooden shaft could be placed through the hole and straightened by applying pressure while holding the shaft over a fire without burning one's hand. Shaft wrenches have also been found in late Pleistocene mammoth-hunter camps of central Europe.

At Blackwater Draw, the remains of *B. antiquus* were found in association with Folsom points stratigraphically above the mammoth and Clovis remains. This established a relative age sequence of Clovis followed by Folsom long before the advent of C14 dating.

Fluted points have been found over most of North America. Archaeologists have recognized regional variations in style, but most points are more similar to the Clovis type than different from one another. Most archaeologists treat fluted points as an index fossil marking the first widely successful peopling of North America. The period characterized by fluted points and a small number of megafauna kill sites is referred to as the Paleoindian (ancient Indian) period. Manufacture of fluted points seems to have stopped by 10,000 years ago. In Michigan and Wisconsin, fluted points, mammoth and mastodon remains, and late glacial boundaries co-occur, indicating a terminal Pleistocene association for fluted points and their makers.

The continentwide distribution of fluted points indicates a rapid spread of humans in the New World. This may have been initially facilitated by unwary game in a landscape devoid of humans, but Clovis people also had to learn the landscape and identify critical resources such as sources of suitable stone to replenish tool kits. Most Clovis points have been found between the Rockies and the Atlantic Ocean. The slightly later Folsom points, however, are restricted to the Great Plains. Fluted points in the East include several varieties, such as Cumberland in the Southeast and Gainey in the Great Lakes region. These varieties may reflect the earliest regional populations, as people adapted to differing ecological regions.

Archaeologists have proposed that migratory but sophisticated hunters and gatherers entered North America from northeast Asia, where their mammoth-hunting traditions have been documented on the Asian steppes at sites stretching back 25,000 years. Upon reaching the American heartland, they would have entered a New World absent of human populations. Geographer Paul Martin has suggested that game in this world would have been completely unaccustomed to human predators. Consequently, animals would not have recognized people as potentially threatening, and approach by hunters would have been relatively easy. Applying their hunting skills to such game, they would have been effective and successful megafauna predators, leading not only to rapid movement throughout the hemisphere but also possibly to the extinction of the very fauna they sought.

If people entered the Americas much earlier than the Paleoindian period, they apparently were not successful and left few traces. The jury is still out on the time of human arrival in the New World. Excavators at a number of sites—such as James Adovasio for the Meadowcroft Rockshelter in southwestern Pennsylvania and Thomas Dillehay for Monte Verde in Chile—interpret these sites as containing remains of human occupations that predate Clovis. Close examination of Meadowcroft, Monte Verde, and other pre-Clovis claims have identified problems, and skeptical archaeologists believe that a smoking gun of pre-Clovis arrival has yet to be found.

The first people to arrive along the banks of the Upper Mississippi River some 12,000 years ago saw and lived in a world hardly recognizable today. At that time, the North American continent remained in the grip of a huge continental glacier that centered on the area of modern Hudson Bay but had at one time spread lobes of ice as far south as Missouri and Ohio. By 12,000 years ago, however, the glacier reached only to northern Minnesota and Wisconsin. To the south of the ice sheet lived a variety of Pleistocene plants and large mammals. These included megafauna, such as the woolly mammoth, mastodon, giant ground sloth, camels, horses, and giant beaver, and modern arctic animals, including musk ox and caribou.

Paleoindians are believed to have organized themselves into highly mobile bands of about 25 people. Based on the study of traditional peoples worldwide who depend on hunting and gathering wild resources as their sole means of subsistence and based on archaeological evidence at Paleoindian sites, these bands were comprised of several cooperating families. They needed to move continually in search of food, and, consequently, clear evidence of their presence often is restricted to a few stone tool types, particularly fluted points. In the upper Midwest, the Paleoindian tradition is generally subdivided into the Early Paleoindian stage, marked by fluted points, and Late Paleoindian. The latter stage is characterized by distinctive unfluted lance-shaped, or lanceolate, points that were used by bison hunters on the Great Plains immediately following the Folsom hunters about 10,000 years ago.

The recovery of fluted points from plowed fields in the Upper Mississippi Valley region attests to the presence of the earliest known North American people (fig. 5.4). Yet fluted points have not yet been recovered by archaeologists from an undisturbed context in the Upper Mississippi River Valley. Nearly all of the known fluted points for this region have been found on upland divides or raised landforms within interior valleys. Barren or prairie-covered ridgetops overlooking rivers would have offered logical foot-travel routes while providing excellent vantage points for locating game in the valleys. Isolated mastodon and mammoth bones have occasionally been found in terrace fills, representing haphazard inclusions with Pleistocene outwash. In the tributary valleys, more complete skeletons of these animals have been found deeply buried. These settings would have been natural locations for Paleoindian kill sites and offer the best opportunity to find undisturbed and well-preserved sites. One such site was found near the town of Boaz in Richland County.

In 1897 four farm boys discovered most of a subadult mastodon skeleton partially uncovered by flash flooding in a headwater tributary stream of the Wisconsin River. The boys informally excavated many of the eroding bones and in the process recovered a Clovis-like fluted point made of Hixton silicified sandstone. The Boaz site is the best candidate for a Paleoindian kill site in the Driftless Area. The Boaz mastodon was purchased by the University of Wisconsin, and the articulated skeleton may be viewed today in the university's geology museum (fig. 5.5). Several other finds of megafauna skeletons have been found in small, tributary floodplains, but none have been formally excavated. While it is probable that sites similar to Boaz exist in the Upper

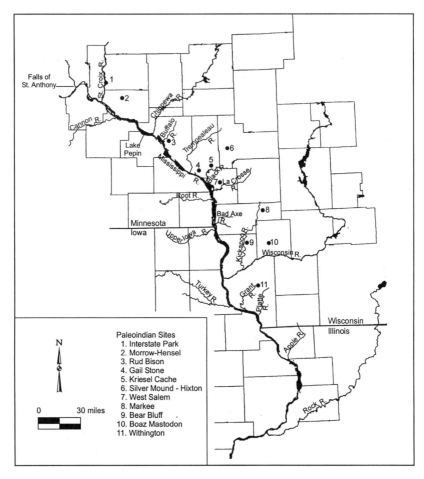

5.4. Key Paleoindian tradition sites mentioned in the text.

Mississippi Valley, their discovery will be complicated by the deep covering of Holocene sediment that blankets most valleys.

A noteworthy Paleoindian locale is Silver Mound in Jackson County, the source of Hixton silicified sandstone. Silver Mound stands out on the surrounding landscape and was found by the earliest Paleoindian peoples who made Clovis-like fluted points. Local workshops have produced numerous broken and worn-out fluted points. These were apparently discarded during retooling visits, when new stone tools were made and exhausted ones discarded. Moreover, a few Paleoindian sites far from Silver Mound contain Hixton fluted points, such as the Withington site in southern Wisconsin and the Morrow-Hensel site to the north. Hixton fluted points are reported to

5.5. The Boaz mastodon on display at Weeks Hall, University of Wisconsin–Madison. Photo courtesy of the University of Wisconsin–Madison Geology Museum.

have been found as far away as southern Ohio and Kentucky. Based on current evidence, Silver Mound was the first location in the Upper Mississippi Valley to which Native people returned on a regular basis, perhaps as part of annual subsistence rounds.

Paleoindians sought and selected the best raw materials within any given region to produce their stone spear points. In the Upper Mississippi River Valley, they used at least two other sources of lithic raw material for fluted point production. One is called Cochrane chert, a glossy red and yellow jasper found on ridgetops and associated ravines in Buffalo and Trempealeau Counties (fig. 5.6). These residual chert deposits were used by some Paleoindian groups to produce fluted points. Cochrane chert was the primary material used for this purpose at the Gail Stone site in Trempealeau County. At other Paleoindian sites in Wisconsin (such as the Aebischer site in east-central Wisconsin), fluted points were manufactured of Moline chert that comes

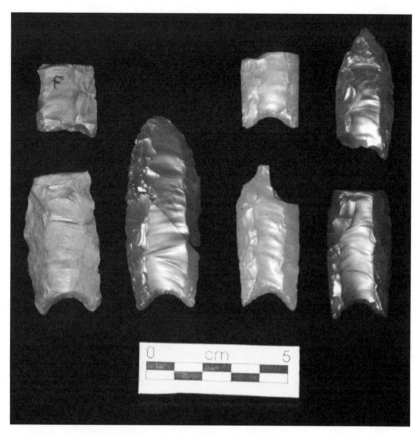

5.6. Fluted points from the Gail Stone site, Trempealeau County.

from limestone outcrops along the Mississippi River near Rock Island, Illinois. A few Moline chert fluted points have been found in the Driftless Area.

Most Early Paleoindian spear tips from the Upper Mississippi Valley are similar to the Clovis type, having relatively short flutes, including a number that are made of Hixton silicified sandstone from Silver Mound. At Gail Stone, portions of at least 11 fluted points have been found on the surface, and these have relatively long flutes that suggest affinities to the Gainey type, a fluted point variant found in the Great Lakes region. Folsom points—which are relatively common on the central and High Plains, where they are associated with extinct bison (*Bison antiquus*)—are rare in the Upper Mississippi Valley, indicating that this region was on the northeastern margin of these Early Paleoindian bison-hunting groups. Indeed, extinct bison remains have been found in bog settings from the headwaters of the Mississippi at Lake Itasca to

Buffalo County in west-central Wisconsin. However, in the rare instances when projectile points have been found with these remains, they are unfluted forms, and these sites appear to date 1,000 or more years after Folsom.

With the retreat of the continental glacier and the beginning of the Holocene about 10,000 years ago, the climate shifted to a regime with sharper contrasts between warm summers and cold winters. This period was dominated by prevailing westerly winds that blocked moist air from the Gulf of Mexico from reaching the upper Midwest. This climate shift is reflected in pollen profiles across the region that show a rapid succession of spruce-fir boreal woodlands being replaced by mixed deciduous hardwoods, then predominantly oak savanna and prairie.

Coinciding with the onset of this dramatic shift in climate and vegetation was the extinction of many species of Pleistocene megafauna. The mammoth, mastodon, sloth, camel, horse, and others vanished from North America at this time. Often, this mass extinction is attributed to the arrival of the first human hunters, and indeed, rapid extinctions also occurred at other places, such as Australia, New Zealand, and Madagascar, shortly after the arrival of people. Another explanation given for the North American wave of extinction at the end of the Pleistocene involves climatic change and fluctuation that may have resulted in lower survivability of the young in winter. Although it was cool in both summer and winter during the Pleistocene, the Holocene brought on warmer summers and colder winters. This may have led to an increase in death among young animals.

At the end of the Pleistocene the people of the Upper Mississippi Valley were adapting to a changing environment. This point of transition is marked by a shift in projectile point styles from the fluted forms to unfluted lanceolate points (fig. 5.7) characteristic of regional Late Paleoindian cultures. The new styles are often grouped into what has been called Plano—a set of point types that includes Agate Basin, Plainview, and Hell Gap—and the Cody Complex, which consists of stemmed lanceolate points such as Eden, Scotts Bluff, and Angostora. Cody also is recognized by a distinctive knife with a tanged stem. Some Late Paleoindian lanceolate points have distinctive flaking patterns that ripple across each face in a diagonal pattern. These are sometimes named Allen/Frederick and include the Browns Valley type, named after a site in western Minnesota. The lanceolate spear tip styles are not as widespread as Clovis, suggesting increased regionalization of human populations in North America. The appearance of these early lanceolate projectile points in the Upper Mississippi River Valley coincided with the replacement of spruce-fir forests with deciduous woods and initial prairie expansion.

5.7. Lanceolate-shaped spear tip. This is typical of Late Paleoindian weapons and compares with the Agate Basin type. The point is about 6 inches long.

Recently, James Stoltman has recognized a southern Wisconsin variant of Late Paleoindian projectile points called Price/Chesrow. This style was once thought to be a later Archaic/Woodland form, but stratigraphic occurrence deep in Driftless Area rockshelters indicates these probably are much earlier. While Chesrow points have been suggested by archaeologist David Overstreet to represent pre-Clovis occupants of southeastern Wisconsin, they have not been found in undisturbed and datable contexts in that region. Price Stemmed and some Chesrow points are comparable with Quad points, a Late Paleoindian style from the southeastern United States and Central Mississippi Valley, which are well dated to about 9,000 years ago. Nearly 15 Price/Chesrow/Quad points have been found on older Mississippi River islands near Prairie du Chien, representing the first apparent human use of the Upper Mississippi River floodplain. These islands are associated with the Kingston Terrace system, which formed sometime after 12,000 years ago but was scoured by later meltwater pulses between 10,500 and 9,200 years ago. Thus the Price/

Chesrow/Quad points found on the islands represent the first recognized human utilization of the Mississippi River bottomland about 9,000 years ago, and these points cannot predate the 11,000-year-old Clovis complex.

The quantity of nonfluted lanceolate projectile points found in the Upper Mississippi Valley is substantially greater than the preceding fluted points, but sites where these have been found in archaeological context continue to be rare. One such site is the Markee site in the Kickapoo Valley of Wisconsin, where a large, resharpened Agate Basin point made of Hixton silicified sandstone was recovered from a feature. Another expended Agate Basin point made of Hixton silicified sandstone is represented by the base and nub of the tip found near Bear Creek, also in the Kickapoo Valley. A number of Late Paleoindian points have been found on the surface of Mississippi River terraces, reflecting what may be the earliest human use of these landforms. Lanceolate point forms have also been recovered from upland ridgetops and in interior stream valleys. In addition, Late Paleoindian artifacts were discovered in undisturbed soil at the foot of Silver Mound during excavations by the University of Wisconsin–Oshkosh.

A unique find of Late Paleoindian artifacts in the Driftless Area is the Kriesel Cache. On a fall day in 1968, David Kriesel was carrying a bee box from the Black River bottoms in Jackson County to his house on an adjacent terrace and decided to take a shortcut up a wooded ravine. Near the top, in the fallen leaves, he spotted a shiny piece of silicified sandstone. Putting down the box, he gently tugged the stone out. It was a beautiful 6-inch-long chipped tool resembling a knife, and Kriesel heard it scrape against another as it emerged from the ground. Pushing away the leaves, he soon had recovered a stack of 74 similar knives, all pointing in the same direction (fig. 5.8). He had found a rare prehistoric cache.

"Cache" is a French word that refers to storing things in the ground. Caches of chipped-stone preforms were buried with the apparent intent of returning when the need for retooling arose. Several Clovis preform caches have been found in the western United States, and a number of Late Archaic/Early Woodland preform caches are documented for the Midwest. The Kriesel Cache preforms are all made of a fine-grained silicified sandstone that is probably from a newly located source in Monroe County. These are long and slender lanceolate-shaped points. Most have collateral flaking, where symmetrical flakes from both edges meet at a central ridge. This type of flaking is distinctive of Late Paleoindian (10,000 years old) spear tips such as Agate Basin points. The lower edges of finished Agate Basin points were usually dulled through grinding to prevent cutting the lashing used to haft these

5.8. The Kriesel Cache of lanceolate points. Scale in centimeters.

onto spear shafts. None of the Kriesel Cache preforms have ground bases, so we presume they were never hafted. The Kriesel Cache is a unique find of a set of Agate Basin preforms that were buried nearly 10,000 years ago. It is the only Late Paleoindian preform cache known, although several Late Paleoindian burial caches are reported for eastern and northern Wisconsin. Why the Kriesel preforms were left there and why no one ever returned to claim and use them are mysteries.

One possible Late Paleoindian bison kill site is located along the St. Croix River. This site was found in 1936 by Civilian Conservation Corps (CCC) workers during construction activities in a peat bog at what is now Interstate State Park. In addition to bison bones, a 10-inch-long copper awl and two stone artifacts were found 40 inches below the surface at the base of the peat. The size and shape of the bony horn cores on the bison skulls indicate that the species of bison was the extinct form *B. occidentalis*. Unfortunately, the possible association of the artifacts with the bones was not professionally documented.

Well-preserved bison bones are relatively common finds in bogs of east-central Minnesota. Excavations at a bog near Lake Itasca found a Quad-like spear tip and several side-notched points in apparent association with *B. occidentalis*. These were radiocarbon dated between 10,000 and 7,000 years ago. The easternmost *B. occidentalis* find is the Rud site located in a small feeder stream of the Buffalo River in western Wisconsin. The Rud site has produced

5.9. Terry Liska holding two of five large basalt adzes he found while installing an underground power cable in his yard near Ferryville.

numerous bison bones that have eroded from the base of a peat deposit since the 1930s. These represent at least five animals, and preservation is so complete that bone marrow was found (fig. 5.2). No artifacts have yet been found with the Rud bison bone bed, but a spurred scraper made of Cochrane chert found nearby may indicate Paleoindian activity at this location.

Late Paleoindian cultures may have ventured into woodworking. In the Central and Lower Mississippi Valley, chipped-stone adzes have been documented with the nearly 10,000-year-old Dalton complex. In the forests west of Lake Superior, three-sided trihedral adzes are thought to be associated with Late Paleoindian camps on ancient beach lines, but these are not well dated. In the northeastern United States and adjacent portions of Canada, ground-stone adzes and gouges are found with later Archaic cultures. A small number of trihedral adzes have also been found along the Upper Mississippi River, indicating possible Late Paleoindian woodworking along the river. These are made of basalt, with a flat base and a highly polished, curved cutting end. Several of the adzes along the Upper Mississippi Valley are nearly a foot long, including a set of three found near Prairie du Chien in the late 1920s; one on the blufftops overlooking Lansing, Iowa; and a cache of five found near Ferryville in 2001 (fig. 5.9). Smaller adzes have also been found in the Kickapoo Valley. The function of the adzes is uncertain, but they may have been used to fashion dugout boats, bowls, or other perishable items.

9,000 B.P.		5,000 B.P.	3,500 B.P.	2,500 B.P.
	EARLY ARCHAIC		MIDDLE ARCHAIC	LATE ARCHAIC

CHAPTER SIX

The Archaic Tradition

The people living during the final phase of the Late Paleoindian period experienced an environment that was rapidly changing. By 10,000 years ago, the Pleistocene megafauna had become extinct, and the habitat of the Upper Mississippi River Valley was becoming essentially modern. These shifts mark the beginning of the Holocene era, which continues today. While regional vegetation communities changed several times over the next 4,000 years in response to the northern contraction of glacial ice, the animals that people hunted for food and hides were modern species. The most important mammals included white-tailed deer, American elk, and, in the less rugged portions of the Upper Mississippi Valley, bison.

The term "Archaic" simply means old; it is assigned by archaeologists to artifact assemblages in eastern North America that share certain characteristics. Archaic people were hunters and gatherers of wild resources who moved seasonally to position themselves at the best locations for harvesting desired plants and animals. The Archaic tradition spans a period of nearly 8,000 years and is subdivided into three stages based on technological innovations and burial patterns.

Archaic societies are often defined on the basis of their tool types, partic-

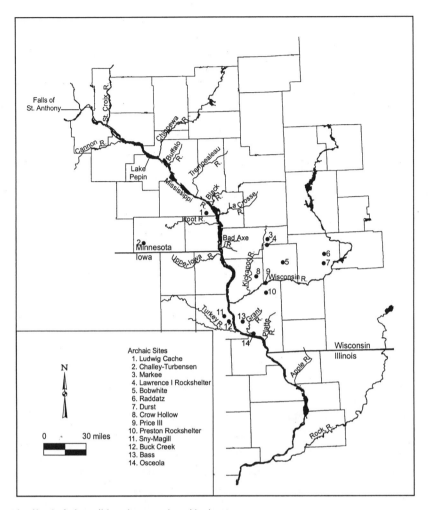

6.1. Key Archaic tradition sites mentioned in the text.

ularly their projectile point shapes. Archaic cultures are generally recognized for the absence of ceramic or pottery cooking vessels; an absence of earth or stone burial mounds; not cultivating domesticated tropical plants such as corn; and initiating small-scale gardening or horticulture of local domesticates at the very end of the tradition. The Archaic began with the Holocene and ended with the adoption of landmark innovations, especially the regular production of pottery containers for cooking, horticulture, and construction of earth mounds to cover the dead.

After 9,000 years ago, increasingly warm and dry conditions allowed prairie vegetation to expand over large parts of the region. This drier period, called the Altithermal, persisted for several thousand years, peaking at about 7,000 years ago. The Altithermal probably led to lower water levels in the Upper Mississippi River proper and may have seen the Mississippi more deeply entrenched and reduced in volume. If the Upper Mississippi Valley experienced these conditions, it seems reasonable to expect that camp sites would have been situated along the lowered shorelines, only to become submerged as moister conditions returned and water levels rose.

Therefore, some Early Archaic sites may have been buried by subsequent flood sediments. Recorded Early Archaic sites are relatively rare in the northern portion of the Upper Mississippi Valley (fig. 6.1). Contemporary sites in Illinois and Missouri show that projectile point styles evolved out of lanceolate forms into stemmed and notched styles referred to by such names as Hardin Barbed, Thebes, and St. Charles. These styles occur in small numbers at surface sites throughout the region, especially in the southern part of the Upper Mississippi Valley. A Thebes point was reported to have been found with the remains of an extinct peccary in a small cave in Grant County. North of the Wisconsin River in western Wisconsin, a number of specimens related to the stemmed types Scottsbluff and Hardin Barbed have been recovered near the Silver Mound quarries in Jackson County (fig. 6.2). Several St. Charles points made of Hixton silicified sandstone have been found throughout the Driftless Area. A heavily reworked St. Charles point was also recovered during excavations at the Challey-Turbensen chert workshop site on the uplands of southeastern Minnesota. This artifact was made from a nonlocal chert and was probably discarded when replaced with a fresh point made from the local chert. The occasional square-notched Thebes points found in the Upper Mississippi Valley are usually made of Burlington chert originating along the Mississippi River to the south.

The Bass Site

The Bass site is an Early Archaic quarry and workshop located south of the Wisconsin River on a high drainage divide near Lancaster in central Grant County. This site was partially excavated by James B. Stoltman in 1976. Good-quality Galena chert was exposed in an upland ravine during the early post-glacial period and found by Early Archaic people. They collected chert from the exposure and carried it to the surrounding higher ground, where it was worked into lighter weight, transportable preforms or finished projectile points. These people produced Hardin Barbed points typical of the style that is widespread in Illinois and Iowa. They seem to have returned to the site many times, perhaps as a part of their annual subsistence round.

6.2. Scottsbluff/Eden point with basal ears made of Hixton silicified sandstone from Jackson County.

Tens of thousands of flakes cover approximately 100 acres at the Bass site. In addition to the flakes and point preforms that broke during manufacture, surface collections found a number of complete Hardin Barbed points (fig. 6.3), numerous end scrapers, and hammerstones. The hammerstones are made of granite and other nonlocal rock that had to have been carried to the site. Moreover, a number of tools were made of Hixton silicified sandstone, the source of which is 140 miles to the north. The presence of end scrapers indicates that animal hides were processed at the site, a task that may be associated with women. This would suggest that families visited the Bass site as part of their band's annual round.

One part of the site had never been plowed. This location produced discrete, intact deposits of chert-knapping debris (fig. 6.4) with associated hammerstones. One debris cluster contained a fine, complete Hardin Barbed point of the local Galena chert and a Scottsbluff-like point basal fragment made of Hixton silicified sandstone. This latter specimen may have been discarded as

6.3. Hardin Barbed spear tips and knives found at the Bass site. The type has been found in Early Archaic stage contexts dating to about 8,000 years ago. The scale is 6 centimeters long. Photo courtesy of Jeffery Behm.

6.4. Concentration of chert-knapping debris in place (profile wall above the trowel) at the Bass site in Grant County. This feature was encountered during excavations by the University of Wisconsin–Madison in 1976 and represents a 7,000- to 9,000-year-old chert extraction workshop.

part of a retooling operation, where the point base was cut from its haft and dropped in the debris.

The use of the Bass site chert source appears restricted to people making Hardin Barbed points who visited for perhaps one or two generations. Site use was discontinued as the dry Altithermal climate caused sediment deposition that buried the chert until it was reexposed by erosion from historic farming.

After 7,000 years ago, the warm and dry conditions of the Altithermal were slowly replaced by increasingly moist weather. Coinciding with this period of increased moisture, the archaeological record shows a greater human use of the landscape. Such use probably reflects several concurrent changes, including an increased human population supported by a greater diversity of natural resources in maturing riverine ecosystems.

The Middle Archaic is defined by several shifts in cultural patterns. Settlements are more conspicuous due to their larger size and higher density of cultural materials. Cultural shifts were perhaps spurred on by the effects of changing mid-Holocene habitats and the availability of new aquatic habitats containing abundant resources, and larger sites seem to reflect reoccupation over long periods of time. The reoccupation indicates a focus on selected, high-quality, dependable food resources. The Middle Archaic also coincides with the first substantial cemeteries in the prehistoric record. A few Middle Archaic sites along the Upper Mississippi Valley have yielded evidence of pit features dug into the ground by the prehistoric occupants for various purposes. Excavations at the Eisele's Hill site found a Middle Archaic layer buried and sealed within an alluvial fan at the base of the bluffs near Muscatine, Iowa. The excavations, done in advance of highway construction that would have destroyed the site, found large roasting pits associated with apparent oval-shaped houses and an extensive midden. These support interpretations from Middle Archaic levels at the well-known Koster site on the Illinois side of the Mississippi River that indicate a prolonged stay and at least seasonal sedentism during this period.

New technological innovations are evident during the Middle Archaic in the form of a variety of ground-stone woodworking tools such as grooved axes (fig. 6.5). The manufacture of side-notched projectile points became common and widespread. Along the Upper Mississippi Valley, these points are commonly called Matanzas, Raddatz, or Osceola (fig. 6.6). Matanzas points are better known for Illinois, where they have been found in several stratified contexts, including the Koster site. These points are well dated in Illinois to around 6,000 to 5,000 B.P. and have only recently been recognized in the Driftless Area. Late 1990s' test excavations by the Museum Archaeology Program at the State Historical Society of Wisconsin at the Crow Hollow site in the lower Kickapoo Valley found several Matanzas side-notched points in a buried soil, and an associated feature produced a radiocarbon date of 4,330 B.P. Raddatz and Osceola points are named after important sites in western Wisconsin. Numerous radiocarbon dates from cultural layers in several rock-shelters that contained Raddatz points are consistently between 5,000 to 3,500 years old. Two dates from the Osceola site in Grant County and another from the Buck Creek site in northeast Iowa, where a Raddatz point was found in a small hearth, agree with this age range. The Eisele's Hill site near Muscatine also produced Osceola points and a series of dates at 4,500 B.P. Side-notched points are commonly found in rockshelters, on upland ridges, on terraces, and at some floodplain locations. They document increased human utilization of Upper Mississippi River islands and indicate greater utilization of aquatic resources.

During this period, artifacts called bannerstones appear across much of eastern North America. Bannerstones are finely ground and drilled artifacts of various shapes, usually made from colorful stone such as banded slate. These have been found in place with hooked bone implements in the south-

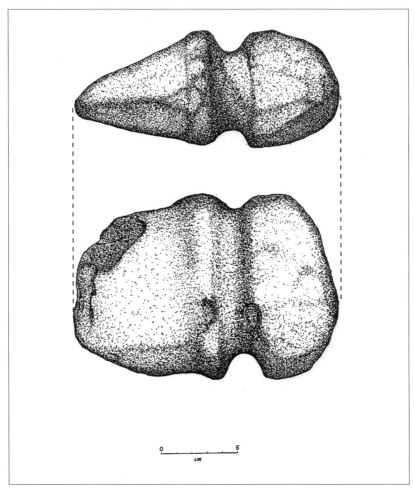

6.5. Side (top) and top (bottom) views of a fully grooved ground-stone ax made from basalt. Drawings by Jiro Manabe.

eastern United States and were almost certainly affixed to wooden spear-throwing sticks called atlatls. The back of the spear shaft sat in the hook, and bannerstones probably served in part as a counterweight to the assembly, adding thrust. Bannerstone shapes probably held symbolic and perhaps ritual significance, and a variety of patterns were crafted, many of which conform to subregions within the eastern Woodlands. Atlatls may have been in use since Paleoindian times or perhaps were introduced during the period when spear tips first became notched during the Early Archaic.

Bannerstones are rare in the Upper Mississippi Valley. A banded slate ban-

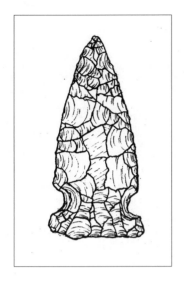

6.6. An example of the relatively common Raddatz side-notched point. This type was first defined from numerous specimens found in the Raddatz Rock-shelter in Sauk County. Side-notched points are typical of the Middle to Late Archaic stages dating from about 5,000 to 3,500 years ago. The point is approximately 2 inches long. Drawing by Jiro Manabe.

nerstone has been found in the Coon Creek drainage of Vernon County (fig. 6.7). A bar-shaped bannerstone made of hard basalt, with an incompletely drilled hole, was found in the Kickapoo Valley, and another was found with a burial at the Bobwhite site in Richland County. One recorded bannerstone appears to have been made of catlinite, a red pipestone from southwestern Minnesota, and atlatls with apparent bannerstone weights are depicted at the nearby Jeffers pictograph site. At Jeffers, these images are interpreted as having been pecked into a hard quartzite exposure by Archaic people based on the depictions of bannerstones and atlatls, which are not known to have been used by succeeding cultures in the region.

Another Middle Archaic innovation was the first regular use of copper for the manufacture of tools and weapons. The so-called Old Copper Culture is defined on the basis of extensive use of native copper by some Archaic societies, particularly in eastern Wisconsin. Great deposits of nearly pure copper occur in portions of the Lake Superior Basin, especially along the Keweenaw Peninsula of Upper Michigan and on Isle Royale in northwestern Lake Superior. This island was extensively mined for veins of copper that were exposed by glacial erosion. Seams of copper were followed, and the resulting pock-marked landscape of ancient quarry pits remains to this day. Archaeological work on Isle Royale indicates that Archaic people were the first to extract copper from this island. Most of the prehistoric mining pits on the Keweenaw Peninsula were obliterated by nineteenth-century commercial mining, although some remain. In northern Wisconsin, considerable amounts of float

6.7. A bannerstone made of banded slate found in Vernon County. Note the drilled hole through the center, indicating this was probably placed on a stick—presumably as part of a spear-thrower, or atlatl.

copper, dislodged and redeposited by glacial ice, could be found in streams and other erosional exposures.

In the late nineteenth and early twentieth centuries, thousands of Old Copper artifacts were recovered by farmers as surface finds, especially in eastern Wisconsin. Artifact collectors such as Henry Hamilton placed ads in local newspapers offering to purchase copper artifacts. Hamilton carefully documented these surface finds, providing an invaluable source of technological, stylistic, and distributional data. His collection of thousands of copper artifacts is now housed at the State Historical Society of Wisconsin. Copper tools are less common in the Upper Mississippi Valley than in eastern Wisconsin, but they occur sporadically across northwestern and west-central Wisconsin, northern Iowa, and north-central Minnesota. Several Old Copper socketed knives or spear tips have been found on blufftops overlooking the Mississippi Valley near La Crosse (fig. 6.8), and records from the 1860s mention three copper socketed axes or spuds that were found during the initial construction of downtown La Crosse. One of these was donated to the State Historical Society of Wisconsin, where it remains. The others were apparently kept by the finders and have long since been lost.

The technology involved in the manufacture of artifacts associated with the Old Copper Culture is well understood from the study of ancient specimens and modern experimental replication of copper tools. Contrary to many claims, copper was not melted and cast in North America. Instead, copper was annealed. Fresh copper was cold-hammered until stress cracks began to

6.8. Socketed copper spear tip. These points are typical of the Middle to Late Archaic Old Copper Culture dating from about 5,000 to 3,500 years ago. They occur across the upper Midwest but are most concentrated in eastern Wisconsin. Photo courtesy of Thomas Pleger.

develop. Then the copper was heated in a fire and quenched in water. This heating and quenching relieved the stress-caused brittleness so that successful shaping by cold-hammering could continue.

Copper spear tips, knives, and other tools have been widely recovered as surface finds but are relatively rare at excavated habitation sites. Most of the archaeologically excavated Old Copper artifacts have been found in association with Archaic burials, such as at the Oconto site on the western side of Green Bay. The use of copper for tools declined substantially by about 3,500 years ago. From then on, copper was more commonly crafted into ornamental bracelets and beads, as seen at the Riverside cemetery, also on the west side of Green Bay. During this part of the Archaic, we see the first long-distance exchange of materials for ritual/ceremonial purposes, and perhaps for the first time the Upper Mississippi River was used as a regular route for transporting exotic materials.

The Osceola Site

The Osceola site is a Middle Archaic cemetery located on a low terrace of the Mississippi River near its confluence with the Grant River in Grant County.

Discovered by people fishing in the area in 1945 as human bones and artifacts eroded from a riverbank, the site was brought to the attention of Robert Ritzenthaler of the Milwaukee Public Museum. Ritzenthaler undertook an excavation that uncovered a burial pit more than 20 feet in diameter and 2 feet in depth. Artifacts included a series of exceptional, deeply side-notched Osceola spear tips (fig. 6.9) and awls or daggers hammered of native copper placed near the remains of the dead. The copper awls suggest association with the Old Copper Culture, which is centered in eastern Wisconsin. Two radiocarbon samples were dated to 4,130 and 3,500 B.P.

The human skeletal remains at the Osceola site were not studied by a physical anthropologist, but Ritzenthaler estimated that the burial pit contained the remains of as many as 500 individuals. The burial of one's ancestors may serve many functions. In traditional societies around the world, systematic disposal of the dead at a particular location may mark a group's territory. A cemetery may serve as an indicator of control of an area that will be defended. Disposal of bodies in a cemetery may mark the center or the margins of band territory. The large number of individuals at Osceola might be thought at first consideration to represent a catastrophic death by disease or warfare. What is clear from similar sites in Illinois and, as we will see, from the Late Archaic Price Site III in Wisconsin is that sites such as Osceola probably represent long-term accumulations of burials of related persons over generations. Artifacts at Osceola and related burial sites tend to be placed with the burial facility (pit) and not with particular individuals. This placement of artifacts suggests that the social group that lived and worked together was more important than any particular individual. These burial locations may have been left open or were reopened periodically to add corpses.

Milling stones for processing seeds, nuts, and other plant foods became abundant during the Middle Archaic. These handheld grinding stones, or manos, mark a shift to the intensive utilization of small-scale resources. The use of coarse grinding stones is reflected in the skeletal remains of Middle and Late Archaic societies, as the teeth of adults are typically ground flat from a high-grit diet.

Several sites excavated in the Upper Mississippi Valley region have produced Middle Archaic side-notched points in undisturbed contexts. These sites include a number of interior valley rockshelters, such as the Raddatz Rockshelter, from which one Middle Archaic point type was named. Native peoples often sought these natural protective settings for seasonal camps as part of their annual round. In the Driftless Area, small-stream valleys often contain rockshelters. Interior valleys off the main stem of the Mississippi

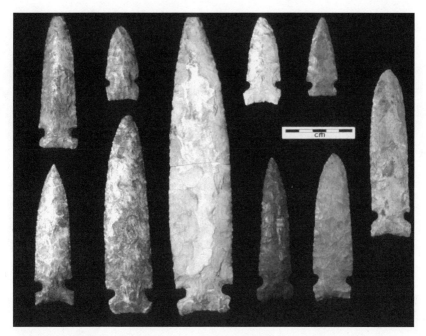

6.9. Osceola points from the Osceola site, Grant County.

were occupied during the fall through spring seasons by family groups or microbands of perhaps 15 to 30 people. These bands focused on the harvest of larger herbivores, particularly white-tailed deer during the fall and early winter months.

Rockshelters are of special interest to archaeologists for a number of reasons. The preservation of organic materials such as bone and carbonized plants is usually good to excellent in rockshelters, permitting an interpretation of the kinds of plants and animals used by the site occupants. The biological remains provide important clues to the region's past natural environments and local habitat. Rockshelters also typically have experienced a buildup in the sediments, creating stratified cultural layers.

The Raddatz Rockshelter

The Raddatz Rockshelter (fig. 6.10) is located in Natural Bridge State Park near the headwaters of Honey Creek, which empties into the Wisconsin River about 75 miles above its junction with the Mississippi River at Prairie du Chien. This is one of several rockshelters selected by Warren Wittry of the State Historical Society of Wisconsin during the mid-1950s in his attempt

6.10. The entrance to the Raddatz Rockshelter at Natural Bridge State Park in Sauk County.

to locate habitation sites with stratification. Wittry knew that shelters, if viewed as favorable by ancient hunters and gatherers, would be returned to over and over again and would likely contain stratified cultural deposits. Indeed, this proved to be the case in numerous Driftless Area rockshelters. The organic remains found in these rockshelters through the Archaic and Woodland traditions are dominated by the bones of deer and by charred nutshells, suggesting fall and winter occupations. The recovery of deer jaws with seasonally distinct erupting teeth demonstrates conclusively a heavy September through November harvest of white-tailed deer at many rockshelters.

At Raddatz, Wittry's work uncovered more than 9 feet of layered Archaic deposits, which he divided into three components. The earliest component was thought to date between 9,000 and 8,000 years ago and was assigned to the Early Archaic, although it contained no diagnostic artifacts. The animal bones indicate that 38 individual deer and one elk had been harvested. Feature 3, a pit containing fragments of two thin corner-notched points that probably represent Early to Middle Archaic Kirk points, was dated to about 5,250 years ago. The majority of the cultural and animal remains from the site (levels 5–12) were assigned to the Middle Archaic and associated with the warm-dry Altithermal climatic regime. In addition to hundreds of stone and bone artifacts, the Middle Archaic layers at Raddatz contained tens of thousands of animal bones that represented at least 203 individual deer and one elk. It is clear that the focus of Middle Archaic fall-winter subsistence activities was the harvest of white-tailed deer. In terms of size, abundance, ease of harvest, palatability, leather for clothing, sinew for strong fiber, and antler for tool-stock, the white-tailed deer was the perfect package. Once it reached abundance during the early postglacial period in the Upper Mississippi River Valley, it remained the principal animal resource for all Native peoples into the historic period.

CHAPTER SEVEN

The First Revolution

The Late Archaic is the final portion of the long, preceramic Archaic tradition in the Upper Mississippi River Valley, dating from about 3,500 to 2,500 years ago. During the Late Archaic, bands of hunters and gatherers manufactured projectile point styles and practiced burial patterns that indicate distinct regional populations and an egalitarian social structure. Late Archaic cultures produced an array of temporally distinct notched and stemmed projectile points, such as Preston Notched and Durst Stemmed. Preston points were found stratigraphically beneath Durst points at the Preston Rockshelter in Grant County and are thought to date from 3,500 to 3,000 years ago. Durst Stemmed points have been found at a number of sites, including the Durst Rockshelter in Sauk County. Stratigraphic evidence, coupled with several radiocarbon dates, indicates that this expanding stemmed type was manufactured from about 3,000 to 2,500 years ago.

Both Preston Notched and Durst Stemmed points (fig. 7.1) are relatively small compared with the lanceolate, large-stemmed and side-notched forms of the preceding Paleoindian through Middle Archaic cultures. Some of the Late Archaic points are so small as to suggest they were made for arrows, which require lighter tips. However, a recent study found that the average

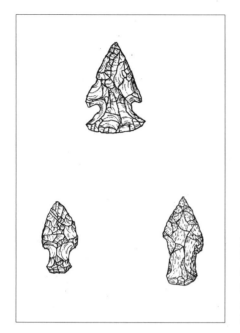

7.1. Preston (top) and Durst points (bottom) are diagnostic of the Late Archaic stage dating from about 3,500 to 3,000 years ago. The Preston point is approximately 2.5 inches long. Drawings by Jiro Manabe.

weight of Durst and Preston points is about .14 ounce, while late prehistoric arrow tips are consistently around .04 ounce. Therefore, the small Late Archaic points were spear tips but reflect a different technology than earlier forms. One possibility is that the smaller spear tips may have been fitted onto foreshafts. Wooden spear foreshafts, sometimes retaining relatively small hafted points, have been recovered from dry caves in the Ozarks and in the American desert Southwest. These points are notched to remain secured to the foreshaft, but the foreshaft itself was designed to detach from the main spear shaft. One advantage of this compound weapon is that a hunter could carry a single spear shaft with multiple foreshaft tips that could be replaced quickly.

Durst Rockshelter

One of the region's most important Late Archaic habitation sites is the Durst Rockshelter. Durst was excavated by Warren Wittry during the 1950s along with Raddatz and three other shelters. The Durst Rockshelter was found to have a substantial Late Archaic component that appears to be a fall through spring seasonal occupation, where the major food resource was white-tailed deer. This component produced a characteristic projectile point type called Durst Stemmed. These relatively small points were found predominantly in

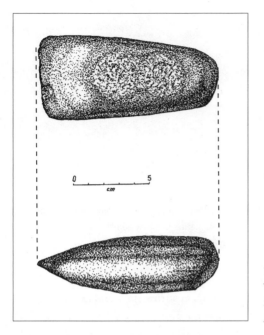

7.2. Top (top) and side (bottom) views of a celt, an ungrooved ground-stone ax. Drawings by Jiro Manabe.

zones four and five and above Raddatz side-notched points and under Woodland tradition points and pottery sherds. Durst Stemmed points are common throughout the Upper Mississippi River Valley and are considered one of the diagnostic types for the Late Archaic.

The Durst Rockshelter contained one of the few human burials to be found in a Wisconsin Driftless Area rockshelter. Although it is certain that many individuals died during the thousands of years these rockshelters were in use, few intentional burials have been encountered. As noted, the remains of individuals who died during the cool-season occupation at shelters were almost certainly removed, to be buried when the larger macroband assembled. The individual at Durst was an adult female having an estimated age at death of 56 to 75 years. Her teeth showed signs of extreme wear, and she had suffered from advanced arthritis. This may have been an individual with relatively lower social status at the end of her life and, as such, did not warrant receiving burial in a corporate cemetery.

Ground-stone artifacts become prominent during the Late Archaic. These include woodworking tools such as grooved axes. At the end of the Archaic tradition, a new form of ax was developed that did not have grooves. These ungrooved axes are called celts (fig. 7.2). Most ground-stone axes have cutting edges but are not extremely sharp. They may have been used to kill trees

7.3. Plummet from Trempealeau County made of hematite, a heavy, iron-rich mineral. Approximately 2 inches long.

by cutting away a ring of bark, or girdling, ensuring firewood in future years. Prehistoric axes and celts in this region are also relatively thick, resembling modern splitting wedges, and battering marks produced by mallets or hammers that are common on the noncutting ends may indicate these were used to split wood.

The Late Archaic ground-stone industry is also represented by special-purpose items like gorgets and plummets. Gorgets are typically flat, oval stones with two or three holes drilled through them for suspension as pendants. Plummets are teardrop-shaped objects with a fine groove cut near the narrow end. They have been interpreted as net weights or possibly bola stones, which would have been tied in sets, spun around a hunter's head, and released to entangle birds or small mammals. Plummets are often made from hematite, a heavy metallic mineral that occurs naturally in many parts of Iowa, Minnesota, eastern Wisconsin, and Missouri. When hematite is ground, the powder creates a useful pigment. Polishing the object creates a lustrous shine. Gorgets and carefully made plummets are usually associated with burials. These artifacts are rare in the Upper Mississippi Valley, although a beautiful hematite plummet was found near Trempealeau (fig. 7.3).

Smoking pipes also first appear in the archaeological record during the Late Archaic about 3,500 years ago. Tobacco seeds are tiny and have only been looked for in the archaeological record since the advent of flotation analysis in the 1960s. Currently, the earliest possible evidence of tobacco seeds are finds dated to 3,400 years ago in Kentucky. The first definite use of tobacco comes from two west-central Illinois sites, where seeds are dated to 1,800

7.4. Tube pipe made of soft red pipestone. Approximately 6 inches long.

years ago. Historic records note that a variety of plant materials were blended for smoking. These include shavings of dogwood and willow bark, known as Kinnikinnick. The earliest pipes are cigar-shaped tube pipes (fig. 7.4) that are often 6 inches long. These are found across northeastern North America by about 3,000 years ago, and are made of a variety of relatively soft stones such as banded slate and catlinite. It appears that some of these were traded long distances and that pipes are also associated with burials. Smoking is a widespread custom among Native American groups that is usually associated with a ritual activity. Since their introduction at the end of the Archaic, pipes were used throughout most of the prehistoric era, becoming common at historic contact. A variety of pipe styles evolved throughout these three millennia.

In the Late Archaic, habitation sites were larger than at any previous time. Camps were seasonally occupied along the Upper Mississippi River Valley and throughout the Driftless Area. These camps were reused many times, and excavations at several Late Archaic sites have revealed prehistoric pits. These pits were presumably dug to store perishable materials and used as miniature root cellars. The trend toward long-term, seasonal reoccupation of single locations indicates selection of the best position to extract the highest quality food resources. The repeated use of specific areas by the same band or closely related bands necessitated territorial boundaries that might have been marked in part by prominent band cemeteries.

The Late Archaic cultures of the upper Midwest developed extraregional exchange networks. These brought marine shell, copper, and exotic lithic materials into the Upper Mississippi River Valley, where they often accompanied the dead in special mortuary settings. For example, a few artifacts made of Knife River Flint, a distinctive root beer–colored stone from western North Dakota, have been found in Late Archaic sites, and a block of the black volcanic rock called obsidian was found at a Late Archaic cemetery along Green Bay. The obsidian came from the Yellowstone area of Wyoming, nearly 1,000 miles to the west.

One Archaic burial pattern that follows Old Copper is called the Red Ocher Culture. Red Ocher cemeteries are more common in the Great Lakes region, and some related finds are known for the Upper Mississippi Valley. These sites are distinctive because human burials and associated artifacts are covered with deposits of a striking blood-red powder. Red ocher is iron oxide made of ground hematite or other iron-enriched minerals, producing a red pigment that may have been applied as a powder or mixed with animal fat or water to make a paint. The artifacts most characteristic of Red Ocher cemeteries are copper items and large flint knives. The copper placed with Red Ocher burials differs from copper from the Old Copper Culture in that, rather than having been manufactured into tools, Red Ocher Culture copper was primarily made into jewelry, such as beads or bracelets. While red ocher was not reported at the Bobwhite site near Richland Center in Richland County (fig. 6.1), a burial there contained a copper bracelet and a bannerstone. This site has been considered as Middle Archaic but is at the transition to Late Archaic.

In addition to copper, Red Ocher cemeteries also contain ceremonial knives, often made of exotic flints, again representing long-distance trade. The obsidian block mentioned earlier was found at a Red Ocher cemetery at the Riverside site on the west side of Green Bay. That site consisted of numerous Red Ocher burials with Lake Superior copper bracelets and beads (sometimes with preserved woven fabric bags in which they had been placed) and chipped knives made of Knife River Flint and a banded, blue-gray chert that originates as cobbles in southern Illinois and Indiana. The latter material, often called hornstone due to the hornlike exterior cortex of the nodule (fig. 7.5), is relatively common at Red Ocher sites. The chalky outer cortex was frequently left at one or both ends, with a bull's-eye banding in the center of the specimen. A few hornstone artifacts have been found in the Upper Mississippi Valley. These include large, bifacially flaked preforms found at island camps between Prairie du Chien and La Crosse and several large, contracting stemmed points that are stylistically similar to Adena points from the Ohio Valley. A few contracting stemmed hornstone points have been found at upland ridge sites in apparent nonhabitation and nonritual contexts. Other Adena-like points in the Upper Mississippi Valley are made of white and pink Burlington chert that originates in southern Iowa and western Illinois. One of these was found on a Mississippi River island

7.5. Hornstone knives from the French Town Mounds in Clayton County, Iowa. Each is about 6 inches long.

near Lansing, Iowa. A cache of nearly ten Adena-like points was found by the Frank Ludwig family near Dakota, Minnesota (fig. 7.6). Most of these were made of silicified sandstone that may have originated at Silver Mound, while one was made of hornstone.

A distinctive Red Ocher style of hornstone knife is pointed at both ends, with corner notches at one end, creating a stem that looks like a plucked turkey tail. These knives are nearly always associated with burials and are more common as burial artifacts to the east of the Driftless Area. A cache of hornstone Turkey-tail points was found near New Lisbon, in the central Wisconsin River Valley, but they are very rare along the Upper Mississippi Valley. Archaeologist Robert Hall has argued that Turkey-tail points did not function as cutting tools or points at all. Instead, Hall suggests that they were used as bull-roarers similar to ones documented in Australia and Africa, where a line is attached to the notched end and then the Turkey-tail could be whirled over one's head to produce a loud whirring sound.

Other artifacts distinctive of the Red Ocher Late Archaic are finely flaked, large flint knives made of Burlington chert from quarries near St. Louis. These remarkable specimens may be up to 17 inches in length. These, too, are rare in the Upper Mississippi Valley, although examples were found in Iowa at Sny-Magill associated with Effigy Mounds National Monument.

A recent analysis of Red Ocher burials by archaeologist Thomas Pleger found that most of the copper ornaments and ceremonial flint knives were found with women and children, including infants. The extensive trade of exotic artifacts that began during the Late Archaic suggests that gifts were exchanged between macrobands to ease tensions as social territories closed. The fact that nearly all of the gifts were then deposited with women and chil-

7.6. Cache of Early Woodland knives from Dakota, Minnesota. Most are made of regionally available silicified sandstone. The dark contracting stemmed knife in the lower left is made of hornstone that originated in southern Illinois or Indiana. The largest ones are about 9 inches long.

dren further suggests that alliances were reinforced through intergroup marriages and adoptions.

Three excavated Red Ocher sites along the Upper Mississippi Valley include one burial area at the Turkey River Mound Group, one at the French Town Mound 10, and one at the Sny-Magill Mound Group, all in northeast Iowa. In addition, excavations at the Price Site III along the Lower Wisconsin River revealed evidence of an earlier variation in Red Ocher burial treatment.

The Price Site III

In 1960–1961 Joan Freeman excavated at the Price Site III as part of the Wisconsin Highway Salvage Program. This site was located on a knoll on the first terrace of the Wisconsin River Valley, 14 miles above its junction with the Mississippi River. The Price Site III contained 21 pits with human burials representing the remains of at least 129 individuals. The site included 40 cremated, 80 secondary, and 9 flexed primary burials. The cemetery included males and females of all ages. Burials were found in two distinct levels in three pits, and one burial pit (Feature 25) contained six levels. Rock slabs covered many individuals, and red ocher was associated with 10 skeletons in two features. A series of radiocarbon dates on carbonized material suggest that the Price Site III was used between 3,700 and 3,100 years ago. The site produced only eight artifacts: four stone projectile points, two antler projectile points, a copper fish hook, and a drilled black bear canine.

The largest of the burial pits at Price Site III, Feature 25, measured 14 by 8 feet and was 3.5 feet in depth with six layers of burials. It was found to contain 88 individuals buried in what Freeman interpreted were 37 separate episodes of interment. This feature contained 15 cremated, 65 secondary, and 8 flexed primary burials. The radiocarbon dating of levels in this feature indicate that this pit was used for the disposal of the dead over a 400-year period. Red ocher was found with nine individuals in the lower levels. Red ocher and rock slabs were mutually exclusive in this feature. One young adult male (Burial 12), in level one of this pit, apparently died as a result of traumatic injury, based on the tip of a projectile point embedded in his spine. The projectile had entered from the left side between the third and fourth ribs and lodged into the third thoracic vertebra.

The majority of burials at Price Site III were of the secondary type. A secondary burial, as mentioned earlier, is one that represents a set of bones brought from another location. They are not in anatomical position and often include only the major bones. Hunters and gatherers moving on an annual cycle may have individuals who die during the winter months. Their corpses may be buried temporarily or placed in a tree scaffold where the flesh would decompose. In the spring or summer, the disarticulated skeletal remains were often bundled and carried by survivors to large encampments where social gatherings took place. At these larger (macroband) aggregations, one important activity of the assembled social groups would be burial of the dead at a designated group cemetery. It is suggested that bodies or, more commonly, the bones of the dead were curated for special treatment. We will see that this practice remained basically unchanged in the Woodland tradition.

The increase in site size with the expansion of Late Archaic populations correlates with increased evidence of violent deaths. Conflict and violence appear with some regularity during the Late Archaic, as indicated by Burial 12 at the Price Site III. Another clear case is represented by a group of adults

7.7. Regional Archaic sites.

who appeared to have died traumatically and were then dismembered. This burial site, called Convent Knoll (fig. 7.7), was discovered during the development of a subdivision in southeastern Wisconsin in 1978. This cemetery includes a pit that contained the remains of six individuals, several of whom had been shot with spears, scalped, and decapitated. This pit was caked in red ocher and contained several marine shell beads. A nearby Red Ocher infant burial contained exotic artifacts, including two large chipped-stone knives, marine shell beads, a copper awl, and an antler tool. Larger populations may have created stress over available resources, leading to higher potential for conflict. Violence was often but not always avoided by peaceful interaction through intergroup marriage, adoption, and gifts, as reflected in exotic materials placed in graves.

Mound 43 of the Sny-Magill Mound Group

In 1952 Paul L. Beaubien of the National Park Service excavated portions of four mounds at the Sny-Magill Mound Group in northeast Iowa. At the base of a conical mound having a height of 5 feet and a diameter of 70 feet, he uncovered four burials with extensive deposits of red ocher. These burials were associated with copper beads, stemmed projectile points, and two Burlington chert knives or daggers. One specimen was 8.5 inches long and the other 7.25 inches long. There were 26 pottery sherds found in the upper portion of the mound, with 25 of these from one Late Middle Woodland vessel.

If Beaubien was excavating a Woodland mound, why did it produce burials with Late Archaic material? The appearance of what might be called cultural stacking of burials from different time periods is well known throughout the Midwest. Archaic people situated burial areas at prominent locations along major stream valleys, particularly where the burial locale would be visible to people passing by. The message would be clear that this territory was owned. The group that claimed it could prove, with the remains of their ancestors, that it was theirs, and it would be defended when necessary. Hundreds or even thousands of years later Woodland people, selecting prominent locations for the same reasons, would build their mounds over these earlier Archaic cemeteries.

2,500 B.P.	1,900 B.P.	1,400 B.P.	850 B.P.
EARLY WOODLAND	MIDDLE WOODLAND	LATE WOODLAND	

CHAPTER EIGHT

The Woodland Tradition

The Woodland tradition, like the preceding Archaic, has been divided into three stages based on technology and burial customs. It was once believed that three characteristics marked the transition from the Archaic to the Woodland tradition: the manufacture of pottery containers, construction of earthen mounds to cover and mark the locations of the dead, and the cultivation of domesticated plants of tropical origin. Now it is understood that these traits moved into regions at different rates and were accepted by societies as desired. Today, the arrival of the Woodland tradition in the Upper Mississippi River Valley is signaled only by the first appearance of pottery vessels.

The manufacture of clay vessels is not a simple procedure. First, a deposit of fine, sticky clay must be found. If this raw clay alone is formed into a pot, air drying will result in shrinkage, producing cracks in the vessel's walls, and it will fall apart before it can be permanently hardened by firing. To prevent cracking of the green ware, a solid material must be added to the raw clay. This material is referred to as temper and may consist of crushed rock (grit), crushed mussel shell, sand, or even crushed potsherds (grog). The type of temper mixed with the clay is often culturally distinct. For example, various Woodland groups used sand, grit, or grog temper, whereas later Oneota people used shell temper. The amount of temper that must be added and kneaded into the clay to prevent cracking from shrinkage is usually 20 to 40 percent of the total volume.

In the Woodland tradition, tempered clay was most commonly formed into vessels by assembling individual coils. After roughly forming the vessel, the coils were kneaded together, often with a paddle wrapped with fibrous cords. The cord-wrapped paddle left distinct impressions of the cords on the exterior surface of the pot. Such vessels, or broken sherds of such vessels, are referred to as cord-roughened or cord-marked. Fragments of Woodland pottery vessels occasionally show distinct breaks at coil junctures. The technique of throwing pottery on a wheel, or for that matter any other use of the wheel, is unknown in the prehistory of the Upper Mississippi Valley.

Vessels were often decorated along the upper portion or shoulder and rim area while the clay was still moist. The decoration was sometimes quite elaborate, and certain styles are common to particular time periods (fig. 8.1). Early pots were decorated by incising fine lines or by fingernail impressions. Later, pots were decorated by using various tools, such as notched sticks or shells, creating toothlike (dentate) stamps. Some of the most elaborate decorations on pottery vessels in the Upper Mississippi Valley occurred during the Late Woodland Effigy Mound Culture. Referred to as Madison ware, the most ornate of this pottery had complicated fabric collars manufactured specifically to be impressed on the still-soft rims.

The firing process is poorly understood. No kilns have been found, and it appears that firing was aboveground. Firing would take place when dried, stacked green ware was surrounded by fuel, which was then ignited. The quality of the vessels must have been heavily dependent on the experience of the potter. Production of pottery containers in most societies is the responsibility of women. The effort to produce pottery containers was perhaps undertaken only once or twice a year during the warm season and may have involved several cooperating women. Pottery-making and decoration traditions would have been passed down from mother to daughter through the generations. The widespread occurrence of similar styles suggests that a woman moved to her husband's group after marriage.

The Woodland tradition in the Midwest can no longer be defined by a simple checklist of archaeological traits. In the Mississippi River drainage south of Rock Island, Illinois, there is evidence of incipient burial mound construction and simple horticultural (gardening) activities during the later portions of the Archaic. Data on the first appearance of these traits and the advent of pottery north of Rock Island are far from clear, but it is generally

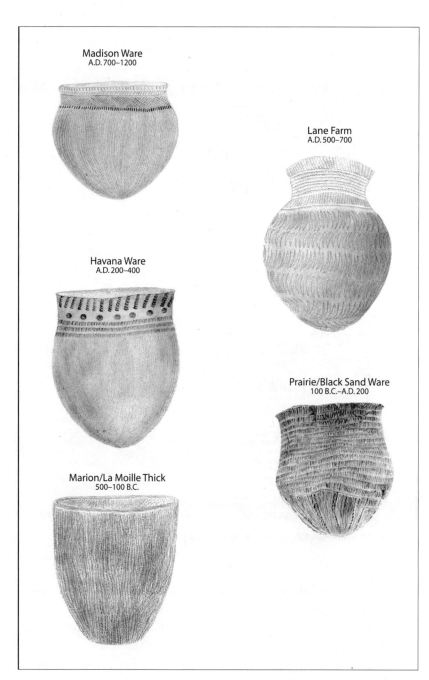

Madison Ware
A.D. 700–1200

Lane Farm
A.D. 500–700

Havana Ware
A.D. 200–400

Prairie/Black Sand Ware
100 B.C.–A.D. 200

Marion/La Moille Thick
500–100 B.C.

8.1. Woodland pottery decorations. Drawings by Madelyn Sarduy.

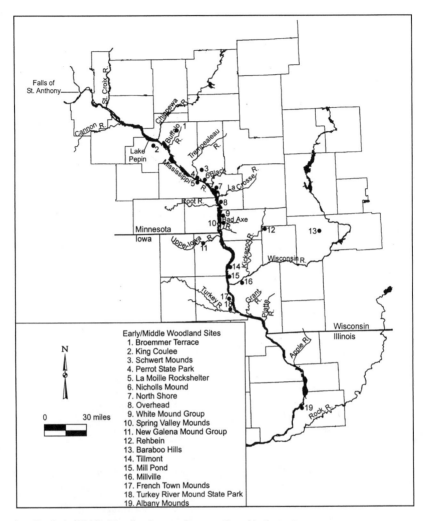

8.2. Key Early/Middle Woodland stage sites mentioned in the text.

Early/Middle Woodland Sites
1. Broemmer Terrace
2. King Coulee
3. Schwert Mounds
4. Perrot State Park
5. La Moille Rockshelter
6. Nicholls Mound
7. North Shore
8. Overhead
9. White Mound Group
10. Spring Valley Mounds
11. New Galena Mound Group
12. Rehbein
13. Baraboo Hills
14. Tillmont
15. Mill Pond
16. Millville
17. French Town Mounds
18. Turkey River Mound State Park
19. Albany Mounds

acknowledged that all three traits have a time-transgressive quality, often with centuries separating the spread and adoption of each practice.

A number of archaeologists have suggested that some Late Archaic Red Ocher burials were covered by low mounds and are attributable to the earliest Woodland. However, evidence for the construction of any earthen burial mounds of noticeable size is not demonstrated in the Upper Mississippi Valley before about 2,000 years ago. The vast majority of the thousands of burial mounds of the region are of Middle Woodland or later age, but some were constructed over Late Archaic (that is, Red Ocher) cemeteries, such as Mound

43 at Sny-Magill. The mortuary practices of Early Woodland people in the Upper Mississippi Valley are unknown at present.

There is also little information on the cultivation of plants by the groups who produced the first pots in the Upper Mississippi Valley. Only one or two occupation sites have been investigated using techniques adequate to recover the carbonized plant remains that can document early plant cultivation. A well-sampled Early Woodland component at the Mill Pond site (fig. 8.2), adjacent to the Mississippi River in southwestern Wisconsin, did not produce evidence of domesticated plants. It would not be surprising, however, to find some early cultigens that are known for this period in the southern Midwest (for example, bottle gourd, squash, and sunflower) in Archaic or Early Woodland deposits of the Upper Mississippi Valley. Analysis of plant remains from the King Coulee site, located at the mouth of a small valley emptying into the west side of Lake Pepin, found squash remains that date to 2,500 years B.P. The bottle gourd and a thin-shell variety of squash probably were first grown in small gardens for use as containers or net floats rather than for food. These plants require minimal maintenance and are well suited for regenerating in disturbed soils such as a regular summer season camp.

Early Woodland pottery is distinctive and relatively similar across large regions. In much of the Upper Mississippi River Valley, two temporally distinct wares are found. The earlier is a thick-walled type called Marion Thick (fig. 8.1) or a variety named La Moille Thick, after a reconstructed vessel recovered by Lloyd Wilford from the La Moille Rockshelter near Winona, Minnesota. These thick pots date to about 500 B.C. and are diagnostic of the Indian Isle phase (formerly called the Ryan phase). Grit-tempered Marion Thick pots are generally cylindrical, with distinctly flat bottoms. Some of these vessels are very large, as exemplified by broken pots excavated in the 1990s at the Tillmont site on an island near Prairie du Chien and at Perrot State Park near Trempealeau.

Another Early Woodland pottery style includes Prairie ware of the Prairie phase dating from around A.D. 1 to 100. Prairie phase pottery is tempered with sand and often has complex exterior decorations that include rows of fingernail impressions and geometric patterns of incised lines (fig. 8.3). These decorations are clearly derived from a slightly earlier pottery style in Illinois called Black Sand. Prairie phase vessels are smaller than Marion Thick and La Moille Thick vessels, with notably thinner walls and cone-shaped bases. Prairie phase pots are more common than the preceding thicker Indian Isle phase forms, and they have been found at many Mississippi River floodplain sites, including the sealed Mill Pond site.

8.3. Prairie phase pot from an island near Prairie du Chien. These Early Woodland vessels are typically decorated with incised lines and rows of fingernail impressions.

The projectile points used throughout the Early Woodland consist of variants of straight-stemmed and contracting-stemmed forms (fig. 8.4) and have been given a variety of type names (for example, Adena, Belknap, Dickson, Gary, Kramer, and Waubesa) reflecting regional variations. This style was widespread during the Archaic to Woodland transition in the Midwest. In the Upper Mississippi River Valley, most of these points are larger than Durst and Preston points from the preceding Late Archaic cultures. For example, the average weight of Waubesa points is over .4 ounce, three times that of the Late Archaic points. This substantial size increase suggests another technological shift. The key to understanding this adaptation is recognizing that the straight and contracting stems of the larger Early Woodland points would serve the same purpose as detachable foreshafts. In other words, relatively large spear tips, designed with contracting stems so that they could be easily removed and refitted onto a shaft, could have replaced a compound setup of a foreshaft tipped with a smaller stone point. If this were the case, one would expect the weight of the Early Woodland points to equal that of a foreshaft mounted with a smaller spear tip. Measurements of foreshafts recovered from dry caves in the Ozarks indicate that they tend to be about 7 inches long and .4 inch in diameter. A wooden dowel of these dimensions weighs nearly .3 ounce, which is exactly the difference between the average weight of Late Archaic Preston/Durst points and Early Woodland Kramer/Waubesa points.

The advantage of switching to detachable larger spear tips includes elim-

8.4. Early Woodland contracting-stemmed points from the Mill Pond site. These points were probably made as expendable spear tips.

inating manufacture of the wooden foreshaft as well as hafting with sinew or other twine. Not only would all three components have been lost by missed shots or wounded game that escaped, but so would the manufacturing labor. In contrast, the loss risk for spears tipped with Kramer or Waubesa points would have been restricted to the stone tip only, and these could be readily replaced by others carried in a pouch. Indeed, many Waubesa points are relatively thick with unfinished edges, giving the impression that they were expediently manufactured as expendable items.

Most Kramer and Waubesa points in the Upper Mississippi Valley were manufactured of local, moderate-quality chert or silicified sandstone. A few were manufactured of nonlocal flints, such as fine gray hornstone from southern Illinois or Indiana or Knife River Flint from western North Dakota. Those made from exotic materials tend to be larger and more carefully manufactured than those of local materials, suggesting a ritual rather than a utilitarian function. As noted earlier, ten large contracting-stemmed points made of Hixton silicified sandstone or Knife River Flint were found near Dakota, Minnesota, and another, made of Burlington chert, was found on a Mississippi River island near Lansing, Iowa. These may be related to Red Ocher ceremonialism. Other large contracting-stemmed points made of Hixton silicified sandstone or occasionally hornstone have been found on upland ridges in the Driftless Area, well away from their sources.

The Early Woodland communities of the Upper Mississippi River Valley were probably composed of egalitarian bands of hunters and gatherers who focused on a combination of upland and riverine resources. These bands were probably involved in seasonal movements, like the preceding and succeeding cultures, to take advantage of shifting resources. Initially, the heavy and easily broken pottery containers might have been important only during the warm season. The acceptance and spread of pottery containers by mobile hunting-and-gathering societies in the Upper Mississippi Valley may have involved several centuries of experimentation with the functional value of such containers. The evidence for winter habitation or use of rockshelters by Early Woodland peoples remains elusive. Indeed, other than at the La Moille Rockshelter adjacent to the Mississippi River, Early Woodland pottery and contracting-stemmed points are remarkably rare at interior Driftless Area rockshelters.

The Mill Pond Site

The Mill Pond site, located on the floodplain of the Mississippi River near Prairie du Chien, was partially excavated in 1980 (fig. 8.5). The site, which lies on a side channel of the Mississippi River, was covered with 4 to 24 inches of sediment. Beneath these flood deposits were more than 3 feet of stratified cultural deposits. Excavations revealed two shell middens, 28 features, and seven cultural components within four major soil zones. The Early Woodland component at Mill Pond was relatively undisturbed. A sample of wood charcoal from a mussel-steaming pit produced a radiocarbon date of A.D. 70. This date is consistent with the Early Woodland ceramic and lithic assemblage from this component and with other Prairie phase dates in the Prairie du Chien locality.

The most striking aspect of the Early Woodland component at Mill Pond was the layer of freshwater mussel shells up to 8 inches thick. Prairie phase pottery sherds found throughout this midden leave no doubt regarding its Early Woodland affiliation. About half of the shell midden was excavated, producing nearly 8,000 individual shells of these bivalved organisms, representing 26 different mussel species. Six species represented 83 percent of all

8.5. The 1980 excavation of the Mill Pond site showing buried shell middens.

identified mussels; one species, the ebony shell (*Fusconaia ebena*), comprised 49 percent of all individuals.

We can learn a great deal about the season of harvest and the habitats exploited by ancient hunters and gatherers by examining specific habitat requirements of ecofacts, such as the discarded mussel shells at Mill Pond. For example, the ebony shell mussel was formerly the most common mussel in the Upper Mississippi River, with many dense populations occurring in beds along the borders of the river and its side channels. Some nineteenth-century ebony shell beds contained millions of individuals, with more than 30 individuals embedded on average in one square yard of bottom sediment. The preferred habitat of the ebony shell was a mixed sand-and-gravel bottom under a rather strong current.

Based on inference from the ethnographic record, the ebony shell mussels were probably collected by women wading in the river during midsummer low-water periods. Harvesting experiments indicate that 175 mussels can be collected by one person in an hour at high-density mussel beds. This means that the 3,500 mussels recovered from the Early Woodland midden might require as little as 20 hours of harvest time, or five people gathering for a single 4-hour period.

A general degradation of the Upper Mississippi River habitat over the twentieth century has resulted in the loss of the ebony shell and many other species once common on the main stem of the river. Ecosystem shifts involved the construction of dams to close side channels, wing dams along the main channel to constrict flow, and, most significantly, the 1930s' construction of a series of locks and dams to enhance commercial navigation. The Upper Mississippi River after 1940 was a slower, muddier stream, carrying ever-increasing loads of agricultural pesticides and sediment runoff as well as urban septic pollution. Changes in resident freshwater mussels of the Upper Mississippi River were dramatic, with once-rare species becoming the most common species because of their capacity to withstand increasingly high silt loads and slower water.

Besides freshwater mussels, a wide variety of fish, reptiles, birds, and mammals were taken for food by Early Woodland peoples. The recovered animal remains, when converted to an estimated amount of food energy in calories and protein, indicate the entire midden at Mill Pond represented a food supply that would support ten people for about three weeks. Freshwater mussels represent about a third of the diet based on the recovered remains.

In addition to the shell midden, there were five Early Woodland features at Mill Pond. These included two clusters of pottery sherds and other refuse and three shallow basins that were filled with burned limestone and wood charcoal. The basins, situated at the edge of the shell midden, appear to have served as steaming pits to cook and open the mussels. One of these was packed with charcoal and contained nearly 50 pounds of burned limestone brought to this island site from the bluffs more than a mile away. Limestone placed in a pit and heated in a wood fire could be covered with fresh mussels and then in turn be covered with moist vegetation to produce a mussel-steaming facility similar to those associated with historic New England clam-bakes. This is the most efficient method to open the strong and thick-shelled mussels of the Upper Mississippi River.

The artifact assemblage in the Early Woodland midden included 3,872 pottery sherds that represented a minimum of 26 different vessels, 5,002 chipped-stone items (mostly flakes), six bone tools, one galena (lead) cube, and ten pounds of cobbles. The decorated pottery sherds were sorted into six stylistic types of the Prairie phase. The chipped-stone assemblage included ten projectile points, all of which are the Waubesa Contracting Stem type. These points and almost all of the flint-knapping debris from this component are of local chert, suggesting little interaction with distant groups.

The Early Woodland occupation at Mill Pond represents a short-term camp and processing area where mussel procurement was an important activity. The specialized nature of the activities are accentuated by an absence or rarity of artifacts usually associated with plant processing (for example, grinding stones) and hide or skin preparation (for example, scrapers). Mill Pond is typical of a pattern of Early Woodland mussel harvesting in the Upper Mississippi River drainage, reflecting the seasonal importance of this food resource 2,000 years ago.

The Mound Builders

There has been a long-standing but incorrect belief that a "race" of people dubbed the Mound Builders constructed the burial mounds of eastern North America. This myth holds that the Mound Builders were earlier, technologically advanced, and separate from the Native American people encountered by Euro-Americans during the settlement era. As detailed by Robert Silverberg and others, this belief began as Euro-American settlers moved west of the Appalachians and discovered large, geometric earthworks that in some cases covered many square miles on the major terraces of the Ohio River and other midwestern streams. In addition to these earthworks were tens of thousands of cone-shaped earthen mounds (fig. 8.6). Some of the mounds were 70 feet high and covered several acres at their base. It was evident that considerable organized labor and skill had been employed in the construction of both the earthworks and mounds.

Mounds of the Ohio Valley contained human skeletons that were sometimes associated with remarkable artifacts: objects made of copper, silver, meteoric iron, finely crafted flint, and polished stone. The tribes that resided west of the Appalachians during the eighteenth century had undergone severe depopulation through the spread of European diseases and intertribal conflict induced by population and power shifts. Native populations in A.D. 1800 may have dropped to 10 percent of their pre-European numbers. The Indian peoples who survived in the Ohio Valley had reverted to hunting and gathering by the time of the Euro-American settlement period, whereas 200 years earlier they had been prosperous village farmers. In part, this economic shift was encouraged by the new fur trade economy. Nonetheless, the incongruity between the ancient mounds and artifacts and the historic tribes—who for the most part did not build mounds, work metal, or carve beautiful stone artifacts—begged for an explanation.

During the Renaissance, Europeans had rediscovered the wonders of ancient Greece and Rome. Western Europe had many ancient earthworks and mounds or barrows that contained the remains of vaguely known peoples.

8.6. Conical mounds at the Fish Farm Preserve near New Albin, Iowa.

Educated European colonists had been disappointed by the absence of any great ancient civilization along the eastern coast of North America. It was clear to the first Euro-American settlers in the Ohio Valley that the local Indian tribes were very different from the unknown builders of the mounds. The mounds and earthworks exhibited evidence of an ability to organize great labor forces, to engage in long-distance trade to acquire exotic materials, and to work these materials skillfully and artfully. Furthermore, when asked, most Native Americans in the early nineteenth century disclosed no oral traditions relating to the mounds. By the mid-nineteenth century, the builders of mounds had become the lost race of Mound Builders. As noted in Chapter 4, the myth of the Mound Builders was ultimately debunked by Cyrus Thomas in his 1894 compendium for the Bureau of American Ethnology.

Middle Woodland and Hopewell

In the Upper Mississippi River Valley, the Middle Woodland commenced about A.D. 100 to 200 with the onset of influences from new cultural developments that were taking place in southern Ohio and central Illinois. The most archaeologically visible portion of this new development, called Hopewell, influenced a broad area of the Midwest.

In eastern North America, the term "Middle Woodland" is applied to a

8.7. Regional Hopewell sites.

wide variety of archaeological manifestations dating from 200 B.C. to A.D. 400, when Hopewell burial ceremonialism occurred. In general, Middle Woodland refers to this period of time, while Hopewell refers to the burial practices of the same people. During these six centuries, specific Hopewell traits were adopted to varying degrees and at different times in different regions. Middle Woodland has been subdivided into regionally distinct ceramic traditions, which in some cases have been divided into temporally distinct phases.

The most outstanding and defining characteristic of Middle Woodland is the elaborate mortuary practices that are collectively called Hopewell. The name derives from a large earthwork complex in southern Ohio on what was the M. C. Hopewell farm in the mid 1800s (fig. 8.7). The Hopewell cultural phenomenon incorporates stylistically similar nonutilitarian artifacts often manufactured of nonlocal exotic raw materials. These exotic artifacts are found with burials or in other ritual contexts in earthen mounds. At least

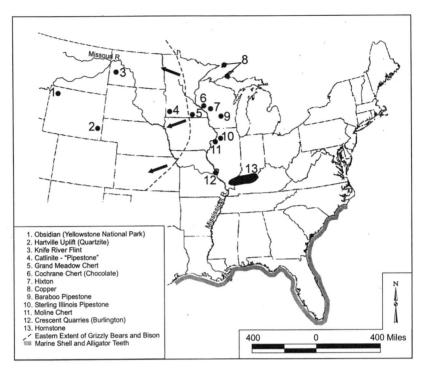

8.8. Raw material sources.

1. Obsidian (Yellowstone National Park)
2. Hartville Uplift (Quartzite)
3. Knife River Flint
4. Catlinite - "Pipestone"
5. Grand Meadow Chert
6. Cochrane Chert (Chocolate)
7. Hixton
8. Copper
9. Baraboo Pipestone
10. Sterling Illinois Pipestone
11. Moline Chert
12. Crescent Quarries (Burlington)
13. Hornstone
Eastern Extent of Grizzly Bears and Bison
Marine Shell and Alligator Teeth

eight regional Middle Woodland cultures stretching from New York to the Gulf Coast were to some degree involved in the elaborate Hopewell burial ceremonialism. Based on the widespread use of exotic raw materials (for example, Rocky Mountain obsidian, Lake Superior copper, and Gulf Coast marine shell; fig. 8.8) and the finished artifact styles destined for mortuary use, some archaeologists have suggested that a Hopewell Interaction Sphere once existed in eastern North America. The Hopewell Interaction Sphere concept proposed to explain the widespread use of exotic raw materials, with associated art motifs and ideology, in mortuary settings among dispersed Woodland populations in eastern North America. In the Upper Mississippi Valley, Hopewell made only a brief appearance, having originated in the Havana Hopewell Culture of central Illinois (named after the small town of Havana along the Illinois River). Ultimately, the origins of Hopewell mortuary behavior embellished with copper, marine shell, and other materials from distant regions can be traced to Late Archaic Red Ocher cultural expressions.

In the Midwest, Middle Woodland cultures are characterized by regionally distinct ceramic styles. In the Upper Mississippi Valley, one finds local variants of the Havana Culture. This Havana influence is found in the Trempealeau phase in western Wisconsin and in the McGregor phase in northeast Iowa. These Hopewell-related complexes seem to date between A.D. 100 and 300.

In the Upper Mississippi Valley, Early Woodland ceramic styles that preceded the Middle Woodland sequence are poorly known. Across southern Wisconsin, including adjacent sections of the Upper Mississippi River, a series of ceramic types called Shorewood Cord-Roughened, Kegonsa Stamped, and Windrow Cord Impressed appear to be regional Havana ware variants. Examples of well-executed Havana styles north of Illinois in the Upper Mississippi Valley are rare but do occur at sites on several major terraces, such as those at Prairie du Chien, La Crosse, and Trempealeau.

The Trempealeau phase is known from a number of mortuary sites in the central and southern portion of the Upper Mississippi Valley. These mortuary sites are represented by multiple burials, often in specially prepared submound tombs, and are frequently found with nonutilitarian artifacts of exotic raw materials. These burials have attracted considerable attention and comment, beginning with the Bureau of American Ethnology research in the 1880s.

A relatively late temporal placement for the Trempealeau/McGregor phase is indicated by Hopewell ceramics associated with burials. Although a number of ceramic vessels have been found in Hopewell contexts north of Illinois in the Upper Mississippi Valley, a distinctive bird motif is not present on any of these vessels. In Illinois, this bird motif appears to be an indicator of Hopewell ware dating to the middle portion of the Havana sequence from about A.D. 1 to 200. Afterward, the bird was replaced with geometric designs. The presence of typical Hopewell cross-hatched rims (fig. 8.9) on vessels with geometric designs seems to indicate a post–A.D. 200 date of the Havana influence in the Upper Mississippi River Valley. Examples of these Hopewell Zoned Dentate pots were found at Prairie du Chien, at the White Mounds at Stoddard, and at the Nicholls Mound near Trempealeau. These pots were tempered with crushed limestone and have polished surfaces, which are characteristics of Hopewell ware in Illinois. In addition, a red-painted (Brangenberg Plain) bowl found by Joan Freeman at the Schwert Mounds near Trempealeau is thought to be a direct import from the lower Illinois River Valley. Red-painted Hopewell pottery also indicates a late date for the Havana Hopewell interaction in the region.

Exotic Hopewell artifacts in the Upper Mississippi River Valley are fewer and less well made when compared to those of the Havana heartland. Some typical Hopewellian items are rare or absent along the Upper Mississippi Val-

8.9. Hopewell zoned pottery from the Upper Mississippi River mound sites. Both have cross-hatched rims and are decorated with geometric zones that are filled with dentate rocker-stamping created by rolling a notched tool back and forth. Top is from the Nicholls Mound near Trempealeau and is about 7 inches tall. Bottom is from the White Mounds at Stoddard and is about 4 inches tall.

ley north of Illinois. For example, marine shell containers are widespread in Hopewell mortuary settings south of Wisconsin, but only a single specimen has been reported north of the Illinois border. Mica sheets, or mirrors, are entirely absent in the Wisconsin area but have been found as close by as Albany Mounds in northwestern Illinois.

Middle Woodland smoking pipes are of two basic forms. The more common form in the Upper Mississippi Valley is the platform pipe, usually carved with a rectangular or oval base and a central cylindrical bowl (fig. 8.10). Some of these are large, with elaborate designs etched into the surface of the platform and bowl. The other form consists of a variety of animals, such as birds and mammals. Hopewell pipes are nearly always found in mounds and are often made from exotic pipestone. In the Upper Mississippi Valley, at least three pipestone sources are known to have been used. A platform pipe from

8.10. Middle Woodland platform pipes. Scale in centimeters.

the Nicholls Mound near Trempealeau is made of catlinite and is one of the oldest artifacts documented from this major pipestone source in southwestern Minnesota. Several platform pipes, including two from the New Galena mounds in northeastern Iowa and possibly a pipe fragment from the mass burial at the Tillmont site, were made from a purple-gray pipestone that has been traced to the Baraboo Hills in central Wisconsin. Several platform pipes from the Spring Valley Mound Group between Stoddard and Genoa are made of an olive green pipestone that has been recently identified as having been obtained from the central Rock River Valley near Sterling, Illinois. The latter material was apparently shipped to the Albany Mounds site in northwestern Illinois, where the pipes were finished and exported. On a few occasions, local materials were used for pipes. For example, a limestone platform pipe was found in a Hopewell tomb at the Overhead site at La Crosse.

It appears that Hopewell in the Upper Mississippi River Valley represents a short time horizon during which some Middle Woodland groups participated in this special form of burial ceremonialism. The association with the Havana Hopewell and the intensity of participation fall off as one proceeds north along the Mississippi River. The Havana expression is very rare north of Lake Pepin, although an affiliated group of mounds is known at Howard Lake in east-central Minnesota.

Trempealeau Hopewell

In 1928 and 1930 Will C. McKern from the Milwaukee Public Museum directed the excavation of a series of mounds near Trempealeau. The cultural materials discovered in these mounds form the basis for what is referred to today as the Trempealeau phase Hopewell, now known to be closely related to the Havana Hopewell of Illinois.

In the 1920s McKern was engaged in examining prehistoric cultural variation from east to west across central Wisconsin. He learned that portions of three pottery vessels had been donated to the Milwaukee Public Museum by Trempealeau resident Ernest Bright. In what is now Perrot State Park, Bright had uncovered four extended burials in a rectangular pit that had been covered by a mound. Along with these burials, he recovered 11 knives made from Knife River Flint, 50 copper beads, two copper ear spools, three drilled bear canine teeth, and pieces of the three pottery vessels.

McKern saw that the type of drilling on the bear teeth, the form of the copper ear spools, and the decoration of the pottery vessels were similar to material reported from Hopewell sites in southern Ohio. He was also aware that Cyrus Thomas reported burials with similar Hopewell remains in mounds along the Mississippi River below Trempealeau. Finally, McKern found reference to excavations by George Squier, who in 1884 donated a portion of a Hopewellian-style vessel he recovered from a mound at Trempealeau to the Peabody Museum at Harvard University.

The Nicholls Mound

Will McKern and his crew from the Milwaukee Public Museum excavated portions of nearly 40 mounds at three different groups in the Trempealeau area in 1928 and 1930. One of the most important of these is the Nicholls Mound, the tallest Woodland mound recorded in Wisconsin. The Nicholls Mound is located on a Pleistocene terrace that is today adjacent to a backwater of the Mississippi River, about a mile east of Trempealeau. When McKern began his excavation, the mound rose 12 feet above the surrounding terrace, and the base was 90 feet in diameter. The excavation consisted of a wide trench cut through the center of the mound (fig. 8.11). The mound base was marked by a distinct humus line. Above that, the mound fill consisted of lens-shaped pockets of different soils representing thousands of basket-loads.

At the center of the Nicholls Mound, a rectangular burial pit was found that measured 7 by 9 feet and extended 2 feet below the mound floor. This pit was flanked on each side by embankments of soil that had been removed in making the pit. These embankments held posts that supported the roof of a tomb structure. The tomb contained the remains of four extended primary adult burials, one infant, and two secondary bundle burials. Artifacts within

8.11. Onlookers at the 1928 excavation of the Nicholls Mound by the Milwaukee Public Museum.

this tomb included copper-covered wooden ear ornaments, silver-covered wooden buttons, six copper celts (axes), a copper breastplate, 20 freshwater pearl beads, and a knife chipped from Knife River Flint. Poles of red oak had covered the burial pit, and the tomb structure was covered with large sheets of bark. The bark roof was several inches thick and covered an area 25 feet in diameter. The species of trees represented by this bark covering include shagbark hickory, hemlock, butternut, black oak, basswood, and willow.

The corrosion of copper slows the decay of organic remains that are in direct contact with the copper. In the Nicholls tomb, salts from two copper celts and the copper breastplate preserved fine, tightly woven fabrics. The fabrics were woven of twisted nettle fibers.

After the tomb was closed, earth was placed upon the central tomb, causing the bark-covered structure to sag and eventually collapse. At the center of the mound, marked by what may have been the depression from the collapse of the central structure, an additional burial was placed about 2.5 feet from the surface. This intrusive burial was an extended primary burial with a host of typical Hopewell artifacts, including a bifacially flaked obsidian knife, a copper disk, a platform pipe made of catlinite, and several large, speckled jasper and gray quartzite chipped-stone knives from sources in eastern Wyoming (fig. 8.12). It is probable that this burial was placed in the upper portion of the mound within 50 or at the most 100 years after construction of the lower central tomb.

8.12. Hopewell artifacts recovered from the Trempealeau mounds by the Milwaukee Public Museum. Chipped knives to the left are made of silicified sandstone, Knife River flint, obsidian, gray quartzite, and dendritic chert. Many of these stone materials were obtained from northern High Plains and Rocky Mountain regions. Platform pipe on top is made of catlinite from southwestern Minnesota. Silver beads beneath the pipe originated in Ontario. Copper axes, breast plates, and tube beads to right and bottom are from the Lake Superior region. Pearls in center are probably from the Mississippi River.

More recent investigations in the Upper Mississippi Valley have documented several Hopewell tombs without mounds. At least two were located at the Overhead site, one at the North Shore site near La Crosse, and possibly another at the Tillmont site. The Overhead site tombs, excavated in the early 1980s in advance of private development, had hundreds of soil-leaching lines called lamellae, indicating that the tombs had been undisturbed since they were filled 2,000 years ago. One tomb contained two primary individuals and several bundle burials as well as several copper buttons, a copper awl, a very small copper ax, several notched points made of Knife River Flint, and a large chipped-stone knife made from a gray quartzite from eastern Wyoming (fig. 8.13). The other tomb at the Overhead site contained a disorganized group of human remains with red ocher staining. The only associated artifacts were a cut portion of a grizzly bear jaw, indicating western trade sources, and three drilled bear canine teeth, possibly from black bear.

The tomb at the North Shore site was also detected by the lamellae in the

8.13. Hopewell artifacts from La Crosse. Drilled bear canine teeth pendants and cut grizzly bear maxilla on left. Chipped-stone knives made of gray quartzite and Knife River Flint. Lake Superior copper buttons, awl, and small ax on the upper right. Limestone pipe and broken clay human figurine on lower right. Cut wolf mandible on lower right beneath the knives. The scale is 10 centimeters long.

soil. A partial clay human figurine was found, depicting the lower half of a person in a kneeling position who is holding a bar across the knees. A skirt or breechcloth is clearly depicted beneath a belt. In accordance with Wisconsin's burial law, the Hopewell tomb was not excavated once burials were encountered. Clay figurines are relatively rare but have been found at the Turner Earthworks and Mound Group in Ohio and at a number of mounds and villages in Illinois, including Baehr, Crabel, Irving, Knight, Macoupin, and Pool, and a set has been recovered in Schuyler County. The figurine at the North Shore site is the northernmost one known along the Mississippi River.

The Tillmont site tomb has not yet been formally reported and was not excavated beyond exposing the top of the grave. Mapping revealed approximately 30 individuals, all buried in the flesh. A few artifacts were noted, including a fine corner-notched point made of chert; a blade core used to produce specialized, long, narrow flakes or blades that are characteristic of Hopewell; and a pipestone fragment that may correlate with the Baraboo Hills source.

8.14. Obsidian disk from Winona County, Minnesota. Approximately 6 inches long.

One role of Upper Mississippi Valley Middle Woodland groups within the Hopewell Interaction Sphere may have been to redistribute high-quality western flints and quartzites. Obsidian found in Hopewell tombs originated in the Yellowstone Park area, where a major outcrop exists at Obsidian Cliff. Root beer–colored, semitranslucent flint or chalcedony artifacts originated from large prehistoric quarries along the Knife River in western Dakota. The speckled jasper and gray quartzite knives found in Upper Mississippi River mounds derive from the Hartville Uplift region in eastern Wyoming, just west of the Black Hills. Obsidian and Knife River Flint knives are known in Ohio and Illinois Hopewell, including major caches of obsidian in mounds at the Hopewell and Mound City sites in Ohio, but the Hartville Uplift material has not yet been identified at Illinois and Ohio sites.

How were these western lithic materials transported to the Midwest? Originally, it was thought the materials would have been boated down the Missouri River to the Mississippi and then shipped to their final destinations in Ohio, Illinois, and the Upper Mississippi Valley. However, a distributional study by Frances Clark found little Knife River Flint at Hopewell sites along the Lower Missouri River in contrast to high frequencies near Trempealeau. Likewise, the gray quartzite and Hartville Uplift chert seem to be most concentrated in the Upper Mississippi Valley. This pattern suggests that at least some of the western flints were transported overland across the Dakotas and Minnesota to the Upper Mississippi River. Contemporary Middle Woodland cultures in the Dakotas and Minnesota are known as Sonota and Malmo, respectively. Sonota is known for mounds along the Middle Missouri River and for a distinctive style of side-notched point. Several of the large knives found in Hopewell mounds of the Upper Mississippi Valley are side-notched, like very large Sonota points. Few if any waste flakes of the western flint materials have been found at Middle Woodland camp sites near the Upper Mississippi Valley mounds, so it appears that the large Hopewell knives were manufactured on the Plains and brought east as finished artifacts. Because Sonota people appear to have been semi-nomadic buffalo hunters, they may have obtained the western flints on annual rounds and carried them eastward to Malmo people in Minnesota, who then brought them to Trempealeau phase Hopewell people in the Upper Mississippi Valley. Contemporary cultures to the west of Sonota in the source area of the western flints near the Black Hills and into Wyoming are known as Besant. Besant flaking technology stands out on the northern Plains as being the most sophisticated since the exquisite flint-knapping of the Paleoindians, and so it seems plausible that these people manufactured large knives.

Most of the obsidian found in Hopewell contexts along the Upper Mississippi River was not finished into tools (fig. 8.14). Several large bifacially flaked disk cores have been recovered from mounds. The inclusion of the obsidian cores in burials not only served as tribute to the dead but removed this material from circulation. This action, then, created demand for more and served to solidify the trade network. It is not known what was exchanged in return, although copper originating from the Lake Superior area has been found across Minnesota and into South Dakota. It is probable that many exchange items consisted of perishable materials such as wood, hide, cloth, feathers, and food that have not been preserved in the archaeological record.

CHAPTER NINE

The Beginning of Tribes

The Hopewell phenomenon ended abruptly across eastern North America by A.D. 400. One example of the demise of Hopewell is the substantial simplification and reduction in the quantity of smoking pipes between A.D. 500 and 1200. During this relatively long period, pipes were small elbow forms (fig. 9.1). Some are made from Baraboo Hills pipestone, and a few of these have decorations, including etched lizards. Most, however, are made of clay tempered with grit, like contemporary pottery, and some have simple decorations made by impressing small tools in the moist clay before firing. Catlinite, which had been used at least sporadically by Early and Middle Woodland peoples, appears to have been virtually unknown during this period.

Likewise, copper, western flints, marine shell, and other exotic materials were no longer traded or even manufactured into elaborate artifacts during the late Middle Woodland and subsequent Late Woodland stages. Indeed, the entire Hopewell exchange network, which formerly reached from the Atlantic Ocean to the Rocky Mountains and from Lake Superior to the Gulf of Mexico, seems to have simply collapsed. Why this happened remains a mystery.

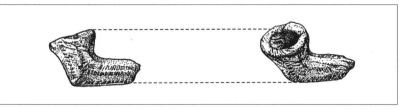

9.1. Clay elbow pipe typical of Late Woodland cultures. Approximately 1.5 inches long. Drawing by Jiro Manabe.

Late Middle Woodland

After the disappearance of Havana Hopewell, or perhaps briefly overlapping it, a new series of ceramics evolved from Havana forms. These late Middle Woodland ceramics characterize what are called the Millville and the Allamakee phases in the Upper Mississippi River Valley. The Millville phase dates between A.D. 200/300 and 500 and is characterized by thin-walled Linn ware, with types such as Levsen Stamped and Levsen Punctated. At the end of this sequence, a ceramic type called Lane Farm Cord Impressed appears to bridge the gap between the late Middle Woodland and the Late Woodland Effigy Mound Culture. During the late Middle Woodland, mounds continued to be built, especially south of La Crosse, though of a smaller conical form and now entirely lacking the exotic Hopewell funerary artifacts.

A number of late Middle Woodland sites have been excavated along the Upper Mississippi River, including mounds and rockshelters in and near Effigy Mounds National Monument in northeast Iowa. These have provided radiocarbon dates and some subsistence information, but major questions remain. For example, the nature of post-Hopewellian Woodland cultures along the Mississippi River north of La Crosse is virtually unknown.

The Millville Site

The Millville site is the most important and remarkable Millville phase occupation thus far known in the Upper Mississippi drainage (fig. 9.2). Millville was excavated in 1962 by Joan Freeman of the State Historical Society of Wisconsin as a salvage project in advance of highway construction. The site is located on the south side of the Wisconsin River 10 miles above its confluence with the Mississippi River at Prairie du Chien. Freeman excavated an area of 90 by 110 feet and uncovered 40 fire pits, 139 refuse pits, 2 burial pits, and 14 house basins.

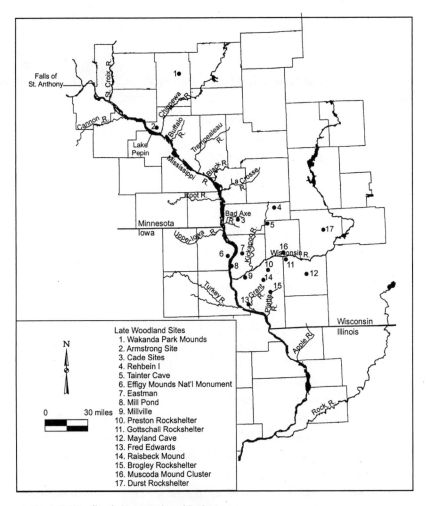

Late Woodland Sites
1. Wakanda Park Mounds
2. Armstrong Site
3. Cade Sites
4. Rehbein I
5. Tainter Cave
6. Effigy Mounds Nat'l Monument
7. Eastman
8. Mill Pond
9. Millville
10. Preston Rockshelter
11. Gottschall Rockshelter
12. Mayland Cave
13. Fred Edwards
14. Raisbeck Mound
15. Brogley Rockshelter
16. Muscoda Mound Cluster
17. Durst Rockshelter

9.2. Key Late Woodland sites mentioned in the text.

The remains of 14 late Middle Woodland houses are unique for the region. These were oval structures created by scooping out a basin up to 10 inches deep and placing upright posts having diameters of 5 to 9 inches around the rim of the depression. The covering material was not preserved, but historic Native American wigwams were often covered with reed mats or sheets of bark. Six of the Millville houses had small additions, marked by extra post stains, that may have been storage areas. The house interiors contained refuse pits that may have been initially storage pits, and several had an interior fire pit. Four houses had been damaged on one side by flood erosion, preventing measurements of the entire structure. In estimating the area of the ten complete house interiors, excluding the storage rooms, four distinct sizes seem to be present. Two were extra large (378 square feet), two were large (247 square feet), three were medium-sized (141 square feet), and three were small (84 square feet). Floor area can help archaeologists gauge the number of individuals that may occupy a house. However, some of the houses have storage/refuse and fire pits that take up portions of the floor. Freeman also found a number of random posts throughout the village area and suggested that these may have linked the circle of houses into a walled compound.

There were four burials with a total of five individuals at Millville, none of which was in a mound. Burials 1 and 4 were newborn infants placed in separate pits that also contained refuse. Burial 2 was a primary semiflexed skeleton of an adult female in an oval pit. Burials 3a and 3b were primary flexed females sharing a common grave. Burial 3b was placed facedown in the pit bottom, and 3a was placed on top of her with her face up. The graves of the three adult females contained no refuse but also no special offerings. All three women were between 40 and 55 years of age at death.

The three adult women had suffered extreme dental wear to the extent that the surfaces of some teeth had eroded into the pulp cavity. All had lost teeth from periodontal disease. The type and severity of dental wear seen at Millville were also observed on individuals at the Rehbein I Mound Group and are represented in most Archaic and Woodland adult populations. Estimates of height were possible for Burial 2, who stood about 5 feet, 3 inches tall, and Burial 3a, whose stature was about 5 feet, 1 inch. The skulls of both these individuals showed evidence of cradleboard deformation. Prolonged binding of an infant's head to a board forming the back of a portable cradle produces a distinct flattening at the back of the skull. In some cases, the front of the skull is also changed by the type of bindings used. Cradleboards are common in cultures where infants need to be transported with their parents either in frequent moves or during work-related activities, and many Native American tribes used these during the historic period.

The ceramic assemblage from Millville is comprised of 925 sherds that include 157 rims. These pottery sherds cover a range of Linn ware types. The 16 projectile points recovered include 14 of the type called Steuben Expanded Stemmed. Additional lithic artifacts include scrapers, drills, and a groundstone ax bit.

The bones from animals that served as food were common in the refuse pits and house basin fills. At least 42 white-tailed deer and five elk are represented at the site. Together, these mammals contribute 95 percent of the usable meat represented by the faunal remains. An analysis of the deer mandibles and the antler-supporting male frontal bones indicates that most deer were taken in the early fall to midwinter.

Millville provides a snapshot of a cool-season encampment of a late Middle Woodland band focused on the harvest of white-tailed deer. This post-Hopewellian settlement shows no signs of exotic raw materials or foreign art motifs. Based on several radiocarbon dates, Millville seems to have been occupied between roughly A.D. 200 and 400. This is the same period when conical mounds were constructed at the Rehbein I Mound Group. As at Millville, Rehbein I contained no trace of a Hopewellian influence, and it is clear that Hopewell's exotic presence was gone from the Upper Mississippi Valley by A.D. 200 to 400.

The Rehbein I Mound Group

The Rehbein I Mound Group (see fig. 9.2) is located in the heart of Wisconsin's Driftless Area. This group of nine mounds includes two linear and seven conicals on a ridge overlooking the Kickapoo River, the largest interior drainage in the Driftless Area. From this location, the Kickapoo flows 45 miles to the Wisconsin River, which in turn continues an additional 15 miles to its confluence with the Mississippi.

Highway construction necessitated salvage of mounds by the State Historical Society of Wisconsin in 1977. Six of the mounds, five conicals and one linear, would be affected by the new road. Several mounds showed evidence of past disturbance, including by railroad workers in 1890.

Barbara Mead directed excavation crews at Rehbein I and recovered the remains of 35 individuals in the six excavated mounds. The data from this site provide a glimpse of the burial types associated with the Millville phase mound burials in the Upper Mississippi River drainage. Artifactual association, radiocarbon dates, and mound shape led Mead to conclude that the linear mounds are associated with the Late Woodland Effigy Mound Culture and the conicals with the preceding Millville phase. Nearly half (16) of the represented population was under 15 years of age at death, with 11 being younger than 18 months. Both males and females were present, with females having a higher mortality between the ages of 20 and 40 years. This is probably related to the risks associated with childbirth under premodern conditions. A brief examination of two of the excavated Millville phase mounds provides a sense of the nature and distribution of burials.

Rehbein I, Mound 1, was a conical 25 feet in diameter and 2 feet high at the time of excavation. Before the mound was constructed, the builders cleared away topsoil and dug a pit measuring 10 by 6.7 feet into the underlying rocky subsoil. The remains of 15 individuals were placed into this pit. Two young individuals, aged 5–18 months and 10–12 years, respectively, were primary burials in the extended position. The remaining 13 were secondary bundle burials. This group included three females aged 20–26 years, 25+ years, and 40–55 years, respectively. One male 60–70 years old was also present. In general, it is not possible to determine the sex of an individual who died prior to maturity based on skeletal remains. Nine individuals could not be assigned a sex. The ages are: 0–6 months = 4 burials, 5–18 months = 1 burial, 16–18 months = 1 burial, 2.5–4.5 years = 1 burial, 10–12 years = 1 burial, and 14–18 years = 1 burial. Three of these show changes in skull shape caused by the use of cradleboards to carry infants.

Rehbein I, Mound 3, was the largest of the group, being 38 feet in diameter and 3.5 feet high. This mound had been heavily damaged by railroad workers, and an 1890-vintage whiskey bottle was found in the looted portion of the mound. Prior to construction of the mound, topsoil had been cleared to the rocky subsoil and replaced with a reddish brown soil. A burial pit was then excavated 1 foot into the subsoil, and the removed sandstone was distributed evenly around the pit, forming a pavement. This pit contained the remains of four individuals. One was an adult female who died between the age of 18 and 25 years. She was extended on her back, and a 6-to-7-month-old fetus that died in utero was associated with her. The burial pit also contained an 18-to-24-month-old infant and a fourth individual represented by fragments of an adult's skull. This burial pit had been disturbed by looters, and the exact size is unknown.

The burials of Mound 3 were covered by birch bark and three evenly spaced oak logs that were 6 to 12 inches in diameter. This covering was at least 10 feet in diameter and was burned. While it still smouldered, a layer of dirt was placed on top, scorching the fresh soil. On this layer was placed a primary burial of a male (?) at least 40 years old and a secondary bundle burial of a possible adult female. Later, 6 inches of new soil was added, and five additional secondary burials were interred, including one female 30 to 40 years of age, a possible adult female, two juveniles, and one infant. At least two adults, one male and one female, exhibited cradleboard modifications to the skull.

Associated with the Mound 3 burials were a vessel and sherds of the Millville phase type Levsen Punctated. The burned roof of the burial feature has been radiocarbon dated at A.D. 260. The fill of this mound and several others produced a small corner-notched projectile point called Honey Creek Corner-Notched, which may be the earliest arrow tip type in the region.

The Rehbein I site burial pattern is informative in that all ages and sexes were included in the mounds. There was high infant mortality, probably reflecting difficulties that accompany weaning. Some adults lived until their 40s or even 60s in one case, but adult females had a high death rate during their child-bearing years. The teeth of adults usually showed extensive wear, and some individuals lost teeth through what appeared to be periodontal disease. However, few cavities were present. A number of skulls showed some modification from the use of cradleboards.

The chronology of the Millville phase is enigmatic. It has long been assumed to follow the Trempealeau phase and Hopewell, yet the relatively few dates from sites such as Millville and Rehbein Mounds overlap the Trempealeau phase between A.D. 200 and 300. This problem presents several intriguing questions: Are the dates accurate? The association of small corner-notched arrow tips and linear mounds at Rehbein suggests a later period, but later dates are lacking. If the Millville phase is contemporary with the Trempealeau phase, how did these cultures interact? What culture occupied the Upper Mississippi River Valley between A.D. 400 and 600? Was the region abandoned for two centuries? If so, why? If not, where is the evidence in the archaeological record? No doubt, future research will clarify the chronological placement of the Trempealeau and Millville phases and the archaeology for the apparent hiatus in the fifth and sixth centuries A.D.

Late Woodland and the Effigy Mound Culture

Beginning about A.D. 600 and accelerating around 800–900, substantial shifts in technology, population, and social structure occurred during the Late Woodland stage. After A.D. 600, the shape of mounds, long restricted to the round conical form, began to include elongated linear forms and those in the shapes of animals, such as birds and mammals. The pottery that is associated with the builders of the new effigy mound forms was decorated by pressing twisted cords or woven fabric into the soft rims and shoulders of clay vessels before firing. Projectile points change from the relatively large Steuben Expanded Stemmed points found at the Millville site to small corner- and side-notched triangular forms, reflecting a widespread shift from spears or darts to the bow and arrow. These three transformations—in mound construction, in pottery manufacture, and the adoption of the bow and arrow—mark the Effigy Mound Culture. This manifestation was restricted to southern and

9.3. Marching Bear Group at Effigy Mounds National Monument is the second largest group of effigy mounds remaining in the United States. This group consists of bear, bird, and linear mounds. They were outlined with lime for this photograph. Photo courtesy of Effigy Mounds National Monument, National Park Service.

western Wisconsin and adjacent portions of Illinois, Iowa, and Minnesota. Other Late Woodland groups in the Midwest did not build mounds in the shape of animals, although they used similar pottery and point types.

The Effigy Mound Culture is widely known for its animal-shaped mounds (fig. 9.3). The variety of shapes and combinations within individual groups has led to a wide range of interpretations of the mounds' ages, functions, and meanings. Only recently have basic distributional patterns been recognized, which suggest distinct regions within the Effigy Mound Culture area, with western Wisconsin assigned to the Eastman phase. For example, long-tailed panther or turtle mounds are common in southeastern Wisconsin but rare in the Driftless Area. In addition, new research indicates that the animal-shaped effigies may be the last type constructed and are one of the first indicators of the development of tribal-level societies (fig. 9.4). One clue for this is that, beginning with Hopewell, conical mounds were positioned along the largest rivers and major prairie-covered drainage divides, such as the Raisbeck Mound Group. Occasional late Middle Woodland (Millville phase) mounds also occur in medium-sized interior valleys, such as the Kickapoo. However, until the end of the Late Woodland stage, mounds were absent from smaller interior valleys like that of the Bad Axe River Valley in western Wisconsin. When they do appear in these remote settings, the mounds consist exclusively of effigy forms.

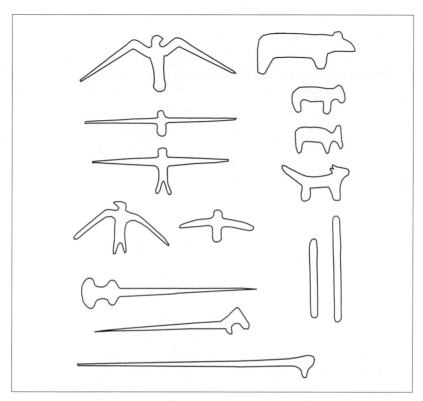

9.4. Selected variations of effigy mound types. Clockwise from top left: birds, mammals, linears, long-tailed "underworld spirits."

The Raisbeck Mound Group

The Raisbeck Mound Group is located on a high, upland ridge overlooking the Grant River (fig. 9.1). Will McKern excavated 20 of the 80 mounds of this group in 1932, and Chandler Rowe published a summary of these excavations in 1956. The Raisbeck group contained 38 conical, 14 linear, 13 bird, 11 canine, 3 oval, and 1 irregular mound. McKern excavated 1 oval, 1 canine, 2 linears, 3 bird, and 13 conical mounds.

No excavated Raisbeck mound showed evidence of stratification, but the observation that all but one of the excavated mounds lacked an underlying humus line indicates that the ground surface was prepared by removing the natural topsoil prior to mound construction. Burials were either primary flexed or secondary bundles. Two of the bundle burials had been partially cremated. No extended burials were present at Raisbeck.

Each burial episode was represented by 1 to 6 individuals, with a range of ages and both sexes represented. An exception is Mound 66, which contained the remains of at least 35 individuals in a single secondary bundle burial. The poor preservation of the skeletal remains does not allow any detailed interpretation of age or health status of this Late Woodland population. At least one adult female showed typical cradleboard skull modification.

The Raisbeck burials were either placed in a shallow pit dug below the prepared mound floor or placed on the prepared surface at what would be the center of the mound. The lack of stratification and the simple construction suggest that these relatively small mounds were built and used only once during a single burial episode because there is no evidence for later use or additions of human remains.

The majority of the excavated Raisbeck mounds contained one or more simple altars made of local sandstone or limestone cobbles or just earth. Mound altars are a characteristic of the Effigy Mound Culture. The evidence from Raisbeck indicates that altars were consistently constructed a few inches above the mound floor, usually at some distance from the burial(s). These platforms were a foot or more in diameter and often show evidence of burning. It appears that the altars were built and burned after the human remains were interred and an initial layer of soil had been placed over the burials.

The conical mounds of the Raisbeck group, like other post-Hopewellian mounds in the Upper Mississippi River Valley, were of relatively modest size. The size McKern recorded for the 38 conical mounds ranged from 18 to 55 feet in diameter, with an average of 28 feet. The height of the 13 excavated conicals ranged from less than 1 foot to 5 feet high, with an average of about 1.6 feet. Artifacts were rare in all mounds. Eight of the 13 excavated conical mounds had simple stone altars, and many of these showed signs of burning. The mass grave of 35 individuals in Mound 66 contained two elbow-shaped clay pipes and a lower turtle shell cut into a rectangular shape. Madison ware pottery was found in two mounds, with Mound 1 containing the remains of one vessel associated with an altar.

One of the most easily recognized mound forms of the Effigy Mound Culture is the bird effigy. The Raisbeck group contained 13 bird effigies. Wingspans ranged from 65 to 180 feet, with an average of 119 feet, and body lengths ranged from 43 to 82 feet, with an average of 56 feet. The maximum height recorded for the three excavated bird mounds ranged from 1.2 to 3.5 feet. In these three mounds, McKern found one or two individuals buried in the heart area. Two of these mounds had burials in pits below the mound floor, and two mounds contained secondary bundle burials, with human remains in the third so poorly preserved that the burial type could not be determined. Each of these bird effigies contained one or two simple altars, like those found in the conical mounds. In one mound, an altar was placed in the center of the bird's head.

The Raisbeck group contained 11 canine effigy mounds. The body length of these ranged from 50 to 132 feet, with an average of 97 feet, and leg-body width ranged from 23 to 60 feet, with an average of 34 feet. The single canine effigy that McKern excavated produced two possible burials indicated by organic staining in subfloor pits, one at the center of the canine's head and the other in the heart-lung region of the upper body. While no clearly defined altars were found, scattered stones may indicate their former presence.

The Raisbeck Mound Group contained 14 linear mounds. This form is often associated with effigy mounds in the Driftless Area. The Raisbeck linear mounds ranged in length from 80 to 158 feet, with an average of 106 feet. The width of these mounds ranged from 13 to 30 feet, with an average of 17 feet. McKern excavated two of these linear mounds. Each contained a burial in a subfloor pit. One was determined to be a young adult male in the flexed position. One linear contained a stone altar, and the other produced scattered stones at each end of the mound that could represent altar remains.

Various Late Woodland societies shared some technological and conceptual ideas, although evidence also suggests territorial and intergroup tensions. Shared concepts are reflected in the transmittal and acceptance of the bow and arrow and the widespread sharing of specific ceramic styles. For example, the motif of alternating triangles is found on Late Woodland pottery from the northern Plains, across the Upper Mississippi Valley, to the eastern Great Lakes. On the other hand, some expressions, such as the effigy mounds themselves, are restricted in space and time. Along the Upper Mississippi River north of the Wisconsin River, the number of animal-shaped mounds drops off dramatically as the valley widens near La Crosse. Indeed, there are 21 reported Effigy Mound groups with at least 69 animal-shaped mounds throughout the Bad Axe River Valley, and only 3 possible effigy mounds in the next drainage to the north, Coon Creek Valley. The edge represented by the spatial difference in effigy mounds between the adjacent Bad Axe and Coon Creek drainages is also apparent in contemporary ceramics and arrow tips and appears to represent a Late Woodland territorial boundary.

Perhaps accentuating this apparent rise in territorialism is the fact that Late Woodland manifestations are the first to show evidence of corn horticulture along the Upper Mississippi River, beginning about A.D. 900. Though not a significant part of the Late Woodland diet, intensified plant cultivation generally corresponds with increased social tension and conflict, in part because it requires greater ties to specific plots of land.

The presence of overlapping warm- and cool-season feature deposits at the Mill Pond site is a significant clue for understanding the end of the traditional seasonal round of alternating interior-floodplain resource exploitation. The floodplain of the Mississippi River appears to have been minimally used during the winter for most of prehistory. Through the first millennium of the Woodland tradition, people congregated along the Mississippi River during the summer and appear to have dispersed into the uplands in family microbands during the fall and winter months to take deer.

Late Woodland at Mill Pond

As noted in the discussion of Early Woodland, the Mill Pond site is located on the floodplain of the Mississippi River near Prairie du Chien in Crawford County. This site was partially excavated in 1980 and was found to contain a series of well-stratified cultural deposits sealed in place by flood sediments. The Late Woodland component at Mill Pond is 8 to 20 inches thick.

Unlike the Early Woodland occupation, the Late Woodland levels did not have a shell midden but contained a small number of freshwater mussel shells as well as a variety of vertebrate remains. Nineteen Late Woodland features were recognized, including four concentrations of cultural debris, six areas of localized burning (surface hearths?), seven well-defined pits filled with cultural debris, and two shallow basins also filled with debris.

Large numbers of Late Woodland pottery sherds were recovered during excavations, including rim sherds representing at least 17 vessels. Five vessels were classified as Madison Cord Impressed (fig. 9.5), five as Lane Farm Cord Impressed, five as Minott's Cord Impressed, and two as Madison Plain. Feature 13 at Mill Pond contained rim sherds of both Madison Cord Impressed and Madison Plain vessels and produced a radiocarbon date on wood charcoal of A.D. 920. Feature 23 produced portions of a Minott's Cord Impressed vessel along with wood charcoal dated to A.D. 1090. These dates are consistent with the ceramic types represented during the latest portion of the Late Woodland occupation.

Nine projectile points were recovered from the Late Woodland occupation at Mill Pond. Three of these are carefully made unnotched triangular points, two of which are serrated. There are two small side-notched Cahokia-like points, one of which is serrated; one, with a missing base, is made of Hixton silicified sandstone (fig. 9.6). This is the only occurrence of Hixton material

9.5. Rim of a Late Woodland pot decorated with cord impressions. From the Late Woodland component at the Mill Pond site near Prairie du Chien. Approximately 6 inches long.

in the Late Woodland component at Mill Pond. The final two points are not easily classified to recognized types.

Although there were thousands of flakes, only a few chipped-stone artifacts were recovered in the Late Woodland levels. These tools include a drill and microdrills, retouched and utilized flakes, biface fragments, chert blocks, and cores. Other tools recovered are a quartz hammerstone, a sandstone shaft straightener, a modified beaver incisor, and a worked deer antler tine.

The Late Woodland occupation at Mill Pond produced carbonized corn in four features, including Feature 23 in association with Minott's Cord Impressed pottery and the radiocarbon date of A.D. 1090 cited earlier. Feature 23 also contained fish remains and some mussel shell, suggesting that it had been filled in the late summer. This stands in contrast to Feature 13, with Madison Cord Impressed and Madison Plain pottery and a date of A.D. 920. Feature 13 also produced carbonized corn kernels, but these were associated with several hundred splinters from deer leg bones, representing portions of at least two individual deer. This type of bone modification is usually associated with winter or early spring occupations where bone is processed to obtain marrow. A more direct warm-cool season feature alternation is apparent with the Feature 15-16-20 sequence at Mill Pond. Feature 15 contained the frontal bone of a male white-tailed deer with scars from dropped antlers, indicating a cool-season kill in the period between January and April. The mar-

9.6. Late Woodland points from the Mill Pond site.

gin of this feature is underlain by a mussel shell (warm-season resource) deposit in Feature 16 and overlain by mussel shell in Feature 20.

Feature 13 at Mill Pond contained two cranial fragments of a large wolf. Wolf remains are rare at sites in the Upper Mississippi River Valley (see Appendix A), so the presence of a complete wolf mandible in Feature 7, an area of localized burned soil, is likewise noteworthy. These are almost certainly bones from the same animal, and it is possible that Feature 7 represents ritual behavior.

To understand why we see overlapping summer-winter features on the Mississippi floodplain at the end of the Late Woodland, it is necessary to recognize several concurrent changes. The Late Woodland period was marked by a series of important innovations that were particularly evident in the upper Midwest during the initial northward spread of Mississippian influences out of the Cahokia region near East St. Louis, Illinois, about A.D. 1000. These changes include: regional adoption of the bow and arrow around A.D. 800 as evidenced by the shift to small, side-notched, Cahokia-like triangular points and often serrated, unnotched triangular points; an apparent sharp regional population increase, requiring new social organization; the construction of effigy mounds, perhaps to mark lineages and clans and territorial boundaries; maize horticulture, demanding warm-season attention that would affect patterns of wild food procurement; and the production of larger, thin-walled pottery vessels.

The bow and arrow offers several technological advantages over spears.

For example, it is easier to carry a bow and quiver with multiple arrows than several spears and perhaps an atlatl or even one spear shaft and several replaceable spear tips, each of which would need to be hafted as others were broken or lost. The bow and arrow also offers increased firepower. As the Spanish conquistador army led by Hernando de Soto learned in the Southeast during the sixteenth century, individual Native American archers were capable of rapid-fire attacks, with multiple arrows finding their target. Atlatls, while effective, cannot match this advantage.

A common misconception is that the small so-called bird points were specifically designed to kill small game. In fact, these points were the right size and weight for arrow tips and were used to kill game of all sizes. For example, small arrow tips are commonly found with late prehistoric bison kills on the Plains, and de Soto's chroniclers recorded the loss of several horses to arrows with small flint tips. The critical factor in killing big animals with an arrow is placing the shot into vital organs.

Chipped-stone arrow tips appear on the Plains about A.D. 500 and in eastern North America by about A.D. 700. It is possible that the bow and arrow was used sporadically earlier in prehistory. However, small, arrow-sized points found in earlier cultures (for example, during the Late Archaic) more likely represent foreshaft tips for compound spears. The first probable arrow points (Honey Creek Corner Notched in the Driftless Area) were notched, a practice that continued until at least A.D. 1000. From A.D. 1050 to 1150, side-notched Cahokia arrow points or the regional variant Grant style arrow points were utilized at Late Woodland sites throughout the southern half of the Driftless Area and westward to the Missouri River. However, nearly all arrow tips after about A.D. 1150 were unnotched triangular Madison points. These points are easy to chip and were the only type of stone arrow tip manufactured by Oneota people who resided in the upper Midwest after that time.

The principal function of notching is to allow the point to be tied securely to the shaft. It is apparent that notched Cahokia points were fixed to arrow shafts. This design has the advantage of causing greater bleeding if the protruding shaft is bumped by the wounded animal. On the other hand, the disadvantage is that shafts might be broken.

Archer Loren Cade replicates Native American bow and arrow technology. His arrow shafts are made from dogwood cuttings with turkey-feather fletching. Cade manufactures chipped-stone arrow tips, which are attached with pitch and sinew. Curing the dogwood shafts requires several months, and the labor to straighten, scrape, abrade, notch both ends, and tie the tip on is much more extensive than that required to chip the stone tip. Cade has successfully hunted deer with his replicated arrows. The first deer he shot with a replicated arrow was hit on the side. The arrow penetrated about 4 inches, and the deer immediately turned, snapping the shaft. The deer ran several hundred yards before dying. When Cade dressed the animal, he found the broken shaft had worked through the chest, rupturing the lungs, so that the point was against the inside of the sternum. Merlin Red Cloud of the Ho-Chunk Nation reports that the Ho-Chunk used willow and hazelnut shoots for arrow shafts and hickory or ash for bow wood.

If notched arrow tips functioned adequately, why then are many Late Woodland and all Oneota arrow tips unnotched and often less well made? One disadvantage of notched points is that the shaft and fastened point tip can be pulled from the wound, facilitating healing. In contrast, unnotched arrow tips were apparently intended to detach from the shaft and remain in the wound. Indeed, Madison points are typically broader at the base than Cahokia points, creating barbs on either side of the arrow shaft. These barbs would not only create a wider cut and increase bleeding but would also ensure the point remained in the wound, thereby complicating healing. While detachable Madison points apparently enhanced hunting, they may have been even more significant in warfare, where wounded enemies could pull out the arrow shaft but not the tip. Historic accounts refer to several Plains tribes that intentionally made detachable points for use in war. Furthermore, recovered arrow shafts could be quickly retipped with points. In this scenario, hunters and warriors could carry a bow and quiver of arrows along with a pouch of lightweight replacement points, substantially enhancing their firepower.

It is not known exactly how unnotched Madison points were hafted, but there is no evidence that they were lashed above the base. Presumably the arrow shaft end was split or notched, the point inserted and fastened, perhaps with heated pine pitch or some other adhesive, and the shaft end then clamped with sinew or other fine cordage to prevent splitting. A method such as this would hold the point securely enough to penetrate with the force of the arrow shot but allow it to detach while catching on the barbs in the wound.

The many advantages of the bow and arrow undoubtedly affected hunting strategies. During the preceding 11 millennia, hunters who used spears had a greater chance of success in group drives, with several hunters getting off single shots. In contrast, the bow and arrow allowed individual hunters to fire multiple shots. The bow and arrow, then, allowed wider coverage of hunt-

9.7. Portion of the deer-hunting scene from Tainter Cave. The central deer has a fetal deer in its abdomen, indicating a late winter–early spring hunt.

ing lands by fewer hunters, although drives were probably still employed in group hunts.

Deer were the most important animal resource in Woodland societies, providing hides for clothing and moccasins, meat for protein, bone and antlers for tools, sinew, and more. In some pre-European periods, the Upper Mississippi Valley may have supported one of the highest densities of deer in America. One estimate for western Wisconsin in 1800 suggests there were 20 to 50 deer per square mile. We have seen from sites such as Millville and the Raddatz and Durst Rockshelters that earlier cultures concentrated their deer hunting in the fall of the year. The bow and arrow allowed increased deer harvests, including the possibility of successful year-round hunting. This is suggested in a pictograph panel at Tainter (formerly Arnold) Cave near the Kickapoo River, where bow hunters are shooting at a series of antlerless deer, some of which are pregnant, indicating a late winter or early spring hunt (fig. 9.7).

An example of the potential aboriginal deer harvest can be seen in a case study of the Bad Axe River Valley, a typical Driftless Area small stream valley in western Wisconsin. If we assume a density of 20 deer per square mile, then a drainage the size of the North Fork of the Bad Axe River Valley (81 square miles) would contain 1,620 deer at any one time. If we allow a modest harvest of 20 percent each year by hunters, then at least 324 deer would be available annually. This number of deer, coupled with the array of other animals and plants (including maize), could easily support a human population of 50 to 100 people year-round.

As populations increased during the Late Woodland, some groups began to take up year-round residence in interior valleys, like that of the Bad Axe River. The combined use of new weaponry and maize cultivation allowed for settlement stability, where individual bands could occupy valleys of 75 to 100 square miles. These resource-rich interior settings provided the necessary animal protein, skins for leather clothing, and rich bottomland soil for garden plots. However, once this new pattern of subsistence and settlement began, groups who continued to follow the traditional annual round (moving from warm-season sites along major rivers into cool-season camps in the dissected interior upland) would increasingly encounter territories occupied year-round by rival groups. The millennia-old pattern of fall-winter microband dispersal into the dissected upland would be disrupted. This is further indicated by the evidence of warm- and cold-season occupation in the Mississippi River floodplain at the Late Woodland component of the Mill Pond site.

Interior valleys had been optimal locations for fall-winter deer harvest and provided shelter, adequate firewood, and numerous perennial freshwater springs. During the Late Woodland stage, many southern Driftless Area valleys became occupied year-round, while some groups remained along the Mississippi River Valley. This is the first time in prehistory in the Driftless Area that all niches of the landscape were occupied at once, indicating a general population increase. Indeed, Late Woodland groups now confined to the Mississippi River Valley were forced to rely more heavily on mussels. Late Woodland intensification of mussel harvesting is reflected in the archaeological record by numerous Eastman phase shell middens located near Prairie du Chien. It is possible that mussels were dried (jerked) and stored to sustain the riverine groups over the winter season.

Once resident populations occupied restricted areas, tensions would naturally increase. One way of demonstrating control and marking territorial ownership was by constructing visible mounds. Often mounds incorporated burials, reinforcing social claim to a territory, but some effigy mounds have no burials, and some (for example, the Raisbeck and Eastman groups) are situated along major ridgetop trails, suggesting their primary purpose was as territorial markers. Appropriately, the Eastman phase is named after a substantial effigy mound group located on the main dividing ridge between the Mississippi and Kickapoo Rivers about a day's walk from Prairie du Chien.

This group of bird, bear, and linear mounds was mapped by Increase Lapham in 1852 (fig. 4.1) and again by Theodore Lewis and a crew from the Bureau of American Ethnology in the 1880s but has since been destroyed by plowing. Historically, this ridge provided the primary route north from Prairie du Chien and today is followed by Highway 27. Isolated effigy mounds were also recorded on a number of side ridgetops, such as a string of widely spaced birds along the ridge overlooking the South Fork of the Bad Axe River.

Conical mounds are absent from most small interior valleys (such as the Bad Axe) and from ridgetop groups (such as at Eastman). There are two possible reasons for this absence. First, conical mounds are generally an earlier form that was replaced by effigy mounds around A.D. 900. Since small interior valleys became occupied year-round only after A.D. 900, all of the local mounds would be effigies by default. Second, population increases leading to year-round settlements likely crossed the threshold from band- to tribal-level societies, and effigy shapes probably reflect the organization of clans in this region. Bird and quadruped forms almost certainly relate to sky and earth clan groupings, which persist into modern times with many midwestern tribes. Furthermore, the common occurrence of bird and quadruped symbols at different Driftless Area valleys probably reflects sodalities that cross-cut and linked various bands of the regional tribe. Thus effigy mound groups represent clan and sodality components of the initial formulation of regional tribes at the end of the Late Woodland stage, replacing conical mounds of earlier band-level Woodland cultures.

2,500 B.P.	1,900 B.P.	1,400 B.P.	850 B.P.
EARLY WOODLAND	MIDDLE WOODLAND	LATE WOODLAND	

CHAPTER TEN

The Second Revolution

By A.D. 1000 the Upper Mississippi River Valley was ripe for another cultural revolution. The bow and arrow had become the weapon of choice, allowing greater deer harvest and tipping the scales in favor of year-round occupation of discrete territories marked by clan-symbol effigy mounds. In addition, corn had begun to be cultivated by local groups, and a major cultural center, Cahokia, was developing to the south near the confluence of the Missouri and Mississippi Rivers (fig. 10.1). Between A.D. 1050 and 1150, these new factors transformed the cultures of the Upper Mississippi from hunter-gatherer-horticulturalists into intensive agriculturalists known as the Oneota. In addition, this change affected how and where people lived and how they interacted with their regional neighbors.

A major factor contributing to the cultural revolution at the beginning of the last millennium was the dramatic increase in corn cultivation. Corn had been domesticated more than 5,000 years ago in Mexico, the native homeland of the antecedent grass teosinte. Through time, 10- and 12-row hybrids developed that survived nontropical climates, and corn appears in the southwestern United States by about 3,000 years ago. Evidence of ritual use of an early 12-row variety of corn occurs in minor amounts as early as A.D. 200 in

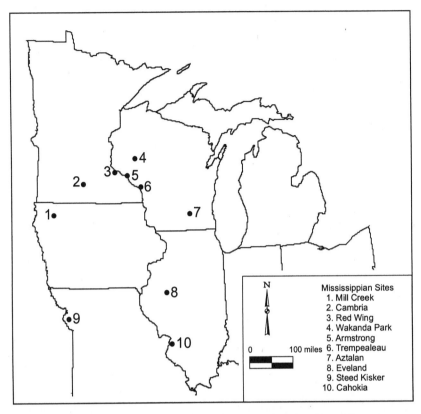

10.1. Regional Mississippian and related sites in the Upper Mississippi River Valley.

the eastern United States, where burned corn has been found at Hopewell sites. It was not until about A.D. 1000, however, that the 8-row hybrid Northern Flint developed, which tolerated shorter growing seasons and allowed relatively reliable harvest across the Great Lakes, throughout the Upper Mississippi River Valley, and along the central Missouri River and its major tributaries.

The spread of viable corn into northern latitudes coincided with a favorable warm and moist climatic regime called the Neo-Atlantic. The precise Neo-Atlantic conditions in the Upper Mississippi Valley are poorly understood, but it was during this period that ice flows in the North Atlantic diminished, allowing safe westward sailing for Norse explorers such as Erik the Red and his sons, Leif, Thorvold, and Thorstein, and daughter, Freydis. Successful Viking colonies were established on Greenland during this period, with outposts as far south as L'Anse aux Meadows in Newfoundland.

Charred corn remains have been found at numerous Late Woodland sites dating from about A.D. 900, including summer camps, such as Mill Pond along the Mississippi River near Prairie du Chien, but the quantity suggests small-scale cultivation. After A.D. 1050, however, corn remains and tools to cultivate and process corn, such as hoes and milling stones, are much more frequent at archaeological sites across this region. Furthermore, large subterranean storage pits become extremely common as sites increased in size and were occupied for longer periods of the year. This evidence indicates a major economic shift from seasonal hunting/gathering and gardening to intensified agriculture, where groups expended much more labor in tilling, planting, weeding, protecting, harvesting, processing, and storing corn.

One consequence of this shift was the need to live at or near the fields during the warm season, and between A.D. 1050 and 1150 there was a dramatic change in the settlement locations of prehistoric people in the upper Midwest. Instead of occupying nearly every niche across the region to exploit the most productive resources seasonally, intensive corn farmers congregated in warm-season settlements at selected localities, leaving vast, uninhabited tracts between. For example, Archaic and Woodland sites are found throughout the small interior drainages of the Upper Mississippi River as well as along its main stem and its major tributaries, such as the Wisconsin. But after A.D. 1150, clusters of intensive corn-farming villages occur only at select places, such as near the mouth of the Apple River in northwestern Illinois and on the extensive terraces at Red Wing, Minnesota. Late prehistoric Oneota remains are exceedingly rare at Prairie du Chien and are virtually nonexistent in the central Wisconsin River Valley and throughout the interior valleys of the Driftless Area. Instead, these unsettled lands were probably visited only on short-term hunting forays by the Oneota.

While corn is nutritious, is high in carbohydrates, and can be grown in sufficient quantities to provide storable surplus for lean periods of late winter, people require a mixed diet to obtain protein and essential nutrients. Consequently, hunting remained an important aspect of the diet, and deer, elk, and other mammal remains reflect this sector of the Oneota economy. However, the optimal warm-season setting for obtaining supplementary dietary resources in the Mississippi River Valley is the floodplain. Rich in protein from fish, mussels, and riparian mammals such as beaver, and supporting a variety of wetland plants such as duck potato and wild rice, floodplains provide the most concentrated and easily exploited niche on any midwestern landscape during the summer (fig. 10.2). It is not surprising, therefore, that Oneota agricultural settlements typically were situated in localities with good tillable soil and extensive wetlands.

10.2. Typical scene of Upper Mississippi River backwater floodplain showing wooded islands interspersed with channels, ponds, and marshes. During the warm season, this is one of the richest econiches for natural foods in the Midwest.

On the other hand, it remains a mystery as to why Oneota settlements did not occupy all such localities. For example, the Prairie du Chien terrace offers nearly identical soils and floodplain resources as Red Wing and La Crosse, and it had been occupied throughout the Archaic and Woodland traditions, yet there were no Oneota villages at Prairie du Chien. One difference is that Prairie du Chien is situated at the mouth of the Wisconsin River. At first glance, this would seem an advantageous location for transportation and commerce. Yet Oneota settlements do not occur at the confluences of most other major tributaries of the Upper Mississippi River, including the Illinois, Des Moines, and Minnesota Rivers. Instead, major Oneota settlements along the Upper Mississippi River were located along midsized tributaries such as the Apple River in northern Illinois, the La Crosse River in western Wisconsin, and the Cannon River in eastern Minnesota.

Another factor affecting the cultural revolution after A.D. 1000 in the Upper Mississippi River Valley was the development and influence of the largest Native American site north of Mexico: Cahokia. Located in the Mississippi River bottoms near the mouth of the Missouri River, this Middle Mississippian settlement emerged between A.D. 950 and 1100 into a complex, stratified society with massive, geometrically positioned mounds and villages com-

10.3. View of Monks Mound at Cahokia State Park near St. Louis. This platform mound is 100 feet high and was constructed with basket-loads of earth between A.D. 1050 and 1200. Photo courtesy of James B. Stoltman.

10.4. Variation of Ramey Incised pottery, the distinctive Middle Mississippian pottery type dating to ca. A.D. 1100–1200. This reconstructed vessel was excavated from Aztalan in eastern Wisconsin. Approximately 12 inches in diameter.

posed of rectangular houses for a population estimated between 10,000 and 40,000 people. The site is centered around a plaza (constructed around A.D. 1025) at the foot of Monks Mound, a 100-foot-high platform (fig. 10.3) that was constructed with millions of basket-loads of earth between A.D. 1050 and 1200. Monks Mound, like many other platform earthworks in the Mississippian world, was probably the residence of a chiefly overseer. This complex was based upon intensive corn agriculture, and satellite communities extended up the Mississippi and Illinois Rivers from Cahokia. Cahokian artisanship and artwork exceeded that of preceding cultures and includes Ramey Incised pottery, a well-made pottery with distinctive curve decorations (fig. 10.4). In addition, a variety of vessel forms were created, such as round jars with angular shoulders, bowls, plates, and long-neck water bottles.

A significant Mississippian technological innovation was the incorporation of crushed shell as a tempering agent for pottery. Platey particles of burned and crushed shell tend to align themselves in a laminated fashion when clay is kneaded, allowing thinner but stronger walls. Consequently,

10.5. The reconstructed southeast platform mound and palisade at Aztalan in eastern Wisconsin.

finer vessels could be made, with improved heat-transfer qualities for cooking or boiling. In addition, cooking in shell-tempered vessels adds some calcium to the diet. Moreover, shell tempering is distinct from grit tempering, allowing archaeologists to recognize Mississippian occupations based on even small pottery fragments.

Middle Mississippian culture developed quickly at Cahokia between A.D. 1050 and 1100 in what is called the Lohmann phase. During this period, there is some evidence for Middle Mississippian outreach up the Mississippi Valley. During the subsequent Stirling phase, from A.D. 1100 to 1200, Cahokia achieved a climax, and there was increased northward expression of Middle Mississippian materials, ideas, and, in some cases, people. Several sites suggest direct contact and perhaps attempted colonization by Cahokians. In central Illinois, a good share of the Eveland site ceramics are clearly influenced by Middle Mississippian designs if not manufacture. In eastern Wisconsin, the site of Aztalan (fig. 10.5), along the inconspicuous Crawfish River, a tributary of the upper Rock River, represents the best example of possible Middle Mississippian colonization. Here, two platform mounds overlooked a palisaded village with a central plaza and rectangular houses whose occupants used Ramey Incised pottery. Aztalan was initially occupied by Late Woodland people who manufactured a distinctive form of pottery (Aztalan Collared) that is similar to forms found in north-central Illinois (Starved Rock Collared), suggesting perhaps a mixed migration. Farther west, Cahokia-

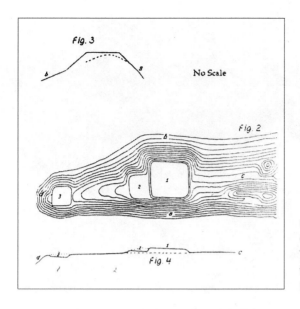

10.6. George Squier's map of the platform mounds at Trempealeau. Taken from the *Wisconsin Archeologist* (1905).

style artifacts occur at complexes along the Missouri River, including Steed-Kisker near Kansas City, Missouri, and the Mill Creek Culture in northwestern Iowa.

Along the Upper Mississippi River, a unique indicator of the initial northward burst of Cahokian influence occurs on the landmark Trempealeau Bluffs. Here, on a narrow bluff spur that overlooks the modern village of Trempealeau, are a series of three connected platform mounds and the borrow pits from which the mound fill was dug. These lie on property that was once owned by George Squier, who mapped and photographed them around 1900 (fig. 10.6). Theodore Lewis had earlier made a detailed map of the site in the 1880s. Squier reported finding distinctive red-painted pottery tempered with crushed shell in his garden located immediately beneath the bluff on which the platform mounds are situated. In an astounding observation for that time, Squier recognized the foreign nature of the pottery and compared it to ceramics described for the Central and Southern Mississippi Valley. In the 1990s test excavations at the Squier Garden site (now a lawn) found additional fragments of red-slipped pottery, and others have been reported from construction sites several blocks away. These are confirmed Lohmann phase Cahokian pottery types dating from about A.D. 1050 to 1100.

South of the Wisconsin River is the Gottschall Rockshelter (fig. 10.7), a site unique for the region due to a wall panel filled with drawings that depict human and animal figures done in a distinctly Middle Mississippian art style.

10.7. Gottschall Rockshelter. Robert Salzer is standing at center in the shelter.

For instance, several of the drawn people have tattoos and spiked circles or sun bursts on their foreheads, and a large bird has a forked eye. These motifs are comparable to Mississippian art in the Central and Lower Mississippi River Valley that is dated at about A.D. 1200. The Gottschall art work (fig. 10.8) has been documented by Robert Salzer, who has excavated the shelter deposits since the early 1980s. Salzer has interpreted the main art panel as a rendition of the Red Horn legend, which was recorded by ethnographers working with the Nebraska Winnebago and the Ioway in the early 1900s. The Nebraska Winnebago separated from the Wisconsin Winnebago (Ho-Chunk) in the late 1800s, and the Ioway speak a dialect of Ho-Chunk and recognize the Ho-Chunk as their parent tribe. If the Gottschall painting does indeed depict the Red Horn legend, the story must have antiquity back to Mississippian times. Salzer has obtained a series of dates from Gottschall and believes the paintings were made by Effigy Mound people around A.D. 900. The stratigraphy at Gottschall is complex, however, and the dating is not certain. For example, Aztalan Collared rims and Cahokia side-notched arrow tips occur in multiple levels above and below those thought to represent the exposed floor when the drawings were made. The distinctive ceramic type Aztalan Collared and Cahokia side-notched arrow tips can be considered archaeological horizon markers, dating to the period from about A.D. 1025 to 1150. Besides occurring at Gottschall, a few Aztalan Collared rims have been found at sev-

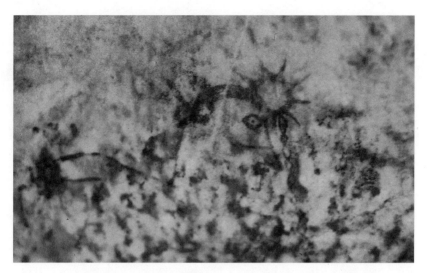

10.8. One of the drawings in the Gottschall Rockshelter showing a human head with a sunburst on the forehead and a chain dangling in front of the face.

eral other rockshelters and open-air sites in the southern portion of the Driftless Area, but this type is not known in the northern portion of the region.

Another Driftless Area site that represents Late Woodland and Mississippian interaction is the Fred Edwards site in Grant County, located nearly 10 miles from the Mississippi River in a remote setting along the Grant River that seems more suited for avoidance than interaction. Excavations were undertaken at the site by the University of Wisconsin in the late 1980s. Late Woodland pottery at Fred Edwards includes Aztalan Collared and cord-impressed vessels. The cord impressions are different from Madison ware, however, consisting of a band of horizontal, triangular, wedgelike areas around the neck of the pots. Similar decoration occurs in the Upper Mississippi Valley at this time, and it appears that this is the last expression of cord impressing in the region. Other pottery from the Fred Edwards site reveals a mixing of grit-tempered Late Woodland wares with shell-tempered Ramey Incised and Ramey-like Middle Mississippian styles. The project director, James Stoltman, analyzed thin sections sliced from some of the pottery under a microscope and identified distinctive paste ingredients that verify that some of the vessels found at Fred Edwards were manufactured at Cahokia.

In addition to finding ceramics with blended characteristics, the Fred Edwards site excavators found rectangular-shaped house floors (fig. 10.9), an architectural form that is distinctly Mississippian, and a palisade line. Fifteen of 18 radiocarbon dates verify that this site represents a short-term village

10.9. Excavations of a rectangular house floor at the Fred Edwards site in Grant County. The square holes around the perimeter are excavated post stains. The larger circles inside are pit features.

dating from A.D. 1050 to 1150, coinciding with the peak of Cahokia. The recovered projectile points from Fred Edwards are dominated by nearly 200 unnotched Madison triangular points, the vast majority of which are made of local Galena chert. Twenty of these were made from Burlington chert that would have been imported from the Cahokia region, and three are made of Hixton silicified sandstone from the north. The point assemblage also contains over 50 side-notched triangular points, which represent variations of Cahokia side-notched points. Most of these are made from local Galena chert, but ten are made from Burlington chert. None are made of Hixton silicified sandstone. Two distinctly Middle Mississippian trinotched triangular points were also recovered at Fred Edwards, both of which are made of Burlington chert.

A similar phenomenon occurs at Hartley Fort on a remote hill 7 miles north of northeastern Iowa's Upper Iowa River Valley, where Middle Mississippian Ramey Incised pottery was found within a Late Woodland stockade. The fortifications at Fred Edwards and Hartley Fort, like Aztalan to the east, suggest that tensions were running high at that time. These are the first forts in this region, and they indicate a new defensive strategy, almost certainly in response to population increases and territorial pressures that coincided with intensified corn cultivation and new warfare capabilities that were accentuated by the bow and arrow. Fortifications substantially enhance a group's ability to withstand attack. Overtaking a fortified village requires a large force, which would undoubtedly suffer substantial casualties in a direct assault. Alternately, an attacking force can lay siege to a fort, overtaking the defenders if critical resources are depleted. Successful defense of a siege is largely accomplished through storage of critical resources, and fortified sites tend to have numerous storage pits inside the palisade walls. We do not know if Aztalan, Fred Edwards, and Hartley Fort were ever attacked, but the introduction of stockaded villages represents a major change in prehistoric warfare in the Midwest at this time.

This sudden and broad northward spread of Middle Mississippian influences deriving from Cahokia provided the catalyst for the end of the Effigy Mound Culture and the emergence of the Oneota in the Upper Mississippi Valley. By A.D. 1150 or 1200 the Native American populations of the Upper Mississippi Valley had begun to congregate at several distinct localities. Initial settlements were located in the lower reaches of the Apple River and near Red Wing above Lake Pepin (fig. 10.10). These Emergent Oneota settlements immediately follow the Late Woodland occupations at Fred Edwards and Hartley Fort yet retain some semblance of Middle Mississippian influences. For example, the pottery is all shell tempered, and designs are clearly derived from the Ramey scroll motif. However, vessel forms are restricted to squat, globular jars that are generally larger than Middle Mississippian vessels.

The transition from Late Woodland to Oneota is best exemplified by the finding of both Middle Mississippian and Emergent Oneota pots in a panther effigy mound at the Diamond Bluff site (see Chapter 11). This site occupies a 220-acre outlier terrace known as Diamond Bluff, or sometimes Mero, across from Red Wing. The Diamond Bluff site, like several in the Red Wing locality, includes substantial village areas interspersed with numerous mounds. At Diamond Bluff, two main habitation areas are minimally 17 acres each and are surrounded by nearly 400 mounds, which were mapped by Theodore Lewis. The majority of the mounds are large, round or oval shapes, with a long-tailed panther, another mammal, and a bird the only effigies represented. Few of the round/oval mounds were excavated, but those that were contained shell-tempered pottery indicating Oneota construction. The panther mound (Mound 26), located at the extreme northwestern end of the terrace, was excavated by the Wisconsin Archaeological Survey under the direction of Moreau Maxwell in 1948. Surprisingly, excavators found both Middle Mississippian and early Oneota pottery forms in this effigy mound.

It is intriguing that the bird mound was constructed at the southeastern

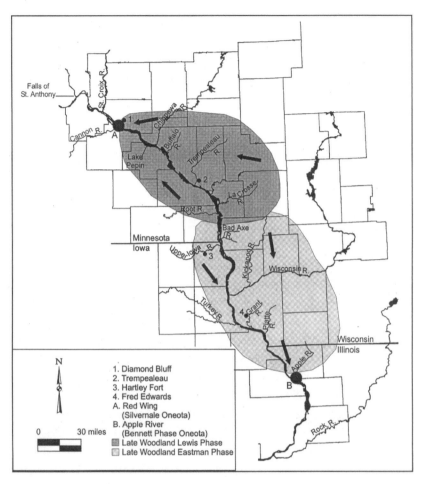

10.10. Transitional settlement shift from numerous interior Late Woodland sites throughout the Driftless Area to nucleated Oneota complexes at Red Wing, Minnesota, and Apple River, Illinois, at either end of the Driftless Area.

extremity of this terrace, so that the bird and panther were situated at opposite ends of this landform, with the quadruped between. Long-tailed mounds are thought to represent underworld spirits. Therefore, the arrangement of the three effigy mounds on the Diamond Bluff terrace may represent the segregation between the sky (bird mound), earth (quadruped mound), and underworld (panther mound). This further suggests contemporaneity with the massive Emergent Oneota settlement here.

Long-tailed panther/turtle mounds were numerous in eastern Wisconsin but rare in the Driftless Area. Indeed, mounds whose tails are as long or longer than the main body are nearly absent in the effigy mound heartland

10.11. Examples of the ceramic type Angelo Punctated. This type is found along the Upper Mississippi River north of La Crosse and is thought to represent the Late Woodland Lewis phase. The carefully applied bands of incised decoration may indicate Great Oasis/Mill Creek Culture influences from northwest Iowa and southern Minnesota. Largest rim to the left is about 5 inches across.

along the Mississippi River south of La Crosse. Lewis's early mound surveys recorded a long-tailed panther effigy at La Crosse and a cluster of nearly 20 at Trempealeau. The Diamond Bluff panther is the northernmost known. In contrast, with one exception, the numerous quadruped animal effigies below La Crosse have tails that are shorter than the body length or no tails at all.

Coinciding with the northerly distribution of long-tailed mounds along the Upper Mississippi River is the occurrence of a distinctive pottery type called Angelo Punctated. This grit-tempered pottery represents a local Late Woodland variety, with carefully incised lines and small punctations decorating the neck area (fig. 10.11). In contrast, the Madison ware pottery of the Effigy Mound Culture of southern Wisconsin, including the Driftless Area below La Crosse, is decorated with cord or fabric impressions rather than incised lines. The closest apparent ceramic relatives of Angelo Punctated are the carefully incised ceramics of the Great Oasis and Mill Creek Cultures to the west. These cultures date from about A.D. 900 to 1200. The Mill Creek Culture is known to have imported pottery and other Middle Mississippian artifacts from the east, and a few Mill Creek pottery fragments have been found at contemporary Mississippian sites such as Eveland in the central Illinois River Valley. Great Oasis sites extend eastward as far as central Minnesota, and a few Great Oasis/Mill Creek–like pottery sherds have been documented in eastern Minnesota and at the Diamond Bluff site.

A key series of sites that blend Mississippian and Great Oasis/Mill Creek traits occur in central Minnesota and are related to the Cambria complex. Archaeologist Lloyd Wilford suggested nearly 50 years ago that these sites may have been antecedent to the Oneota sites at Red Wing. As such, the restricted distribution of Angelo Punctated and long-tailed effigy mounds between La Crosse and Red Wing may reflect a major territorial division within the Effigy Mound Culture. The northern group is referred to as the Lewis phase, and these people may have adopted Middle Mississippian traits through contact down the Mississippi River and with Mill Creek and Cambria Cultures to the west. In doing so, it appears their culture rapidly transformed into Silvernale Oneota, with a major center located at Red Wing. Besides the Emergent Oneota panther mound at Diamond Bluff, the same kind of unusual cord-impressed pottery found at the Fred Edwards site was found at the Bryan site, a palisaded Silvernale phase village at Red Wing. The Bryan site was partially excavated in the 1950s by Wilford and again in the 1980s by the Institute for Minnesota Archaeology but has since been obliterated by a sand-and-gravel quarry.

Downriver from the Red Wing area, Eastman phase effigy mound groups in the southern portion of the Driftless Area may have initially rejected Cahokian incursions. Other than a few occurrences of Middle Mississippian pottery on Mississippi River floodplain islands, there is currently minimal evidence for Cahokian activity at the major Effigy Mound center at Prairie du Chien. However, immediately after the Fred Edwards and Hartley Fort occupations, a major settlement arose at the mouth of the Apple River on the southern margin of the Driftless Area in northwestern Illinois. Archaeologist Thomas Emerson interprets the Apple River complex to represent two sequential phases. He named the first one the Bennett phase in honor of John Bennett, an early archaeologist who had worked in the area. Emerson interpreted the Bennett phase as dating from A.D. 1050 to 1200 and correlated it with the Silvernale occupations at Red Wing. Indeed, ceramics from Bennett and Silvernale are similar. Significantly, Emerson recognized extensive Late Woodland interaction with the Mississippian-oriented Bennett phase people. The subsequent occupation at Apple River is called the Mills phase, dated between A.D. 1200 and 1300, and Emerson compared Mills phase people to Oneota groups in adjacent regions, including the Upper Mississippi Valley.

Emerson suggested that the Bennett phase people were decidedly not Oneota. Likewise, some do not consider the comparable Silvernale phase to be Oneota but rather northern expressions of Middle Mississippian. There is no question, however, that cultures that evolved from the Silvernale phase are Oneota. Likewise, the Mills phase, which succeeds the Bennett phase at Apple River, is an Oneota variant. Therefore, we prefer to acknowledge the related Silvernale and Bennett phases as the earliest expressions of Oneota. It is intriguing that each is situated along the Mississippi River on either end of the Driftless Area. Once these Oneota bases were established, Prairie du Chien and all other effigy mound locales in the Driftless Area became virtually abandoned for several centuries.

Thus the second major cultural revolution along the Upper Mississippi River witnessed the rapid shift from the Woodland to the Oneota tradition between A.D. 1100 and 1200. This metamorphosis followed the year-round occupation of substantial portions of the Driftless Area landscape and the end of the ancient annual subsistence cycle. Ecological and archaeological information from Wisconsin's Driftless Area increasingly points to periods of catastrophic collapse of white-tailed deer populations, and such events could have provided a final catalyst for a major cultural shift. Woodland tradition populations in this region were dependent on deer for most of their winter supplies of protein, fat, and skins for clothing. Hunting methods that included widespread use of fire in drives by hunters armed with bows and arrows led to an overharvest of deer and winter fuelwood in an increasingly denuded landscape. The final blow to both humans and deer probably came as desperate, terminal Late Woodland hunters killed late-winter herds of deer trapped and unable to flee in deep, crusted snow, an event that may be rendered in the hunting scene in Tainter Cave (see Appendix B). This is precisely how the early Euro-American settlers destroyed the deer and elk populations in the Driftless Area during the winter of 1856–1857. In historic accounts compiled by A. W. Schorger, trapped animals were often killed without firearms by cutting their throats with a knife or employing an ax. Following this harvest, deer were not abundant in the region again for decades. Moreover, the disappearance of earlier groups, such as those Archaic peoples who made Raddatz and Durst points, may reflect comparable stress on the local deer population.

The Oneota revolution was based on intensification of corn-based agriculture, which not only tied groups to particular localities during the growing season but also allowed larger population aggregations. Furthermore, surplus crops could be stored for the lean late-winter months. This shift to a reliance on corn closely corresponds with the peak of the Middle Mississippian center at Cahokia and a widespread northward expansion of Mississippian ideas. The expression of Mississippian intrusion is observed in the appearance of shell-tempered pottery, a technological innovation that facilitated the cooking of corn. Within this 100-year period, ceramics shifted from grit to shell-tempered, effigy mound building ceased, and populations abandoned vast areas to cluster in major agricultural villages at Red Wing and Apple River. From this point to the first contact with Europeans, the Upper Mississippi Valley was dominated by the Oneota Culture.

CHAPTER ELEVEN

The Oneota Culture

The Oneota Culture was born of the marriage between Late Woodland people and Middle Mississippian ideas. Local groups appear to have selectively adopted Mississippian cultural aspects, such as intensified corn agriculture and shell-tempered pottery. The resulting Oneota are sometimes referred to as Upper Mississippian. The Oneota, however, never became fully Mississippianized. Missing from the Oneota cultural repertoire are stratified societies and platform mounds that served as elite residential substructures. After about A.D. 1200, Middle Mississippian influence waned as Cahokia went into decline, but Oneota persisted, lasting until European contact in the seventeenth century.

The Oneota Culture was not stagnant for the six centuries that it inhabited the Upper Mississippi Valley (fig. 11.1). Populations congregated in distinct localities and periodically moved, while ceramic styles evolved with uncanny similarity across the broad region from Lake Michigan to the Missouri River. Despite maintaining distinct settlements, these groups were clearly interacting on a regular basis.

Although sharing basic subsistence economies focused on corn agriculture and wetland resources, Oneota groups located east of the Driftless Area

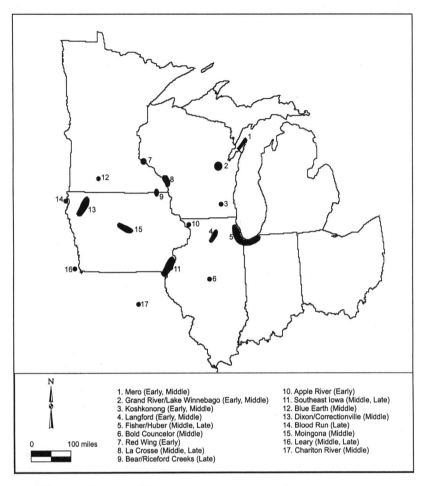

11.1. Oneota localities through time.

were more adapted to the resources of Lake Michigan and eastern Wisconsin's inland rivers and lakes. To the west, Oneota groups were increasingly more reliant on Plains resources, particularly buffalo. Groups that settled at Mississippi River localities such as Red Wing, Minnesota, La Crosse, and southeast Iowa were strategically located to take advantage of resources from both the river and prairie environmental zones through travel or interaction. Furthermore, Oneota people located along the Mississippi River could take advantage of the natural north-south highway presented by this major artery. This crossroads location played a critical role at the end of prehistory, during the final cultural revolution experienced by Native American societies.

Interaction between Oneota settlements along the Mississippi River and

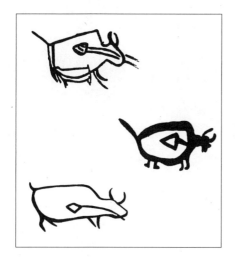

11.2. Drawings of buffalo carvings, or petroglyphs, from Driftless Area rockshelters with arrows or heart lines entering the chest area from the mouth. These were almost certainly carved by Oneota artisans.

those in the glaciated region toward Lake Michigan probably occurred through river systems such as the Fox-Wisconsin and the Des Plaines–Illinois routes. These routes were later followed by French explorers. Western interaction is reflected in the presence of buffalo shoulder blade hoes, engraved buffalo artwork, and red pipestone (most of which originated at the catlinite quarries of southwestern Minnesota) at Oneota sites along the Fox Valley in eastern Wisconsin and at others near Chicago. In addition, some pots found at eastern Wisconsin sites have decorations that mimic those found at western Oneota sites, while a few vessels found at La Crosse appear to have been manufactured in eastern Wisconsin.

Evidence for interaction between Oneota groups on the Mississippi and areas to the west is stronger, with more buffalo shoulder blade hoes, catlinite, and artistic depictions of buffalo. Carvings and drawings of buffalo have been found at several western Wisconsin rockshelters, each of which has produced evidence of minor Oneota occupation (fig. 11.2), and in etchings on rare pipestone tablets found at Oneota village sites (see Appendix B). The high degree of Plains influences, including the accurate portrayal of buffalo, suggests that some of the Mississippi River Oneota ventured onto the eastern Plains, obtaining resources themselves. Other shared traits, such as near-identical ceramic decorations and common lithic resources, suggest exchange between the Mississippi River Oneota and Plains groups. For example, between about A.D. 1250 and 1400 Oneota potters at Red Wing and La Crosse employed decorations that are nearly identical to those found at settlements in the Blue Earth River Valley of south-central Minnesota and the

11.3. Marine (saltwater species) shell beads from La Crosse Oneota sites. These are one indication of trade with groups in the Lower Mississippi Valley.

Dixon/Correctionville locality of northwestern Iowa. The Red Wing, early La Crosse, and Blue Earth settlements also shared a unique flint resource, Grand Meadow chert. This gray flint occurs as small nodules that were mined from an upland locality in southern Minnesota, about midway between the La Crosse and Blue Earth settlements.

North-south interaction along the Mississippi River corridor is reflected in shared ceramic styles between La Crosse and southeastern Iowa over several hundred years. In addition, some Burlington chert from the southern locality is found at nearly all La Crosse Oneota sites. Exchange is also indicated by the recovery at many Oneota sites of a few beads (fig. 11.3) made from *Prunum* (formerly *Marginella*) shells, a marine snail that inhabits the Atlantic Ocean and Gulf of Mexico. Another southern indicator is a single alligator tooth found at the State Road Coulee site in La Crosse County, which probably derived from the Lower Mississippi Valley. Finally, southern artistic motifs such as the mace (fig. 11.4) have been found at Oneota sites. The maces were manufactured of copper and pipestone, both northern resources. Carved monolithic mace axes have been found at late prehistoric Mississippian sites in the southeastern United States, where this crosslike ax was also rendered in the hands of dancing bird-men warriors at late Mississippian town sites. At upper midwestern Oneota sites, the mace generally occurs individually as a pendant but was also depicted in rock art and incorporated into tails of sheet-copper birds and as heart lines within buffalo etched onto catlinite tablets (see Appendix B).

Leather string

11.4. Mace pendant made from sheet copper. Note the preserved leather string at the top. Found at the Oneota Tremaine site north of La Crosse. Approximately 2.5 inches long.

Another indication of Middle Mississippian influences among Oneota groups in the Upper Mississippi Valley is a type of ear ornament made of shell or copper that was formed into what is known as the long- or short-nosed god mask. These distinctive objects occur at Middle Mississippian sites throughout the central United States, including Aztalan in eastern Wisconsin and peripheral sites such as Diamond Bluff (Mero) near Red Wing. Based on carvings and etchings, they appear to have been worn on the ear by males. Robert Hall has associated these small masks with the Ho-Chunk and Ioway mythical hero Red Horn, or He Who Wears Human Heads as Earrings.

Because Oneota settlements were typically larger than those of prior cultures, there tends to be more artifacts at Oneota sites. Furthermore, the more recent Oneota artifacts and ecofacts tend to be better preserved. Oneota settlements have been extensively researched, particularly over the past two decades, in advance of modern development at both Red Wing and La Crosse. For example, salvage excavations have been undertaken at the Bryan and Energy Park sites at Red Wing and at Valley View, Sand Lake/Krause, Pammel Creek/Overhead, State Road Coulee/Trane, Gundersen (Sanford), Midway/

11.5. Oneota artifacts. From left to right: pottery vessels, bison scapula hoes, deer jaw tools, and grinding stones (mano/metate). Scale in centimeters.

Tremaine/OT/Filler, and others at La Crosse. In addition, major recovery excavations have been undertaken at the Wever site in southeastern Iowa, and studies have been initiated near Lima Lake on the Illinois side of the Mississippi River. Consequently, archaeologists have a greater understanding of Oneota artifacts and lifeways than they do of earlier cultures.

Ellison Orr, Charles R. Keyes, Mildred Mott Wedel, and Will C. McKern first distinguished Oneota through distinctive artifact traits. Key diagnostic artifacts continue to form the basis for attributing archaeological sites to this culture: round to oval shell-tempered pots (fig. 11.5), sandstone abraders, circular manos, celts (ungrooved axes), bison scapula hoes, sheet-copper pendants, and catlinite disk pipes (fig. 11.6). The broad distribution of assemblages containing these artifacts led to the recognition that the Oneota Culture spanned the upper Midwest from Lake Michigan to the Missouri River. However, Oneota settlements tend to cluster in particular localities: southern Lake Michigan, the west side of Lake Winnebago, La Crosse, Red Wing, the middle reaches of the Upper Iowa and Blue Earth River Valleys, the central Des Moines River, southeastern and northwestern Iowa, and the Chariton

11.6 Oneota disk pipes with macelike projections. These pipe bowls would have been attached to long wooden handles. The lower pipe is approximately 8.5 inches long.

River of Missouri. Between these Oneota localities were vast, unoccupied tracts that presumably were used as hunting territories.

By the end of the twentieth century archaeologists had obtained more than 400 radiocarbon dates from Oneota sites. Among other insights they offer, these dates have allowed the establishment of regional chronologies based on styles of decorative motifs found on Oneota pots and on styles from a select group of other time-sensitive artifacts. Ceramic motifs seem to mark a sequence of Oneota horizons. Copper coil earrings and rib rasps first occur in the proto-historic period, the brief span of time during which European-manufactured items, such as glass beads, were traded to groups through Native exchange systems before these groups were directly contacted by Europeans. Manufac-tured trade items mark the beginning of the historic era and the concurrent demise of traditional Oneota material culture.

Based primarily on contemporary shifts in common ceramic decorations across the Oneota Culture, archaeologists have tended to subdivide the cul-ture into a series of horizons. The earliest is often referred to as Emergent Oneota, followed by the Developmental Horizon and then the Classic Hori-zon, which extends into the era of European contact. As more data become available, the horizon model is continually being refined, but the broad out-line remains the same.

The origins of the Oneota Culture have been debated for years. The argu-ments generally revolve around whether the earliest Oneota sites predate the peak Middle Mississippian occupation at Cahokia and its northward burst of influence around A.D. 1050–1150 as witnessed by sites such as Aztalan. Some eastern Wisconsin Oneota sites and, more recently, minor Oneota evidence at the Gottschall Rockshelter have been interpreted as representing a pre–Middle Mississippian emergence of Oneota, perhaps through early migrations of people from Illinois. The dating of all of these sites remains tenuous, however. More certain is the emergence of Oneota settlements along the Mississippi River that were influenced by Cahokia at about A.D. 1150. The earliest Oneota complexes from that period are located at the mouth of the Apple River in northwestern Illinois and on both sides of the Mississippi River near Red Wing. Both complexes share distinct early Oneota styles and exhibit undeniable Cahokian influences, such as the scrolled Ramey design. Apple River and Red Wing are situated on the margins of the Driftless Area, which for all practical purposes had become abandoned by A.D. 1150 or 1200.

Where did the Effigy Mound people go? Data from the Fred Edwards and Hartley Fort sites suggest that in the southern Driftless Area, Late Woodland groups were being transformed from the Eastman phase through contact with Cahokia, blending Late Woodland and Middle Mississippian pottery and architecture. Yet their remote, interior settings and fortifications imply that their residents were defensively minded. Something was perceived as a threat, and then the people were gone. Immediately thereafter, populations congregated at Apple River and at Red Wing, maintaining contact with Cahokia, suggesting that by around A.D. 1150 Eastman and Lewis phase peoples had converted to Upper Mississippian lifeways.

Lewis phase Effigy Mound people in the northern Driftless Area appear to have distinguished themselves from Eastman phase people around A.D. 1000. In this segment of the Upper Mississippi River Valley, Lewis phase settlements, recognizable in part by the presence of Angelo Punctated pottery, were relatively sparse and were involved with Plains-oriented Great Oasis/Mill Creek groups. However, they were also involved with Late Woodland people in eastern Wisconsin, where long-tailed panther mounds are most concentrated. In addition, a high incidence of unnotched silicified sandstone arrow tips at Aztalan reflects interaction with Late Woodland groups in the northern portion of the Driftless Area. Early Middle Mississippian influences in the northern portion of the Driftless Area are also represented by a grit-tempered pot with angular shoulders and a rolled rim found by Warren Wittry in Mound 8 at the Wakanda Park Mound Group in Dunn County. These mounds also contained Lewis phase Angelo Punctated pottery. The transition from the Lewis phase to Emergent Oneota is best demonstrated at the Silvernale phase Diamond Bluff site in the Red Wing locality, where Middle Mississippian and early Oneota pots were found in a long-tailed panther mound.

In 1973 Robert Alex of the University of Wisconsin–Milwaukee conducted excavations in the village area of the Diamond Bluff site and documented an intensive Oneota habitation. These excavations were subsequently synthesized by Roland Rodell. Alex's excavations revealed numerous storage pits and an apparent small, oval house basin. The pots are round, shell-tempered Oneota forms with curved decorations that were derived from the Ramey scroll motif. Projectile points include a mix of side-notched Cahokia and unnotched Madison forms. Stone tools were chipped both from locally available chert and regionally available silicified sandstone. These traits, supported by a suite of radiocarbon dates, allowed correlation of Diamond Bluff to similar sites in the Red Wing locale that have been designated the Silvernale phase. The Institute for Minnesota Archaeology has also undertaken test excavations at Diamond Bluff as well as at the Bryan and Energy Park sites on the outskirts of Red Wing, but these await final descriptive reporting.

In sum, the answer to the question of where the Driftless Area Effigy Mound people went is one previously offered by James Stoltman. They became Oneota, abandoning the filled landscape, where horticulture supplemented hunting and gathering, in favor of concentrated agricultural settlements at Apple River and Red Wing. As discussed earlier, the Eastman phase people probably had little choice after deer herds were depleted. Presumably, former Eastman phase people established the Apple River settlements, while descendants of Lewis phase people settled at Red Wing. Once established as Oneota, these two groups interacted with one another on a regular basis, as evidenced by shared ceramic styles and the occurrence of silicified sandstone at both Red Wing and Apple River.

By about A.D. 1300 and after Cahokia had fallen into a period of decline known as the Moorehead phase, Oneota complexes along the Mississippi River changed. The Apple River center was abandoned, while major settlements sprang up in southeastern Iowa—for example, the Wever site and Burlington phase, central Iowa (Moingona phase), northwestern Iowa (Dixon/Correctionville phase), and south-central Minnesota (Blue Earth phase). Settlements remained at Red Wing for a time, such as at the Bartron site on Prairie Island, but soon shifted down the Mississippi to a series of sites, such as Armstrong at the mouth of the Chippewa River, and then to Trempealeau, as represented by the Shrake-Gillies site adjacent to Perrot State Park and the Schoolyard site within the modern village of Trempealeau. As Red Wing was completely abandoned by about A.D. 1350, major villages were established at the Olson/North Shore site on Brice Prairie near La Crosse and the Sanford Archaeological District (including the Gundersen locale) on the La Crosse

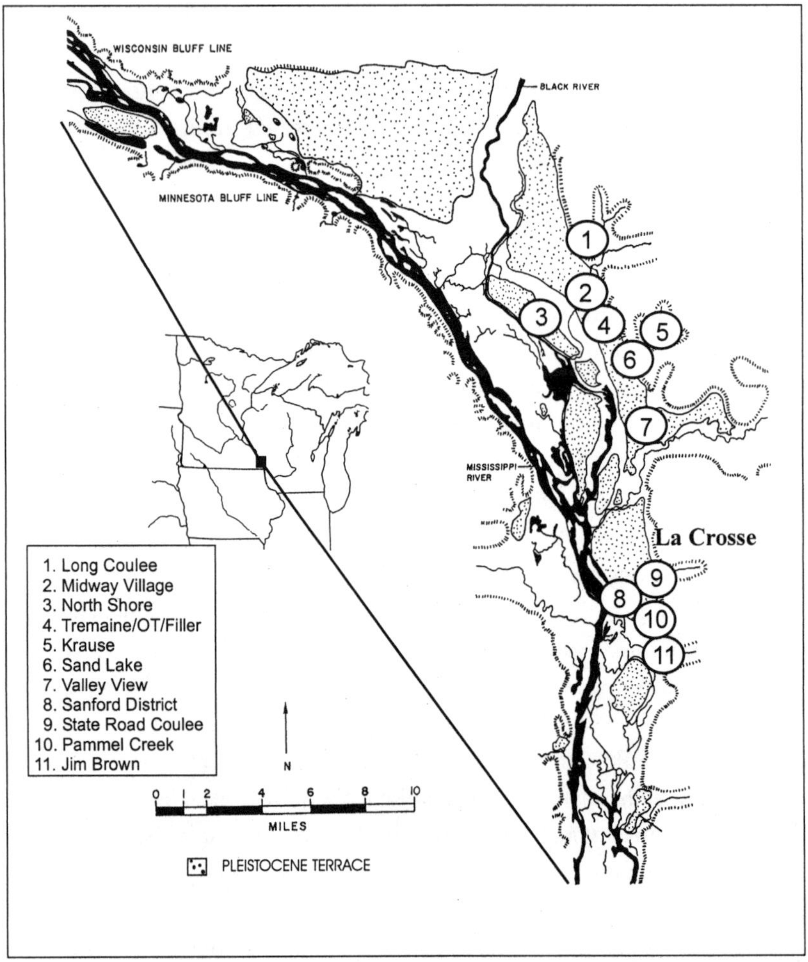
WISCONSIN BLUFF LINE
BLACK RIVER
MINNESOTA BLUFF LINE
MISSISSIPPI RIVER
La Crosse
1. Long Coulee
2. Midway Village
3. North Shore
4. Tremaine/OT/Filler
5. Krause
6. Sand Lake
7. Valley View
8. Sanford District
9. State Road Coulee
10. Pammel Creek
11. Jim Brown
N
0 1 2 4 6 8 10
MILES
PLEISTOCENE TERRACE

11.7. Oneota sites in the La Crosse locality.

terrace (fig. 11.7). Midway Village and Tremaine also were established at this time, making La Crosse the most intensively populated locality on the Upper Mississippi by A.D. 1400. At La Crosse, these initial Oneota settlements represent the local Brice Prairie phase.

Initially, the La Crosse Oneota interacted with settlements at Blue Earth and southeastern Iowa. This interaction is seen in part by shared ceramic decorations at all three localities that differ from the preceding Silvernale styles. Interaction is also indicated by the presence of Grand Meadow chert at contemporary Blue Earth and La Crosse sites and by Burlington chert at Oneota sites in La Crosse. The Grand Meadow chert source location is between La Crosse and the Blue Earth Valley, and presumably the groups met periodically, perhaps during seasonal buffalo hunts. During such rendezvous, intergroup marriages could be arranged in which potters (presumably women) might move to the other locality, fostering similarities in ceramic styles across large areas. It is also possible that entire Oneota families may have chosen to move between localities for particular years, again leading to a blending of artifact styles across broad regions. Burlington chert was locally available to southeastern Iowa Oneota people, and the occurrence of this material at all La Crosse Oneota sites probably reflects continuous contact along the Mississippi River.

Soon after A.D. 1400, the Blue Earth Oneota complex ended, coinciding with the apparent abandonment of Oneota settlements in central (Moingona) and northwestern (Dixon/Correctionville) Iowa. Oneota centers were maintained at La Crosse and in southeastern Iowa (Kelly phase), each persisting until shortly before European contact. The Oneota villages at La Crosse during this period fall within what is called the Pammel Creek phase, which persisted until about A.D. 1500. During this phase, ceramic styles changed again as settlements began to shift from the edge of the Mississippi River toward the bluff base on the eastern margin of the La Crosse terrace. This movement may have been to take advantage of the very rich black soil that is concentrated along the bluff base. Here, La Crosse Oneota people tilled extensive ridged agricultural fields in rich bottomland soil at the mouths of small valleys such as Sand Lake.

Sand Lake

The Sand Lake site is located near Onalaska, north of La Crosse, at the mouth of a small, spring-fed valley called Sand Lake Coulee. Sand Creek is blocked from the Mississippi River floodplain by the mile-wide Onalaska terrace, and, consequently, the stream simply "sank" into the sandy terrace. However, the mouth of Sand Lake Coulee also developed an extensive floodplain that became a low prairie, which was only seasonally wet. The soils of this floodplain are silty and black from organic enrichment, forming some of the richest farmland in the region. The Oneota recognized the agricultural potential of this floodplain and began farming at Sand Lake around A.D. 1400. Occupations soon covered the surrounding land, including the terrace margins and an adjacent loess-capped bluff. The settlement quickly became so intensive that erosion began to have devastating effects on the agricultural fields. Gulleys formed in the highly erodible loess, and Sand Creek became

11.8. Cleaning the profile of a deep excavation unit at the Sand Lake ridged field site near On-alaska. The trowel is at the top of a ridge constructed of the original black floodplain soil. The banded soil above is redeposited loess and sand that eroded from an adjacent hillside, sealing the ridged fields beneath an alluvial fan.

choked with sediment. One consequence was the formation of a massive gulley and an alluvial fan that covered at least 13 acres of the ridged fields. By A.D. 1450 the fan had stabilized, and the Oneota used it as a habitation area.

Archaeologists from the Mississippi Valley Archaeology Center (MVAC) excavated at Sand Lake in 1982, 1984, and 1986. The first excavations were preceded by a surface collection of the modern field, which revealed the intensity of the Oneota village on the alluvial fan. Initial excavations were undertaken to investigate the village, as the excavators had no idea that preserved agricultural fields lay beneath. As the excavations proceeded through the light-colored redeposited loess, Oneota artifacts continued to be found at surprisingly great depths, until the soil changed to black floodplain sediments. Not only were Oneota artifacts found on the black surface, but the surface undulated in a series of regular ridges and swales. These represented an Oneota ridged-field system (fig. 11.8), created by using bison scapulas to build the floodplain sediments into parallel ridges.

The ridged fields at Sand Lake were preserved with amazing detail due to the extensive upland erosion brought on during their use. In fact, MVAC archaeologists found individual planting hills placed at regular intervals along the edges of the ridges in zigzag patterns, permitting optimal use of the ridge surfaces. Evidence of compost in the form of ash and other refuse was scattered through the fields. The ridges were rebuilt at least ten times, as the alluvium covered them between A.D. 1400 and 1450. So important were the fields at Sand Lake that Mississippi River resources such as clams and fish, including a 50-pound catfish, were carried several miles to be cooked and eaten at this center of spring and summer agricultural activity.

The shift away from the Mississippi River edge may also reflect defensive posturing as a reaction to conflict. Excavations by the State Historical Society of Wisconsin at the Tremaine site in the Highway 53 corridor between Onalaska and Holmen found a series of post stains that formed large ovals (100+ feet by 30 feet), which represent the outlines of long structures, like those of the Iroquois. These buildings were attributed to the Pammel Creek phase based on radiocarbon dates and diagnostic pottery. Although habitation features were found, the structures also contained over 80 burials placed inside and generally oriented perpendicular to the walls. Five of the Tremaine burials had experienced traumatic death, revealed by the presence of an arrow tip embedded in the spine of a 25–35-year-old male and scalping marks on the skulls of at least four individuals.

After about A.D. 1500, the transitional Pammel Creek phase gave way to the Valley View phase at La Crosse. Named after the Valley View site, this phase is distinguished by distinctive pottery types such as Allamakee Trailed and Midway Incised, which are found at other Oneota locales in the Midwest, particularly in southeastern Iowa (Bailey Farm phase), and along the Missouri River at sites like Fanning in northeastern Kansas. Direct interaction between southeastern Iowa and La Crosse is also reflected in the presence of Burlington chert at Valley View phase occupations at La Crosse. Clearly, Oneota people continued to maintain contact over broad areas, and the main mechanism may have been rendezvous scheduled to coincide with annual bison hunts.

During this final period of prehistory, the Oneota increasingly obtained, exchanged, and exported catlinite from southwestern Minnesota in the form of disk pipes and tablets. Many tablets are etched, and a few have been found along the Upper Mississippi River Valley. These include a large tablet found on the New Albin terrace at the mouth of the Upper Iowa (formerly Oneota) River. The tablet has a human figurine with a hawk head and forked eyes on one side, while the other side has a series of symbols that include maces (see Appendix B). A replica of the tablet can be viewed at Effigy Mounds National Monument. Sheet-copper mace pendants have been found at several Oneota villages along the Upper Mississippi River, including Diamond Bluff at Red Wing and the Tremaine site at La Crosse (fig. 11.4). In eastern Wisconsin, the mace was incorporated into the tail of a sheet-copper raptor, and this symbol was also used as a variation of the heart-line motif drawn from the mouth into the chest area of bisonlike animals etched on a catlinite tablet from the Midway site (see Appendix B). The symbolism extends even to the flaring top of catlinite disk pipes (fig. 11.6), which archaeologist Bob Hall has correlated with a long tradition of adoption ceremonies to foster intergroup peace as culminated in the calumet ceremonies documented by Europeans throughout eastern North America in the seventeenth and eighteenth centuries.

More conventional heart lines, consisting of arrows entering the mouth and chest, are rendered on buffalo carved into the walls of several Driftless Area rockshelters, such as Samuels Cave, Gullickson's Glen, and Bell Coulee in western Wisconsin and La Moille Rockshelter in southeastern Minnesota. These are presumed to have been carved by Oneota people based on the presence of a few Oneota sherds at most rockshelters and the recovery of bison bones at regional Oneota sites to the exclusion of bison remains at preceding Woodland and Archaic sites. Oneota occupation of rockshelters was never as intensive as preceding Woodland and Archaic occupations, and Oneota use may have been more for ritual purposes, such as vision questing. Nonetheless, the realistic depictions of buffalo at these sites strongly suggest that the Oneota knew bison firsthand, probably from communal hunts to the west.

Despite indications of interregional exchange, the Valley View phase reveals evidence of continued conflict. For example, major settlements such as Valley View and State Road Coulee continued to be pulled back from the Mississippi River edge, and the Valley View site was fortified with a palisade. Unlike nearly all other Oneota sites at La Crosse, excavations at Valley View found only one fragment of catlinite and relatively few hide scrapers. La Crosse Oneota sites typically have many more scrapers than arrow tips. The high frequency of scrapers at these sites suggests that dried buffalo hides were carried back to La Crosse from seasonal hunts on the prairies to the west. Evidence that the dried hides were scraped for final processing at La Crosse is found in distinctive patterns of wear polish visible under a microscope. Presumably, the cleaned hides were used to make moccasins, as tarps, and for many other purposes, but all have decomposed through time. The lack of catlinite and the low incidence of scrapers at Valley View suggest that during the occupation of this palisaded village, contact with the peoples to

11.9. The 1978–1979 excavations at the Valley View site during early construction of the Valley View Mall between La Crosse and Onalaska.

the west was interrupted. This site is thought to be the last Oneota occupation at La Crosse.

Valley View

The Valley View site was noted by Joseph Nicollet, who in 1839 sketched the first detailed map of the lower La Crosse River Valley. Nicollet noted abandoned American Indian ruins about 6 miles from the Mississippi River. Theodore Lewis mapped the site in 1885, depicting an oval berm of earth on a narrow peninsula that extended into the La Crosse River floodplain. Lewis also reported that one side of the berm was being cultivated for the first time and that numerous artifacts of village refuse were exposed. For much of the twentieth century the site was hunted by private collectors, until 1978 when the Dayton-Hudson Corporation obtained the land for construction of the Valley View Mall. A year earlier, archaeologist James Gallagher, learning that the site was being disturbed by the initial grading, called for volunteers to help rescue the archaeological record. Dayton-Hudson cooperated, supporting two seasons of excavation (fig. 11.9), which were described in a University of Wisconsin–Madison dissertation by Katherine Stevenson and in a series of spin-off articles.

The excavations found that Valley View was a fortified Oneota village occupied around A.D. 1600. Inside the stockade lines were hundreds of storage and refuse pits, as well as probable house remains. Although the occupation was intensive, it appears to have been short-lived, as the site was abandoned before the arrival of French explorers in the mid 1600s. The Oneota residents farmed and exploited resources from the adjacent La Crosse River floodplain. Some interaction with contemporary Oneota groups in southeastern Iowa is indicated by the presence of Burlington chert, but catlinite is extremely rare. The lack of catlinite contrasts with its widespread use at this time in most of the region. Furthermore, Valley View is anomalous in having very few end scrapers. The fortified nature of Valley View on a defensively situated peninsula well away from the Mississippi River suggests social tensions, and the lack of catlinite and end scrapers suggests the residents were cut off from their traditional access to the Plains and bison resources. This breakdown of centuries-old patterns occurred just before the abandonment of La Crosse by the Oneota and the beginning of European exploration of the Upper Mississippi Valley.

CHAPTER TWELVE

The End of Prehistory

While the people whom archaeologists call Oneota were thriving at La Crosse and other localities in the upper Midwest, Europeans were discovering, exploring, and settling the Atlantic seaboard. Within 30 years of Columbus's initial voyage to the New World, Spanish armies had conquered the Aztec state in Central America. A few decades later, Spanish expeditions cut across the southeastern Woodlands and penetrated to the center of the Great Plains. While Hernando de Soto's 1539–1541 march of conquistadors wreaked havoc on southeastern Indians from Florida to Arkansas, his vision of riches died with him on the banks of the Mississippi River. Francisco Vásquez de Coronado's 1541 probe into Kansas, which also failed to find cities of gold, was less devastating to indigenous people. Nonetheless, the Spanish had set the stage for European colonization with the aid of an unseen ally: germs.

Having been essentially isolated from the Old World for nearly 12,000 years, Native Americans had never been exposed to measles and smallpox prior to 1492. When these diseases were carried to the New World on European ships, epidemics struck the Native population full force. Typical of childhood and endemic in Europe, these diseases killed Native people by the tens of thousands but also conferred resistance to the survivors. It is difficult to discern the direct impact of the first waves of disease across the Americas because there are few written records for the coastal areas and none for the interior regions. Nonetheless, diseases probably spread between Native groups via existing exchange networks, affecting the Upper Mississippi River Valley long before direct European contact. Certain estimates place the disease-induced population decline in some parts of the Americas as high as 90 percent.

Such uncontrolled and unexplainable devastation left Native American societies in a quandary. Survivors integrated into other groups or moved, and entire regions were abandoned, allowing game to replenish and expand in those areas. As the Ohio Valley became depopulated around A.D. 1600, buffalo expanded eastward as far as Virginia.

In the 1500s the Dutch, English, French, and Spanish colonial powers explored the eastern seaboard and exploited pristine fishing grounds, such as the Grand Banks off the mouth of the St. Lawrence River. English colonies were attempted in the early 1600s, with Jamestown in Virginia the first permanent settlement. The Dutch followed at New York, and the French explored the St. Lawrence and established settlements at Montreal and Quebec, realizing the economic bounty of the fur trade. This trade was based on Native peoples' harvest of pelts, which were exchanged at rendezvous points for European-produced items such as iron knives and axes, brass kettles, glass beads, and guns. Within decades, eastern tribes had abandoned stone tools for iron and earthen pots for brass kettles. The colonial powers vied to establish contact with western tribes both to expand fur production and to search for a northwest passage that could provide a shorter route to the Orient.

French control of the St. Lawrence River allowed them to send explorers and missionaries to the Great Lakes region. In 1634 Jean Claude Nicolet, dressed in oriental garb, arrived in what is now Wisconsin seeking to expand the fur trade and searching for an overland route to rumored western saltwater. It is not clear exactly where Nicolet landed or how far he traveled. He almost certainly met with the Ho-Chunk and Menominee along Green Bay, and he may have ventured up the Fox River to its short portage with the Wisconsin River and then down to the Mississippi River.

French exploration into the western Great Lakes and Mississippi River Valley was interrupted in the 1640s by the eruption of the Iroquois Wars. Increasing European demand for furs created hunting pressures that resulted in overexploitation. The fur trade led to competition for new hunting territories, inevitably creating conflict. The Iroquois Confederacy, situated south and east of Lake Ontario, was allied with the Dutch and English, while the

French had allies in the Algonkian-speaking tribes north of the St. Lawrence as well as with the Huron, who occupied the enviable central portion of the Great Lakes region and, along with the Ottawa, controlled access to the western Great Lakes.

From 1640 to about 1670 the Iroquois periodically attacked French-allied tribes along the St. Lawrence and Great Lakes. These attacks nearly annihilated the Huron and caused abandonment of what is now Michigan by the Chippewa, Kickapoo, Sauk, Meskwaki (Fox), and Potawatomie. These groups fled to the west side of Lake Michigan, into Wisconsin, where Iroquois raiding parties continued to pursue them. In the 1650s Huron refugees ventured to the Upper Mississippi River, where they settled for two years with the Ioway. During this period, the brothers-in-law Pierre Esprit Radisson and Sieur de Grosseillers made several expeditions to the western Great Lakes and perhaps the Mississippi Valley. Their accounts refer to buffalo and red pipestone and the initial contact between the westward-migrating Chippewa and the indigenous Dakota Sioux. This contact soon led to intertribal conflict. It is unclear what became of the Ho-Chunk during this period, although French accounts and oral tradition refer to a catastrophic decline due to disease and warfare with the Illinois Confederacy.

When the Iroquois Wars subsided around 1670, the French once again focused their attention on the western Great Lakes and Mississippi River. In 1673 Father Jacques Marquette and his guide, Louis Jolliet, made the first certain European observation of the Upper Mississippi River. They reached the mouth of the Wisconsin River on June 17, proclaiming: "The Mississippi River takes its rise in various lakes in the country of the Northern nations. It is narrow at the place where the Miskous [Wisconsin] empties; its Current, which flows southward, is slow and gentle. To the right is a large Chain of very high mountains, and to the left are beautiful lands; in various Places, the stream is Divided by Islands."

A few years later, Father Louis Andre established a mission at Green Bay and in 1676 was visited by a family of Ioways, whom he remarked were rich in buffalo hides and red pipes. By 1677 Réne-Robert Cavelier, Sieur de La Salle, was seeking wealth in minerals and buffalo hides throughout the Upper Mississippi Valley. He sent samples of blue clay to France from southern Minnesota hoping that the color indicated a rich copper ore, and legend has it he may have even visited the Silver Mound quarry site, leading to its historic name. La Salle's prospecting efforts were unproductive of minerals, but hides were real and his enterprise acquired many. He sent trader Michel Aco to live with the Ioway for two years, securing buffalo hides for commercial purposes. La Salle was joined by the missionary Louis Hennepin who, with Aco, was captured in 1680 by a band of Eastern Dakota Sioux. The accounts of La Salle's expedition and Hennepin's captivity refer to specific places along the Upper Mississippi River and various aspects of tribal life, including buffalo hunting and the use of earthen vessels. Hennepin's account mentions Lake Pepin and groups of buffalo at what is likely the Buffalo River in Buffalo County.

In 1685 Nicolas Perrot set out for the Upper Mississippi River in search of the Ioway, who as Father Andre had reported, were buffalo hunters. Perrot was guided by a party of Ho-Chunk hunters who knew, presumably from past contact, how to find the Ioway. Like Marquette and Jolliet, Perrot approached the Mississippi from the Wisconsin River, but at the confluence he turned upstream. At some point, perhaps near Trempealeau (fig. 12.1), he waited while the Ho-Chunk went off to locate the Ioway. Two weeks later, the guides returned with word that the entire Ioway village was coming to meet Perrot. When the Ioway were a short distance away, Perrot went to meet them and was treated to the calumet ceremony, in which his hosts weeped over him, carried him on a prepared buffalo hide, smoked a red pipe, and ate buffalo tongues cooked in a great earthen pot.

Historical records are not precise enough to pinpoint the location of Perrot's 1685–1686 wintering post or the Ioway village(s) that he and Aco visited. Based on the description of Perrot's post at the foot of a "mountain," behind which was an extensive prairie teeming with game, historians inferred that the post may have been located at the foot of the unique Trempealeau bluffs. The discovery of the remains of a French post during the 1888 construction of a railroad along the base of these bluffs seemed to confirm this interpretation, and for more than a century this site was attributed to Perrot. However, mid-1990s' excavations there found that the site was not occupied in the late 1600s but rather around 1730. Therefore, the site at which Perrot awaited word of the Ioway has not been found. The generic description of a "mountain" and adjacent plain could, in fact, be almost anywhere along the west side of the Upper Mississippi River, as French mapmakers of the period, relying on reports from explorers like Marquette and Jolliet, often depicted the western margins of the Upper Mississippi as a mountain range.

The La Crosse Oneota sites have produced no early historic European trade artifacts, nor do the French mention villages at any place that can be recognized as La Crosse. Therefore, this locality must have been abandoned before the encounters between Aco, Hennepin, and Perrot and the Ioway in this region in the late 1600s. However, early in the twentieth century Ellison Orr

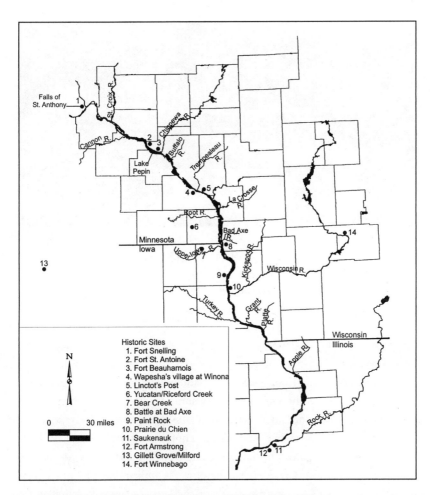

12.1. Some important historic sites in the Upper Mississippi River Valley.

Historic Sites
1. Fort Snelling
2. Fort St. Antoine
3. Fort Beauharnois
4. Wapesha's village at Winona
5. Linctot's Post
6. Yucatan/Riceford Creek
7. Bear Creek
8. Battle at Bad Axe
9. Paint Rock
10. Prairie du Chien
11. Saukenauk
12. Fort Armstrong
13. Gillett Grove/Milford
14. Fort Winnebago

and Charles R. Keyes found iron knives, brass kettle parts, and glass beads in direct association with distinctive shell-tempered pottery at a series of sites along the Upper Iowa River. This river had formerly been called the Oneota River after the geologic Oneota dolomite formation through which the river carved deep bluffs, and the archaeological culture with shell-tempered pottery was thus named Oneota. In 1938 Mildred Mott Wedel brought together the archaeological record and early historical documents to support a compelling argument that these early historic-contact Oneota sites can be identified as the Ioway villages visited by the French in the late 1600s.

Many of the early historic Oneota sites in the Upper Iowa River Valley were clustered at the mouth of Bear Creek, a small tributary located about 10 miles

12.2. Rib-bone rasp (top) and bone whistle (bottom) from Oneota sites in the Upper Mississippi River Valley. The rasp is probably made of a bison rib and was recovered from the Farley Village site in Houston County, Minnesota. The whistle is made from naturally hollow bird bone and was excavated from the Pammel Creek site at La Crosse.

upstream from the Mississippi River. Similar early contact-era Oneota sites have been found in Minnesota near the head of Riceford Creek, a tributary of the South Fork of the Root River that is immediately north of Bear Creek. The pottery at many of these sites is very similar to that of the latest prehistoric Oneota villages at La Crosse, such as the Valley View site. In addition, distinctive protohistoric artifacts, such as copper coil earrings and rib-bone rasps (fig. 12.2), have been found at the latest La Crosse Oneota sites and at the Bear and Riceford Creek sites. Therefore, it appears the Oneota shifted from the Mississippi River terraces at La Crosse to interior valley sites to the west. But why?

Oneota people had settled at La Crosse about A.D. 1300, apparently having migrated down the Mississippi River from Red Wing, Minnesota. Once at La Crosse, they established large summer villages, harvested massive quantities of food from the Mississippi River floodplain, tilled extensive ridged-field systems, and buried their dead. For 300 years, La Crosse was home to a large population. Then, just before direct French contact, they left.

Oneota populations moved periodically throughout prehistory for unknown reasons. Perhaps they ran out of critical resources such as wood for fuel. Perhaps their crops failed for a series of years. Whatever the reasons, one of the major documented relocations was from Red Wing to La Crosse, and another is from La Crosse to Bear and Riceford Creeks. The first went from one Mississippi River terrace complex to another and consequently did not affect a major portion of the subsistence economy. At both Red Wing and La Crosse, the Mississippi River floodplain provided an incredible abundance of food throughout the warm season, and the Oneota were clearly adept at harvesting fish, mussels, turtles, beaver, waterfowl, crawfish, wild rice, and other natural resources.

The second move, from La Crosse to Bear and Riceford Creeks, was very different. These interior valleys are deep and narrow with small floodplains, offering few of the wetland and riverine resources that were abundant in the Upper Mississippi. In moving there, the Oneota were, in effect, giving up the ability to exploit the Mississippi Valley at will. Why? Why live in these particular small valleys out of the hundreds of similar valleys on both sides of the Mississippi? And why move in the mid 1600s, just as the French were about to meet them?

Perhaps the La Crosse Oneota had used up available wood or had spoiled the ground near their villages so that they could not open new storage pits without contaminating the food. La Crosse was a prairie, and wood may have been scarce. Nonetheless, islands in the adjacent Mississippi floodplain would have been full of trees, and driftwood would have been continually available. Furthermore, one of the last Oneota villages at La Crosse was the Valley View site, which was protected by a stockade built of timber, suggesting that wood was not scarce. Yet the Valley View site is located at the eastern edge of the La Crosse terrace prairie, overlooking a gallery forest in the adjacent floodplain. Then again, because the vast majority of Oneota activity at La Crosse was during the warm season, wood supplies may not have been overexploited for fuel. Clean soil for storage pits was clearly a concern, and the La Crosse Oneota seem to have extended their storage areas outward from village centers over time to avoid digging new pits where old ones were spoiled by garbage and rodents. But while the Oneota dug pits over large portions of the La Crosse terrace system, they did not use all of it. Moreover, if these were critical problems and if the people desired to maintain connections with the Mississippi River, why not simply move to another unoccupied terrace such as at Prairie du Chien?

It is possible that European disease had spread along trade systems and reached the La Crosse settlements, devastating the population. Marine shell beads indicate connections with the Gulf of Mexico, and de Soto had reached the Lower Mississippi by 1541, providing an opportunity for measles and smallpox to have infiltrated Upper Mississippi populations. Based on Spanish accounts from a few decades later, we know that nine of ten Native villages along the Middle Mississippi Valley ceased to exist in the 50 years after de Soto. There is no direct evidence for epidemics at La Crosse, however. Infections that kill in a matter of days or weeks do not leave marks on bone, and no mass graves have been found at La Crosse. On the other hand, when faced with catastrophic death, many cultures simply cannot maintain traditional burial practices, and corpses may be left on the surface.

Pressures from the Iroquois Wars may have influenced the Oneota to shift westward. These prolonged mid-seventeenth-century conflicts caused a number of eastern tribes to move westward, including the Huron, who took refuge with the Ioway around 1650. Seventeenth-century French accounts describe extensive intertribal warfare in the Upper Mississippi Valley, largely between the Dakota Sioux and eastern groups. For example, Radisson and Grossiellers report conflict between the Sioux and Chippewa in the late 1650s. In 1669 the Jesuit missionary Claude Alloez found the Meskwaki occupying a massive village in eastern Wisconsin that was fortified out of fear of Sioux attack. Three years later the Meskwaki sent a war party to eastern Minnesota to attack the Sioux but were repulsed and lost over 30 warriors. In 1676 both the Ho-Chunk and Ioway were said to be at war against the Sioux. In 1680–1681 a combined Sioux and Chippewa war party of over 800 warriors set out to attack the Meskwaki in eastern Wisconsin but were unsuccessful. And in 1686 a large war party consisting of Meskwaki, Kickapoo, and Mascoutin attacked a French trading post called Fort St. Antoine on Lake Pepin. The Meskwaki also attacked a Chippewa camp in western Wisconsin in 1687 and overran a Sioux hunting camp in west-central Wisconsin in 1690. That same year, the Sioux gathered a force of 400 to counterattack another Meskwaki war party in western Wisconsin. In the mid 1690s the Meskwaki and Mascoutin again attacked a Sioux village at Lake Pepin, and the Mascoutin are reported to have killed more than 200 captives.

These accounts demonstrate that warfare was ongoing at the time of the first French record of the Upper Mississippi River. Furthermore, the warfare sometimes involved hundreds of warriors who traveled great distances. One response to this situation was the establishment of fortified villages, which implies siege warfare tactics. French accounts of this period document several sieges and reveal that these were generally won or lost depending on which side had the greatest reserves of food and water. Because of the heavy losses that would have been incurred by the attackers, fortifications were only rarely attacked directly. It is not known if siege warfare was practiced in prehistory, but fortified sites begin to appear in the archaeological record of the Midwest about 1,000 years ago, including such sites as Aztalan, Fred Edwards, Hartley Fort, and the Bryan site. Along the Missouri River, the fortified Crow Creek site has been made infamous by the discovery of nearly 500 mutilated bodies found in a gully. Crow Creek is interpreted as having been attacked around A.D. 1325 while its stockade was under construction. The attackers are lost to prehistory, but they must have been a substantial force.

The fact that the residents of the Valley View site surrounded themselves with a stockade indicates at least a perceived threat from a substantial enemy. It is not known if Valley View was actually besieged or attacked, but given the record of the subsequent century, this may have been enough to cause the La Crosse Oneota to abandon their 300-year-old home and the graves of their ancestors. The remoteness of their subsequent villages at Bear and Riceford Creeks also suggests the occupants were hiding.

An alternative factor in the shift from La Crosse to the west may have been economic incentives. As mentioned earlier, Father Andre in 1670 noted the Ioway's wealth in buffalo hides and red pipestone. Based on local depictions of buffalo, the presence of buffalo shoulder blade hoes, and the large quantity of end scrapers for processing hides, the La Crosse Oneota were actively involved in bison hunting. Indeed, based on the overall lack of evidence for large Oneota populations living at La Crosse during the late fall and early winter months, it is inferred that most of the people migrated west to hunt buffalo at this time of year. Some La Crosse Oneota sites, particularly late ones, also have produced numerous red pipestone artifacts, most of which were made from catlinite.

By the time La Salle sent Aco to live with the Ioway in the late 1670s, La Salle was specifically licensed by the French government to procure bison hides. Indeed, bison hides had been a commodity of trade across both the eastern and western margins of the Plains for at least a century. Spanish chroniclers in the Southwest and others with de Soto recorded exchange of various goods for bison hides in the 1500s. Thus, as the doors opened to direct French contact and commerce with Upper Mississippi River tribes in the late 1600s, the incentive to provide buffalo products in exchange for European goods may have proved to be the catalyst for abandonment of La Crosse and the Mississippi River in favor of more direct access to the Plains.

By 1700 the Ioway had shifted farther onto the prairies, settling briefly near a series of prairie lakes in north-central Iowa. There, the Milford and Gillett Grove sites have produced Oneota pottery and European trade items. This move presumably was influenced in part by European economic incentives to trade buffalo hides. One of the common precontact Oneota artifact forms that reflects bison hide processing is the end scraper, and one would expect an increase in the quantity of these tools as buffalo hides became a trade commodity with the French. Yet at Milford, typical Oneota end scrapers are almost nonexistent. The likely reason: stone scrapers were quickly replaced by iron tools that kept an edge longer.

Indication of the rapidity of the material culture change is revealed by Hennepin's acknowledgment that Upper Mississippi River Valley groups were still using earthen pots and chipped-stone tools in 1680, though by 1690–1691 Perrot stated: "You have forgotten that your ancestors in former days used earthen Pots, stone Hatchets and Knives, and Bow; and you will be obliged to use them again, if Onontio abandons you."

In eastern Wisconsin, the Meskwaki controlled the Fox-Wisconsin water-way, in effect blocking French traders from conveniently reaching rich fur markets along the Mississippi River where the Sioux and Ioway lived. Consequently, much of what is known about tribal activity along the Upper Mississippi River during the first half of the eighteenth century is through French records that tend to emphasize problematic relations with the Meskwaki. In 1716 the French sent an army into eastern Wisconsin, which failed in laying siege against the well-provisioned Bell site. The next year, the French court decided to shift the control of its interests in Illinois Country from Canada to Louisiana, in effect pitting its New World colonies against one another, and for several years northern tribes raided the Illinois and collaborating French traders with little discouragement from Quebec. A consequence of these raids was for the Illinois to turn to tribes along the Missouri River, including the Osage, Missouri, Oto, and Ioway, who were drawn into the conflict. For example, in 1725 the Meskwaki raided the Oto and Missouri. That year the Meskwaki also formed an alliance with their former enemies, the Sioux, and the French court finally intervened to stop the attacks on the trade in Illinois. One tactic was to break the Meskwaki-Sioux alliance by having a French officer named René Godefroy, Sieur de Linctot, negotiate peace between the Sioux and the Chippewa. In 1726 the French established a post at Lake Pepin called Fort Beauharnois after Charles de la Boischer, marquis de Beauharnois, the new governor of New France.

The next year Governor Beauharnois chose to wage war against the Meskwaki and in 1728 sent an army consisting of 1,650 French, Ottawa, Potawatomie, Chippewa, and Huron to Green Bay. This time the Meskwaki, Ho-Chunk, and Sauk abandoned the area and fled to the Mississippi River. That fall the Meskwaki had camps along the Mississippi River below the mouth of the Wisconsin River and 60 lodges at Lake Pepin with some Ho-Chunk.

In the fall and winter of 1728–1729 the Meskwaki made a series of political blunders, not the least of which was killing two Kickapoo and Mascoutin hunters, members of tribes that had long been allies. As a result, the Kickapoo and Mascoutin formed an alliance with the Illinois against the Meskwaki, and by the fall of 1729 the Ho-Chunk had also turned, joining the Ottawa, the Chippewa, and some Menominee in raids against the Meskwaki. The Meskwaki were now isolated, and the majority of the tribe chose to attempt an eastward exodus that ended in disaster on the prairies of eastern Illinois. The remaining Meskwaki established a village along the lower Wisconsin River and several smaller camps at Prairie du Chien and near Trempealeau. Even then, the Meskwaki village on the lower Wisconsin was attacked and overrun by a Huron and Iroquois war party in December 1730. Only then did some tribes take pity on the few remnant Meskwaki, and soon thereafter the Sauk assisted the Meskwaki, with both tribes moving to northwestern Illinois in the mid-eighteenth century.

Following the crushing defeat of the Meskwaki, the French once again infiltrated the Upper Mississippi River Valley, with military and commercial posts established at Trempealeau and Lake Pepin. As noted earlier, the excavations at what had been thought to be Perrot's 1685–1686 wintering post instead found evidence of a 1730s' French occupation, with glass beads, gun flints, a brass ring, and quantities of bone from large mammals such as bear and buffalo. This post is thought to have been commanded by Linctot.

From 1720 to 1760, the Sioux and Chippewa had an ongoing conflict, creating an area in northwestern Wisconsin in which hunting and raiding parties could venture but settlements were too risky. The Sioux gradually shifted to the southwest, encouraged by the establishment of a French settlement at Prairie du Chien in the 1750s, which became the principal point for annual intertribal trade fairs or rendezvous. By the end of the century, the Sioux established a series of villages along the west side of the Mississippi from Minneapolis to Red Wing and south as far as Winona, Minnesota, where Wapesha's band lived. These villages countered the Chippewa expansion into western Lake Superior and beyond, leading to a century of periodic conflict and maintaining the uninhabitable land in northwestern Wisconsin.

By the mid 1700s the horse had become incorporated into the ways of Upper Mississippi tribes. Until then, travel primarily had been on foot or by watercraft. The introduction of the horse through the Spanish in the Southwest had completely transformed Native American life on the Plains but was less a factor in the rugged Driftless Area. The Sauk-Meskwaki alliance in the late 1700s led to the establishment of the principal Sauk village of Saukenuk at the mouth of the Rock River in Illinois and to Meskwaki villages in adjacent portions of eastern Iowa. From there the Sauk and Meskwaki rode horses on annual buffalo hunts and inevitably encountered Sioux hunting parties from Wapesha's village at Winona doing the same. Conflicts resulted, and for the next 50 years the Meskwaki and Sioux skirmished along the modern Iowa-Minnesota border.

During the middle portion of the eighteenth century, various tribes lived briefly at certain locations in the Upper Mississippi Valley. The British explorer Jonathan Carver, for instance, noted Meskwaki settlements at Prairie du Chien in 1766. While Britain gained control of the fur trade in the region following the 1763 British victory in the French and Indian War, regional European settlers along the Upper Mississippi River were nearly all French. Prairie du Chien had become a key settlement on the Upper Mississippi River, with annual rendezvous where tribes from far and wide brought pelts and other items for exchange. During the late 1700s, the tribes became dependent on British supplies.

By 1788 Julien Dubuque had obtained permission from the Meskwaki to mine lead on their land in northeastern Iowa. About this time the Ho-Chunk experienced a rejuvenation, and their settlements spread south along the Rock River and west to La Crosse, in effect controlling the major portion of the lead-bearing formations east of the Mississippi River. Given their proximity, members of the La Crosse band of Ho-Chunk intermarried with members of Wapesha's Sioux band at nearby Winona, while those on the Rock River became aligned with the Sauk and Meskwaki.

Following Thomas Jefferson's negotiation of the 1803 purchase of the Louisiana Territory from Napoleon, Zebulon Pike led an American expedition up the Mississippi in 1805. However, the region remained controlled by the British trade network out of Canada, and most European residents remained French. It was not until the War of 1812 that the United States began actively asserting influence along the Upper Mississippi. At the start of the war, Americans quicky constructed a fort at Prairie du Chien, but this was almost immediately captured by a combined force of British troops, representatives from many of the regional tribes, and local French Canadian residents. The British force maintained control of the Upper Mississippi throughout the war, turning the fort over to the Americans only after the conflict had ended.

In order to maintain control over the Upper Mississippi, the Americans soon constructed forts at Rock Island (Fort Armstrong), Prairie du Chien (First and Second Fort Crawford), and the Falls of St. Anthony (Fort Snelling). During this period, stores were established adjacent to the forts through the American factory system. These supported American, British, and French

Canadian traders but continued to rely on Native American hunters and trappers, who were kept in constant debt through a credit system controlled by the Americans.

In 1823 the passage of the *Virginia*, the first steamboat to ply the Upper Mississippi, signaled a new era. J. C. Beltrami recorded his observations on this trip, including a reference to a rock above Prairie du Chien that was annually painted red and yellow by Native inhabitants and to a prairie fire along the bluffs that extended for 15 miles. The *Virginia*, or another steamboat shortly thereafter, was apparently recorded by a Native American who carved a depiction of a steamboat on Paint Rock near Waukon Junction, Iowa.

American forces were garrisoned at forts along the Upper Mississippi for the next 30 years, during which time the Native American tribes of the Upper Mississippi River Valley lost their lands in a series of conflicts and treaties. The major event during this period was the 1832 Black Hawk War, which was spawned by cultural misunderstandings that began 30 years earlier. These conflicts intensified with the lead-mining boom of the 1820s, which saw a large influx of Americans to the Driftless Area, many in direct violation of existing treaties. By 1830 the Ho-Chunk had ceded much of the lead district south of the Wisconsin River, and the Sauk were forced to comply with an 1803 treaty to move to the west side of the Mississippi River. This split the Sauk tribe, and in 1831 and 1832 attempts by Black Hawk's "disaffected" band to return to Saukenuk and their Ho-Chunk neighbors at Prophetstown were met with an aggressive response by Illinois state militia and U.S. Army regulars. In 1832 U.S. forces trapped Black Hawk's band in the upper reaches of the Rock River. Black Hawk then attempted to skirt around the northern portion of the lead district, below Fort Winnebago at Portage, cutting across the Driftless Area south of the La Crosse Ho-Chunk and Wapesha's Sioux. Many Sauk died of starvation en route, and the remnant band was caught on the banks of the Mississippi near the Bad Axe River, just below the modern town of Victory. There, a rearguard decoy deflected most of the pursuing army, but a militia force happened upon the main band. In the resulting battle, Sauk resistance quickly deteriorated, and the conflict turned into a massacre. Approximately 150 Sauk were killed, including women and children. Survivors regrouped on the Iowa side of the river, only to be hunted down by Sioux warriors from Wapesha's village, who killed another 60 to 80 people near the Cedar River. Black Hawk was subsequently captured by Ho-Chunk from La Crosse and turned over to American authorities at Second Fort Crawford, a recently excavated site in Prairie du Chien (fig. 12.3).

The decisiveness of the American victory over Black Hawk's band led to

12.3. Stone foundation walls of Second Fort Crawford (1829–1864) being exposed after 140 years beneath Beaumont Road in Prairie du Chien.

new treaty negotiations in which the Sauk and the Meskwaki ceded all of eastern Iowa, and in 1837 the Ho-Chunk gave up their remaining land in western Wisconsin. In 1840 the federal government began removing Ho-Chunk families from western Wisconsin, settling them at a school, agency, and mission complex near Fort Atkinson in northeastern Iowa. The soldiers at Fort Atkinson had the job of forcing the Ho-Chunk to live in the narrow zone between the antagonistic Dakota Sioux and the Meskwaki. Many Ho-Chunk people filtered back to western Wisconsin throughout the 1840s. The government repeatedly removed them, first to a series of reservations in Minnesota and then finally in Nebraska. Those who moved to Nebraska formed the Nebraska Winnebago Nation. For those who had come back to Wisconsin, the government offered recognition of their homesteads in the 1870s. These tracts were clustered near Black River Falls, but several were located along the Upper Mississippi from Trempealeau to De Soto.

By 1851 the federal government had negotiated Sioux removal from the Upper Mississippi River Valley, and Wapesha's band had left Winona. By that time the land was being surveyed for public sale, and American settlers of European descent quickly arrived on hundreds of steamboats each year. Only the Prairie Island band of Dakota Sioux was able to maintain a land-hold along the Mississippi River near Red Wing.

Approximately 12,000 years ago the first people laid eyes on the Upper Mississippi River Valley. The landscape at that time would have been hardly recognizable to us. The region would have resembled the subarctic, and the people would have seen not only caribou and musk ox but also mastodons and mammoths, relatives of the modern elephant; giant ground sloths; 400-pound beavers; and huge buffalo with straight horns. To the first people in this region, these sights were normal, and the people were perfectly adapted to surviving in that environment. They and their ancestors had been living along glacial margins of the last Ice Age for thousands of years, hunting megafauna all the while.

The Upper Mississippi region was, however, new land, and the initial colonists had to find critical resources, such as supplies of stone for making their weapons and tools. They also had to quickly learn the landscape in order to return to these sources periodically. It must have been an amazing process to wander through this absolute wilderness in a continual pursuit of game and food to forage and yet be able to find the way back to places like Silver Mound. The first people here certainly established landmarks, and the vast outwash gorge of the Mississippi River undoubtedly became a principal locational feature, as it remains today.

Despite the difficulties that the first people must have faced for survival,

13.1. Salvage excavations at the Midway Village site north of La Crosse in advance of gravel quarry operations.

they were adapted to the cold periglacial environment with its associated wildlife. Living through the climate changes that mark the onset of the Holocene and the concomitant mass extinctions of the megafauna must have been somewhat disconcerting to Paleoindian hunter-gatherers, even though this shift may have occurred over a thousand-year period involving nearly 50 generations. On the other hand, dramatic changes may have been experienced within individual lifetimes. During this transition, people adapted to new environments, first the replacement of the tundra with spruce-fir forests, followed by deciduous forests and later a major expansion of the prairies and eastward migration of buffalo. After people had successfully adapted to these environmental waves, the climate of the Upper Mississippi region shifted once again in the late Holocene, witnessing the retreat of the prairies. Again the inhabitants changed and survived.

The human adaptations to the environmental changes are reflected in the archaeological record by technological innovations that archaeologists use to mark the sequence of cultural traditions and stages for this region. The first people, those of the Paleoindian tradition, were bands of Ice Age hunters and gatherers following herds of mammoths and other large game across a tundra-like landscape. Their descendants, the people of the Archaic tradition, hunted deer and elk and gathered nuts and other food in recognizable territories. Late in the Archaic, people began to cultivate simple gardens, and this begat

13.2. Left to right: Jerry Greendeer, Merlin Red Cloud, and George Garvin of the Ho-Chunk Nation at Tainter Cave in 1998.

Woodland tradition people, who added pottery to the material culture and marked formal cemeteries with earthen mounds. The Archaic to Woodland transition is signaled by wide-ranging trade systems and extensive ritual ceremonialism. The Woodland tradition in the Upper Mississippi Valley experienced a series of fluctuations, ending 1,000 years ago at the time intensive corn agriculture was adopted in the region. This was a period of conflict, and the newly introduced bow and arrow provided a far superior weapon that played a role in the development of the first fortifications. Groups consolidated, tribes were born, and the Upper Mississippian, or Oneota tradition, came into being. These people renewed an interest in hunting bison on the nearby eastern margins of the Plains, and it was the Oneota who were here when the French explored and provided the first written records in the mid 1600s. Despite the incredible and sudden disruption caused by the arrival of Europeans, Native people have survived.

Native people have a long story, and it is rarely told from beginning to end. Indeed, the story has no end but continues in the lives of Native people today and as the archaeological record continues to be explored and deciphered. The story is inevitably incomplete. Much has been lost through the natural processes of time, but even more has been lost within the last 150 years as the landscape has been artificially modified for agriculture, lumbering, town and city development, and, most recently, urban sprawl (fig. 13.1).

Increase Lapham recognized the threat in the 1850s, and Theodore Lewis lamented the destruction of mounds in the 1880s. Charles Brown, Ellison Orr, and Charles R. Keyes began archaeological preservation efforts in the first half of the twentieth century, and the second half saw federal regulations that have spurred American archaeology since the 1970s. Still, most of the archaeological record is located on private land and is largely unprotected save for the stewardship of individuals. In 2001 archaeologists and Native Americans teamed up to promote a local ordinance in the city of La Crosse that recognizes the archaeological resources remaining within that municipality. "Smart Growth" measures are being introduced, which often encourage local governments to consider cultural resources in long-range plans. There is precious little remaining of what was here only 150 years ago. The future of the archaeological record for the Upper Mississippi River Valley depends upon preservation and recovery, and that will happen only through the mutual efforts of archaeologists, Native Americans, and the public (fig. 13.2).

Included among the rich harvest of archaeological materials recovered from archaeological sites in the Upper Mississippi River Valley are the shells and bones from the animals that provided animal protein for the region's Native Americans prior to the arrival of Europeans. In addition, remains of small vertebrates recovered occasionally during archaeological work provide a glimpse of animals that were not used for food but were simply part of the local environment.

This summary is directed toward documenting which species of animals were present in the Upper Mississippi River Valley during the 5,000 years prior to European arrival. The 190 species listed here were recovered as bones and shells from 32 Native American habitation sites, the majority of which are located in western Wisconsin (see figs. A.1 and A.2 and table A.1). Persons interested in the references for specific sites and assemblages should see the report by Theler (2000) in the *Transactions of the Wisconsin Academy of Sciences, Arts and Letters*.

Because these remains have passed through a series of "human filters," archaeological faunal assemblages do not constitute statistically representative samples of local animal populations at the time the sites were occupied. First, these species were selectively chosen by ancient peoples for their suitability as food, clothing, and tools. Second, the archaeological recovery process itself can be selective for both the size and the type of faunal material recovered. Third, the existing archaeological faunal assemblages have been analyzed by people with varying levels of expertise. Nonetheless, these faunal remains provide a wealth of information on the animals used by Native Americans and also serve as a valuable general index for the species once present in the region.

TABLE A.1. Archaeological Sites with Identified Animal Remains

Abbreviation	Site Name	Site Number	Location
ONEOTA SITES			
PC	Pammel Creek	47Lc61	La Crosse Co., WI
VV	Valley View	47Lc34	La Crosse Co., WI
GU	Gundersen	47Lc394	La Crosse Co., WI
MV	Midway Village	47Lc19	La Crosse Co., WI
NS	North Shore	47Lc185	La Crosse Co., WI
JB	Jim Braun	47Lc59	La Crosse Co., WI
TS	Tremaine	47Lc95	La Crosse Co., WI
SR	State Road Coulee	47Lc176	La Crosse Co., WI
LC	Long Coulee	47Lc333	La Crosse Co., WI
KS	Krause	47Lc41	La Crosse Co., WI
SL	Sand Lake	47Lc44	La Crosse Co., WI
OT	OT	47Lc262	La Crosse Co., WI
FS	Filler	47Lc149	La Crosse Co., WI
AR	Armstrong	47Pe12	Pepin Co., WI
FV	Farley Village	21Hu2	Houston Co., MN
WOODLAND AND ARCHAIC SITES			
CR	Carrol Rockshelter	13Db486	Dubuque Co., IA
QR	Quall Rockshelter	47Lc84	La Crosse Co., WI
VR	Viola Rockshelter	47Ve640	Vernon Co., WI
CS	Cade sites	47Ve631, 643, 644	Vernon Co., WI
MS	Millville	47Gt53	Grant Co., WI
SF	Stonefield Village	47Gt1	Grant Co., WI
PR	Preston Rockshelter	47Gt157	Grant Co., WI
RR	Raddatz Rockshelter	47Sk5	Sauk Co., WI
DR	Durst Rockshelter	47Sk2	Sauk Co., WI
BR	Brogley Rockshelter	47Gt156	Grant Co., WI
MP	Mill Pond	47Cr186	Crawford Co., WI
MC	Mill Coulee	47Cr100	Crawford Co., WI
LR	Lawrence I Rockshelter	47Ve154	Vernon Co., WI
ML	Mayland Cave	47Ia38	Iowa Co., WI
BS	Bluff Siding	47Bf45	Buffalo Co., WI
JD	John Deere Harvester	11Rl337	Rock Island Co., IL
AM	Albany Mounds	11Wt1	Whiteside Co., IL

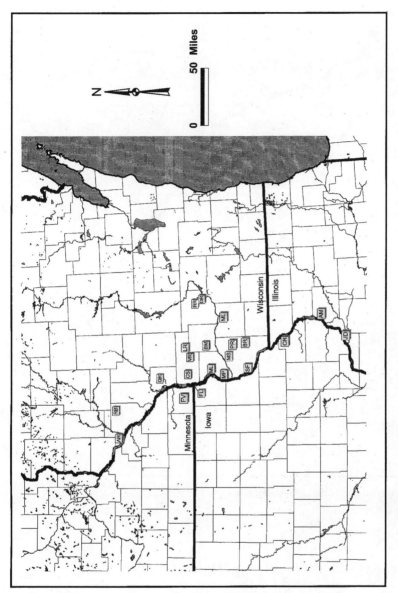

A.1. Archaic and Woodland sites and selected Oneota sites outside of the La Crosse locality. See table A.1 for site key.

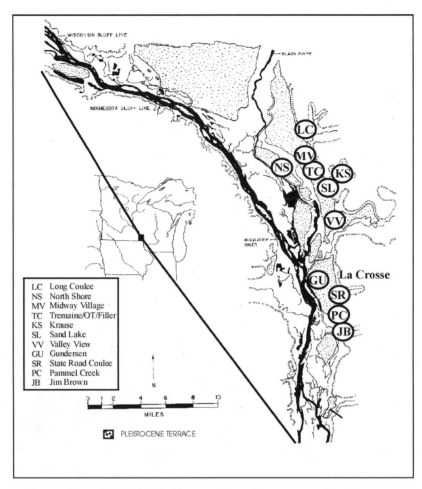

A.2. Oneota sites at the La Crosse locality.

LC Long Coulee
NS North Shore
MV Midway Village
TC Tremaine/OT/Filler
KS Krause
SL Sand Lake
VV Valley View
GU Gundersen
SR State Road Coulee
PC Pammel Creek
JB Jim Brown

MILES

PLEISTOCENE TERRACE

Recovery and Identification of Animal Remains

During the past 50 years, as archaeologists have become increasingly interested in understanding the contents of habitation sites, they have generally used some type of screening device to separate artifacts and animal remains from the excavated soil. An archaeological screen is an open-topped box with wood sides and a metal screen attached as the bottom. Screen mesh sizes depend on the excavators' objectives and soil types. Some excavators in the past used screen with a half-inch mesh, but today the minimum standard is quarter-inch mesh. Since the 1970s many archaeologists have employed finer screens with a mesh size of one-sixteenth inch or less to recover both animal and carbonized plant remains. The recovery method is a critical factor in the types and frequencies of animal species recovered. Relatively few fish or small mammal remains are recovered with a half- or quarter-inch screen.

Another critical factor is how the animal remains are identified. The remains Theler analyzed in this summary were identified through direct comparisons of the archaeological specimens to modern specimens of known species. Collections of reference skeletons and shells used in these analyses are housed at the University of Wisconsin–La Crosse and at the zoology museum at the University of Wisconsin–Madison. Other experts provided identifications for specimens that were difficult to identify because of a lack of reference material and/or expertise.

Archaeological specimens for which species identification was ambiguous are not included in the tables accompanying this summary, although they are listed in the original reports. Most faunal analysts note ambiguous identifications by the use of "cf.," which indicates that a specimen "compares favorably" but cannot be definitely assigned to the species. Mallards, for example, are often cited as "mallard (?) cf. *Anas platyrhynchos*" or "probable mallard, *Anas* cf. *A. platyrhynchos*," because most mallard bones are difficult or impossible to distinguish from those of the black duck (*Anas rubripes*). The presence of "cf." mallard is documented at many archaeological sites in the Upper Mississippi region, but these identifications are not included in this summary, causing mallards to appear rather uncommon in the tables.

Animal Remains Excluded from This Appendix

Bone, antler, and shell of many animal species were commonly used as tool stock or raw material for making tools and ornaments. Bone tools, even if identifiable to species, were not included in this summary because the materials were often collected or retained in a very different way from animal products used for food. Certain skeletal elements, such as antlers dropped by elk and deer in midwinter, appear to have been collected and saved for future conversion into tools. During certain periods in pre-European times, bones and shells of some species seem to have been traded as raw materials for tool manufacture.

One example of bones that were traded are the shoulder blades (scapulae) of bison, used for the manufacture of agricultural hoes. The latest prehistoric people in the La Crosse area were the Oneota, agriculturalists who grew domestic plant crops in the region between A.D. 1300 and 1650. The most common large Oneota bone artifact is the bison scapula hoe, with nearly 100 specimens recovered at local sites. Unworked nonscapula bison bones, however, are very rare at all sites in the La Crosse area, indicating that live bison were uncommon locally. The most likely source of Oneota bison bone was west of the Mississippi River in Iowa and Minnesota.

This summary does not give the number of recovered bones for each animal species or the number of individual animals, although that information is usually available in the original reports. There is evidence that many groups deboned large mammals at the kill location, retaining only selected bones to be used as tool stock or leaving smaller bones on the hide to aid in carrying the meat and hide bundle back to the camp or village. Elk and white-tailed deer seem to have been consistently deboned in the field during the later prehistoric period.

Two other types of remains are also omitted from this summary. The first are animal remains occasionally found as possible ritual items placed with human burials. The second are faunal materials that represent long-distance trade, such as marine shell (*Prunum apicinum*; formerly called *Marginella apicina*) beads recovered at the Overhead and Sand Lake sites and a single, unworked American alligator (*Alligator mississipiensis*) tooth from the State Road Coulee site.

Results

Mammals

There are 44 species of mammals represented at the 32 archaeological sites covered in this summary (table A.2). The human remains listed in table A.2 do not represent burials but rather isolated bones or teeth that are occasionally found during excavations of habitation areas.

It is clear that the most economically important animal utilized by all pre-European groups in the Driftless Area was the white-tailed deer (*Odocoileus virginianus*). The remains of this species are especially numerous at Archaic and Woodland fall-winter occupations in western Wisconsin rockshelters. The occupation zones in these rockshelters often contain hundreds or thousands of deer bones, consistently broken open for extraction of the fat-rich marrow. The fall-winter white-tailed deer provided a perfect package, in both size and quality, of meat, fat, and hide. While not nearly as abundant as deer, a few bones of one or two elk (*Cervus canadensis*) are present at most sites. These bones are usually from the hoof. Presumably, they were left on the hide to help transport the hide and meat bundle, while most of the skeleton was left at the kill location.

The situation for bison (*Bison bison*) is similar to that for elk, though bison is found at fewer sites. The few unmodified bison bones at Oneota sites on the La Crosse terrace are mostly hoof bones (phalanges). Bison remains are almost unknown at sites in Wisconsin's Driftless Area, with an exception in the Archaic component at Preston Rockshelter in Grant County. At the Carroll Rock Shelter, a Late Woodland site in Dubuque County, Iowa, a different pattern is represented, with bison apparently taken close to the occupation area and the meat along with some associated bone returned to the site.

The remains of black bear (*Ursus americanus*) are widely but thinly represented, particularly at La Crosse–area Oneota sites. Most of these remains are mandible or maxilla sections or bones associated with leg extremities (for example, metacarpals, metatarsals, and phalanges), presumably bones left on the skin. The presence of bear skull parts seems to relate to an interest in acquiring the animal's large canine teeth.

Mustelids, members of the weasel family, are rare at all the sites and often are represented only by skull parts (mandibles or crania). River otter (*Lutra canadensis*) and mink (*Mustela vison*) remains are found at many Oneota sites in the La Crosse area. It is possible that the particular elements represented relate to special or ritual use of these animals.

Other mammals of some importance are the muskrat and beaver. The remains of

TABLE A.2. Mammals

Common Name	Scientific Name	Oneota	Woodland	Archaic
Opossum	*Didelphis virginiana*		QR/PR	
Masked Shrew	*Sorex cinereus*	FV		
Short-tailed Shrew	*Blarina brevicauda*	VV/SR/FV	VR/CR	PR/RR
Prairie Mole	*Scalopus aquaticus*	PC/VV/FV/ SR/SL/MV	QR/MS/PR/CR	PR/RR
Big Brown Bat	*Eptesicus fuscus*			RR
Eastern Cottontail	*Sylvilagus floridanus*	VV/SR	QR/VR/PR/ DR/ML	PR/RR/DR
Eastern Chipmunk	*Tamias striatus*	VV/MV/FV	QR/VR/MS/ PR/DR/MC	CS/PR/RR/ DR
Woodchuck	*Marmota monax*	VV/MV	QR/VR/MS/PR/ DR/MP/ML	PR/RR/DR
Thirteen-lined Ground Squirrel	*Spermophilus tridecemlineatus*	PC/VV/FV/ KS/OT	QR/PR/AM	PR
Gray Squirrel	*Sciurus carolinensis*	VV	VR/MS/PR/ DR/ML	PR/RR/DR
Fox Squirrel	*Sciurus niger*	VV		
Red Squirrel	*Tamiascirurus hudsonicus*		QR/AM	PR/RR
Flying Squirrel	*Glaucomys volans*		QR/PR	PR/RR
Plains Pocket Gopher	*Geomys bursarius*	VV/GU/MV/FV/ SR/SL/OT/AR	QR/VR/CS	
Beaver	*Castor canadensis*	PC/GU/MV/JB/ SR/FV/SR/KS/ SL/OT/FS/AR	QR/VR/CS/MS/ PR/DR/MP// ML/AM/CR	PR/RR/DR
Deer Mouse	*Peromyscus maniculatus*	PC/KS		
White-footed Mouse	*Peromyscus leucopus*		CS	
Meadow Vole	*Microtus pennsylvanicus*	PC/FV/KS/ SL/FS	CS	
Prairie Vole	*Microtus ochrogaster*	KS/SL	CS	CS
Southern Bog Lemming	*Synaptomys cooperi*		CS	RR

Common Name	Scientific Name	Oneota	Woodland	Archaic
Muskrat	*Ondatra zibethicus*	PC/VV/GU/MV/ TS/SR/FV/SR/ KS/SL/OT/AR/ FS	QR/VR/CS/ MS/PR/DR/ MP/ML/AM	CS/PR/ RR/DR
Meadow Jumping Mouse	*Zapus hudsonius*	KS		
Porcupine	*Erethizon dorsatum*	VV	VR	
Domestic Dog	*Canis familiaris*	PC/GU/MV/ KS/OT	MS	
Coyote	*Canis latrans*		DR	DR
Wolf	*Canis lupus*	PC	QR/MP	PR/RR/LR
Red Fox	*Vulpes vulpes*		DR/AM	
Gray Fox	*Urocyon cinereoar- genteus*		PR/AM	
Black Bear	*Ursus americanus*	PC/VV/GU/MV/ JB/TS/FV/SE/ KS/SL/AR	DR/ML	LR
Raccoon	*Procyon lotor*	PC/VV/GU/JB/ FV/KS/SL/MV	ML/AM/QR/VR/ MS/PR/DR/MP/ MC	CS/PR/RR/ DR
Pine Marten	*Martes americana*	MV		RR
Fisher	*Martes pennanti*		QR/PR/DR	RR/DR
Long-tailed Weasel	*Mustela frenata*		PR	PR/RR
Mink	*Mustela vison*	PC/VV/GU/SR/ SL/AR	MS/DR	
Badger	*Taxidea taxus*	VV/FV/SR	QR/MS	
Striped Skunk	*Mephitis mephitis*	OT	QR/PR	PR
River Otter	*Lutra canadensis*	PC/VV/GU/SR/ SL/FS	MS/PR/DR	
Mountain Lion	*Felis concolor*			RR/LR
Bobcat	*Lynx rufus*	GU	MS/AM	RR
American Elk	*Cervus canadensis*	AR/PC/VV/GU/ MV/JB/TS/FV/ SR/KS/SL/OT	JD/BS/VR/CS/ MS/PR/DR/MP/ AM	CS/PR/RR/ DR

Common Name	Scientific Name	Oneota	Woodland	Archaic
White-tailed Deer	*Odocoileus virginianus*	OT/FS/AR/PC/ VV/GU/MV/NS/ JB/TS/SR/FV/ KS/SL	MC/LR/ML/AM/ JD/QR/VR/CS/ MS/PR/DR/MP	LR/ML/CS/ PR/RR/DR
Moose	*Alces alces*	FV		
Bison	*Bison bison*	PC/VV/MV/JB/ SR/KS/OT/AR	CR	PR
Human	*Homo sapiens*	PC/MV/TS/SR/ KS/SL/OT/AR	QR/CS/PR	

both of these riparian species were widespread at regional sites. At La Crosse–area Oneota sites, beaver are represented largely by skull parts. Numerous lower jaws (mandibles) of beaver have been found with the incisors carefully removed. This pattern may be related to the use of beaver incisors as woodworking tools.

In pre-European times, the dog was the only domestic animal in the Upper Mississippi River Valley. Domestic dogs were associated with Native peoples throughout most of North America over the past 10,000 years. Dogs were important in Native societies as pack animals, assistants in the hunt, village alarm systems, disposers of unused food, and sometimes a food resource. Dog remains have been found at a number of archaeological sites where dogs appear to have been used as food. A complete set of four discarded lower leg extremities (paws) was found adjacent to a refuse pit at the Pammel Creek site, and another set was found in pit fill at the Krause site. Two dog skulls were recovered in a refuse-filled pit at the OT site. Intentional dog burials appear to be very rare at Oneota or Woodland sites of the Upper Mississippi River Valley. One dog burial was found in a conical mound at the Late Woodland Raisbeck Mound Group in Grant County.

Birds

In all, 51 species of birds are represented in the 32 faunal assemblages (table A.3). The most widely represented bird species is the wild turkey (*Meleagris gallopavo*). In southwestern Wisconsin, turkey remains are represented by a range of skeletal elements. They are fairly abundant at both Archaic and Woodland sites south of a line from Green Bay to Prairie du Chien that marks the species' distribution before European contact. Ten La Crosse–area Oneota sites have produced turkey remains. These bones are primarily those from the wing tips (carpometacarpus, phalanges, and digits) that support the stout primary feathers. Primary feathers are the best choice for arrow fletching, according to Loren Cade, an archery enthusiast. This distribution of

TABLE A.3. Birds

Common Name	Scientific Name	Oneota	Woodland	Archaic
Common Loon	*Gavia immer*	W/AR		
Great Egret	*Casmerodius albus*	SL		
American Bittern	*Botaurus lentiginosus*	SR/AR		
Tundra Swan	*Cygnus columbianus*		AM	PR
Trumpeter Swan	*Cygnus buccinator*	MV/SL/AR	AM	
Canada Goose	*Branta canadensis*	PC/VV/MV/SR/ KS/FS/AR	QR/MS/DR/ PR/AM	RR
Wood Duck	*Aix sponsa*	PC/VV/GU/MV	AM	RR
Green-winged Teal	*Anas crecca*	GU/AR	QR/ML	
Blue-winged Teal	*Anas discors*	MV	MS	
Mallard	*Anas platyrhynchos*	MV/SR	MS/DR/ML/AM	RR
Northern Pintail	*Anas acuta*		AM	PR
Northern Shoveler	*Anas clypeata*	VV		
Gadwall	*Anas strepera*		PR	
Redhead	*Aythya americana*	VV	MS	
Ring-necked Duck	*Aythya collaris*	VV	ML	
Common Goldeneye	*Bucephala clangula*		ML	
Bufflehead	*Bucephala albeola*	GU/AR	CR	
Common Merganser	*Mergus merganser*	PC	MS/AM/CR	
Hooded Merganser	*Lophodytes cucullatus*	VV/AR		
Turkey Vulture	*Cathartes aura*			RR
Northern Harrier	*Circus cyaneus*	SL		
American Kestrel	*Falco sparverius*			PR
Merlin	*Falco columbarius*	VV		
Peregrine Falcon	*Falco peregrinus*	FS		
Red-tailed Hawk	*Buteo jamaicensis*	AR	PR	RR/PR
Bald Eagle	*Haliaeetus leucocephalus*		VR	
Red-shouldered Hawk	*Buteo lineatus*		DR	
Ruffed Grouse	*Bonasa umbellus*		DR/ML/PR	RR/DR/PR

Common Name	Scientific Name	Oneota	Woodland	Archaic
Greater Prairie Chicken	*Tympanuchus cupido*	MV	PR	PR
Wild Turkey	*Meleagris gallopavo*	PC/VV/GU/MV/ TS/SR/FV/SL/ OT/FS	VR/MS/DR/ ML/PR/AM/ CR	PR/CS/RR/ DR/LR
Virginia Rail	*Rallus limicola*	AR		
Common Moorhen	*Gullinula chloropus*	AR		
Sora	*Porzana carolina*	VV/GU/MV		RR
American Coot	*Fulica americana*	GU/TS/SR/ KS/AR	PR/AM	RR
Sandhill Crane	*Grus canadensis*	PC/VV/SR/ FS/AR		
Upland Sandpiper	*Bartramia longicauda*	VV		
Passenger Pigeon	*Ectopistes migratorius*	VV/FV/SR/MV	VR/DR/PR	RR/PR
Sharp-tailed Grouse	*Pedioecetes phasianellus*		QR/MS/DR/ ML/PR	RR/DR/PR
Eastern Screech-owl	*Otus asio*	VV	PR	RR
Great Horned Owl	*Bubo virginianus*	VV/SR		
Barred Owl	*Strix varia*	VV		RR
Belted Kingfisher	*Ceryle alcyon*	VV		
Red-headed Woodpecker	*Melanerpes erythrocephalus*	PC/SR		RR
Northern Flicker	*Colaptes auratus*	VV/GU	PR	
Blue Jay	*Cyanocitta cristata*	AR		RR
American Crow	*Corvus brachyrhynchos*	VV	AM	RR
Common Raven	*Corvus corax*	VV		
Red-bellied Woodpecker	*Centurs carolinus*		VR	
American Robin	*Turdus migratorius*		PR	PR
Red-winged Blackbird	*Agelaius phoeniceus*	PC/GU/MV/TS/ FV/KS/SL	VR	RR
Northern Cardinal	*Cardinalis cardinalis*			RR

bones seems to indicate that turkey wing tips, with the primary feathers attached, were saved during seasonal travel or hunts or perhaps traded into the La Crosse area during the Oneota occupation.

Waterfowl are present at many sites, with Canada geese and dabbling ducks being most common. Canada geese are the most widespread, with both bones and eggshell having been recovered. Analysis of bone size and eggshell structure indicates the Canada geese harvested in the La Crosse area were the "giant race" (*Branta canadensis maxima*). Mallards (*Anas platyrhynchos*) and wood ducks (*Aix sponsa*) have been found at several sites. The presence of eggshell and medullary bone, occasionally observed inside long bones as the source of calcium for eggshell formation, indicates spring harvest of waterfowl eggs and nesting birds. The trumpeter swan (*Cygnus buccinator*) is represented at three La Crosse–area Oneota sites.

A wide range of raptorial birds (for example, hawks and owls) as well as crows and ravens show up in small numbers at archaeological sites. It is well known that Native Americans often assigned ritual significance to certain bird species. Although not included in the tables, two burial sites in the Upper Mississippi River Valley contain interesting bird remains. A "headdress" found with a human burial in a Sauk County mound included the remains of two bird skulls and portions of four wing bones from the common raven (*Corvus corax*). At the Flynn site, a protohistoric Oneota cemetery uncovered during road construction in Allamakee County, Iowa, a raven skull was also associated with a human burial.

Small species of perching birds (Passeriforms) are rare or absent in the faunal assemblages from sites of all time periods. The single exception is the red-winged blackbird (*Agelaius phoeniceus*), represented at seven Oneota sites in the La Crosse area. The bones of this species are sometimes found charred, indicating the bird's probable use as food. Red-winged blackbirds are a noted agricultural pest and would have been a common summer resident near Oneota villages and cornfields.

Fishes

There are 35 species of fish represented at the 32 archaeological sites (table A.4). The most widespread species is the freshwater drum (*Aplodinotus grunniens*), and the most common are the catfishes, particularly the black bullhead (*Ictalurus melas*). Many fish species, including northern pike (*Esox lucius*) and members of the sucker family (Catostomidae), were taken during spawning periods. Others (gar, bowfin, and bullheads) were taken during the summer months by seining or trapping in shallow backwaters along the Mississippi River. The thick, durable rhombic scales of gar (Lepisosteidae) are present at most sites along the Mississippi River, but well-preserved skull bones are necessary to separate the longnose gar (*Lepisosteus osseus*) from the shortnose gar (*Lepisosteus platostomus*). The exterior surfaces of gar scales often exhibit evidence of being burned or scorched, an indication that entire fish may have been roasted in their armorlike scale covering.

Exceptionally large flathead catfish (*Pylodictis olivaris*) of 50 pounds or more and large channel catfish (*Ictalurus punctatus*) are present at many Woodland and Oneota sites adjacent to the Mississippi River. These catfish were probably harvested from their nest sites during the midsummer. There is no indication based on estimated size

Common Name	Scientific Name	Oneota	Woodland	Archaic
Lake Sturgeon	*Acipenser fulvescens*	PC/VV/MV/FS		
Shovelnose Sturgeon	*Scaphirhynchus platorynchus*	PC		
Paddlefish	*Polyodon spathula*	SL		
Shortnose Gar	*Lepisosteus platostomus*	PC/MV		
Longnose Gar	*Lepisosteus osseus*	PC/MV	MS	
Bowfin	*Amia calva*	PC/VV/GU/MV/ NS/JB/TS/SR/ KS/SL/OT/FS	QR/MS/MP/MC	CS
Northern Pike	*Esox lucius*	PC/GU/SR/KS/ OT/FS		
Bigmouth Buffalo	*Ictiobus cyprinellus*	PC/VV/SR		
Smallmouth Buffalo	*Ictiobus bubalus*	VV/SL	MC	
Quillback	*Carpiodes cyprinus*	VV/OT		
River Carpsucker	*Carpiodes carpio*	VV		
Black Redhorse	*Moxostoma duquesnei*	PC/KS		
Golden Redhorse	*Moxostoma erythrurum*	PC/VV/KS/SL	VR/MC	
Silver Redhorse	*Moxostoma anisurum*	PC		
Shorthead Redhorse	*Moxostoma macrolepi- dotum*	PC/VV/MV/TS/ FV/SL/FS	QR/VR	
River Redhorse	*Moxostoma carinatum*	VV/KS		
Northern Hog Sucker	*Hypentelium nigricans*	OT		
White Sucker	*Catostomus commersoni*	PC/VV/FV/ SR/OT		
Black Bullhead	*Ictalurus melas*	PC/VV/GU/MV/ NS/TS/KS/SL/ OT/FS	PR	
Brown Bullhead	*Ictalurus nebulosus*	PC/VV/MV/NS/ TS//KS/SL/OT		
Yellow Bullhead	*Ictalurus natalis*	PC/VV/MV/NS/ TS/KS/SL/OT/FS		
Channel Catfish	*Ictalurus punctatus*	PC/VV/GU/MV/ JB/TS/FV/SR/ KS/SL/OT/FS	VR/PR/MP	

TABLE A.4. (continued)

Common Name	Scientific Name	Oneota	Woodland	Archaic
Tadpole Madtom	*Noturus gyrinus*	PC/KS		
Flathead Catfish	*Pylodictis olivaris*	PC/VV/MV/JB/ SR/SL/OT	MP/MC	
Smallmouth Bass	*Micropterus dolomieui*	VV/GU		
Largemouth Bass	*Micropterus salmoides*	PC/MV/RB/SL	MP/MC	
Green Sunfish	*Lepomis cyanellus*	VV/GU		
Pumpkinseed	*Lepomis gibbosas*	PC/VV/KS/SL		
Bluegill	*Lepomis macrochirus*	VV/MV/KS		
Rock Bass	*Ambloplites rupestris*	VV/MV/FV/ST		
White Crappie	*Pomoxis annularis*	VV/KS		
Black Crappie	*Pomoxis nigromaculatus*	PC/VV/MV		
Walleye	*Stizostedion vitreum*	PC/VV/GU/KS/ FS		
Yellow Perch	*Perca flavescens*	PC/VV/GU/MV/ FV/SR/SL	QR/MS	
Freshwater Drum	*Aplodinotus grunniens*	PC/VV/GU/ MV/NS/JB/TS/ SR/FV/KS/SL/ OT/FS/JD	QR/MP/MC	CS

or species distribution that gill nets were used or swift waters fished. For example, juvenile individuals of the flathead and channel catfish, which are typically associated with relatively swift water, are almost unknown from the late prehistoric sites of the Upper Mississippi River Valley.

There is little evidence for ice fishing in the Upper Mississippi River Valley during the pre-European period. However, fish lures made of mussel shell that imitate small fish are fairly common at some Oneota sites in eastern Wisconsin. It is presumed that these lures were dangled through the ice to invite the strike of aggressive large predatory fish such as the northern pike. Only one site in the La Crosse area, State Road Coulee, has produced shell lures, and these are perhaps imports from the eastern Oneota. It may be the case that for most of prehistory no people lived on the backwaters of the Mississippi or Wisconsin Rivers during the winter months when such lures would have been effective. Among the eastern Oneota living adjacent to lakes such as Winnebago, a winter residence pattern and a focus on the harvest of northern pike are more likely.

Amphibians

The bones of frogs, toads, and salamanders are occasionally found by fine-screen recovery techniques. In most cases these remains appear to be part of the natural rain of small-scale fauna preserved at some sites rather than a regular part of the human diet. Four amphibian species are represented at the sites considered here (table A.5).

Two occurrences of amphibians are worthy of mention. The skeletal remains of nine leopard frogs (*Rana pipiens*) were found in the bottom of a refuse-filled pit at the Tremaine site, an Oneota site on the La Crosse terrace. It is unclear whether these individuals represent a natural inclusion or were brought to the site as food items. The rock fill at the base of the pit lay directly on the bones of these frogs.

Also of interest are the skeletal remains of at least four tiger salamanders (*Ambystoma tigrinum*) recovered from pit fill at the Krause site, an Oneota habitation area on the La Crosse terrace. The zone of pit fill that contained the salamander bones also produced more than 14,000 bones representing more than 300 individual fish of 16 species (most individuals were black bullhead). Thrown into this mix were crawfish remains, the bones of a coot (*Fulica americana*), and the paws of a dog. This deposit is thought to represent a seining episode in a backwater habitat. The occurrence of the tiger salamander is of interest given the historic absence of the species from the unglaciated Driftless Area of southwestern Wisconsin, except for one historic report.

Reptiles

The remains of turtles occur at many of the 32 archaeological sites, with nine species represented (table A.5). They are typically represented by segments of the upper and lower shells (the carapace and plastron, respectively). Turtle remains appear most frequently at the open-air Woodland and Oneota sites found adjacent to the Mississippi River and its wetlands.

The most widespread turtle remains are those of the snapping turtle (*Chelydra serpentina*). Although the remains are present at many sites, only one or two individuals are represented in most of the site assemblages. Scorching on the exterior of many shell fragments indicates that, when captured (perhaps during spring egg-laying on dry land), turtles were cooked in their shell. The softshell turtle (*Trionyx*) is also widespread, but few individuals are represented. The softshell turtle is easy to identify to the genus level by the distinctly sculptured exterior surface of its shell, but it is difficult to distinguish between the two species (*Trionyx spiniferus* and *Trionyx muticus*) found in the Upper Mississippi Valley. Therefore, the tables include this common taxon only at the genus level. The ornate box turtle (*Terrapene ornata*) has been recovered at archaeological sites (for example, Preston Rockshelter in Grant County) adjacent to this species' historically known range on the sand terraces along the lower Wisconsin River. The box turtle is absent from archaeological sites on the Prairie du Chien and La Crosse terraces. A variety of other turtles show up infrequently. The Blanding's turtle (*Emydoidea blandingi*) has been found at a few sites, and its deeply cupped upper shell was sometimes modified for use as a container.

The vertebrae of five species of snakes have been recovered. Snakes probably were part of the natural accumulation of small vertebrates that can become incorporated

TABLE A.5. Amphibians, Reptiles, and Crawfish

Common Name	Scientific Name	Oneota	Woodland	Archaic
AMPHIBIANS				
Eastern Tiger Salamander	*Ambystoma tigrinum*	KS		
American Toad	*Bufo americanus*	SR/KS		
Northern Leopard Frog	*Rana pipiens*	MV/TS/SR/KS	VR	
Green Frog	*Rana clamitans*	MV		
REPTILES				
Snapping Turtle	*Chelydra serpentina*	AR/JD/PC/VV/ GU/MV/NS/SR/ KS/SL/OT/FS	QR/VR/MS/ DR/AM	RR/DR
Stinkpot Turtle	*Sternotherus odoratus*		MP	
Wood Turtle	*Clemmys insculpta*		VR	
Blanding's Turtle	*Emydoidea blandingi*	TS/SR/AR	MS/DR/MP	RR/DR
Ornate Box Turtle	*Terrapene ornata*		PR/DR/AM	RR/DR
Painted Turtle	*Chrysemys picta*	PC/VV/GU//MV/ JB/SR/OT/AR	QR/VR/MS/ PR/AM	RR
Map Turtle	*Graptemys geographica*	PC/VV/MV/SR/ OT	QR	
False Map Turtle	*Graptemys pseudo-geographica*	PC/GU		
Softshell Turtle	*Trionyx*	JD/PC/GU/MV/ JB/TS/SR/KS/SL/ OT/FS	QR/MS/DR/ MP/AM	
Bullsnake	*Pituophis melanoleucus*	PC/GU/MV	QR/VR	
Garter Snake	*Thamnophis radix*	KS		
Timber Rattlesnake	*Crotalus horridus*		QR/VR	
Eastern Hognose Snake	*Heterodon platyrhinos*	SR		
Fox Snake	*Elaphe vulpina*	SR	VR	
CRAYFISH				
Papershell Crayfish	*Orconectes immunis*	PC		
Northern Crayfish	*Orconectes virilis*	PC		
Devil Crayfish	*Cambarus diogenes*	PC		
White River Crayfish	*Procambarus acutus*	KS		

into archaeological site deposits. There is no indication that snakes were harvested for any reason by Native Americans of the Upper Mississippi River Valley. The late prehistoric Oneota sites on the La Crosse terrace do show several occurrences of the bullsnake (*Pituophis melanoleucus*). The bullsnake's presence is not surprising given that many La Crosse–terrace Oneota sites contain bones and burrows of the Plains pocket gopher (*Geomys bursarius*), a common prey species of the bullsnake.

Crayfish

Crayfish remains have been recovered from refuse-filled pits at the Krause and Pammel Creek sites, both Oneota villages (table A.5). At Pammel Creek, hundreds of burned crayfish carapace fragments occurred in ash zones that also produced red-winged blackbird bones and carbonized wild rice (*Zizania aquatica*) grains. These three food items may have been harvested during the midsummer period at a single floodplain habitat.

Freshwater Mussels

There are 39 species of freshwater mussels represented at the 32 archaeological sites (table A.6). Many Native peoples of the Upper Mississippi River Valley harvested large numbers of freshwater mussels as a seasonal food source. One Woodland-period shell midden near Prairie du Chien is estimated to contain more than a million shells, the result of many seasons of use. Although mussels were used primarily as food, their shells were sometimes converted into tools and crushed into the tempering agent used in Oneota shell-tempered pottery. In a few cases, attractive shells such as the elephant-ear (*Elliptio crassidens*) were buried with the dead.

While the shells of large, heavy mussels such as the washboard (*Megalonaias nervosa*) were sometimes traded or carried over some distance, most shells were evidently discarded near the body of water from which they were harvested. These shells accumulated to form middens or were used as fill for storage pits that had fallen into disuse. The archaeological record of freshwater mussel distribution provides a unique view of the geographic distribution of these animals prior to European disruption of the native aquatic ecosystems. A case in point is the assemblage of mussels from the Brogley Rockshelter, located along the Platte River in Grant County. Brogley Rockshelter produced thousands of shells of more than 20 mussel species. This site demonstrates the rich freshwater mussel fauna that occupied the small, interior streams of western Wisconsin's Driftless Area prior to the arrival of Europeans. The two most abundant species at Brogley were the spike (*Elliptio dilatata*) and the ellipse (*Venustaconcha ellipsiformis*). These species, along with an array of other small-stream mussel taxa (for example, *Alasmidonta viridis*, *Lasmigona compressa*, and *Villosa iris iris*), are unknown in the region today and illustrate the importance of the archaeological record for producing well-dated assemblages to aid in an accurate biogeography.

Summary

The ancient Native peoples of western Wisconsin followed an annual round to harvest subsistence resources. This round involved a scheduled movement to place peo-

TABLE A.6. Freshwater Mussels

Common Name	Scientific Name	Oneota	Woodland	Archaic
Cylindrical Papershell	Anodontoides ferrussacianus		QR/PR	PR/BR
Giant Floater	Anodonta grandis	PC/VV/GU/MV/NS/SR/SL/FS	QR/VR/PR/BR	PR/BR
Squawfoot	Strophitus undulatus	VV/SR/FV	QR/VR/DR/MP/BR/BS	BR
Elktoe	Alasmidonta marginata	PC/GU/MV/AR	VR/MS/BR/JD	BR
Slippershell Mussel	Alasmidonta viridis		BR	BR
Rock-Pocketbook	Arcidens confragosus	NS	MC	
White Heelsplitter	Lasmigona complanata	PC/VV/GU/SR/SL/AR	BS/QR/PR/DR/MP/AM/BR/JD	
Fluted-Shell	Lasmigona costata	GU/AR	QR/VR/MS/DR/MP/BR/BS	BR
Creek Heelsplitter	Lasmigona compressa	FV	BR	BR
Washboard	Megalonaias nervosa	VV	MS/BR/JD	BR
Pistolgrip	Tritogonia verrucosa	PC/VV/GU/MV/SR/SL/FS	MS/SF/MP/MC/JD/BS	
Maple Leaf	Quadrula quadrula	PC/VV/GU/MV/NS/LC	MS/MP/MC/JD/BS	
Winged Maple Leaf	Quadrula fragosa	GU/MV	MP/MC/BS	
Monkeyface	Quadrula metanevra	PC//VV/GU/NS/JB/LC/SR/FS/AR	MS/SF/MC/AM/JD/CR	RR
Wartyback	Quadrula nodulata		MP/MC/JD	
Pimpleback	Quadrula pustulosa pustulosa	PC/VV/GU/MV/NS/JB/LC/SR/SL/FS	MS/SF/MP/MC/AM/JD/BS/CR	
Threeridge	Amblema plicata	PC/VV/GU/MV/NS/JB/SR/LC/SR/SL/FS/AR	QR/MS/SF/PR/DR/MP/MC/AM/BR/JD/BS	DR/BR
Ebonyshell	Fusconaia ebena	PC/VV/GU/MV/NS/JB/SR/LC/SL/FS	QR/MS/SF/MD/MC/AM/BR/JD/CR	
Wabash Pigtoe	Fusconaia flava	PC/VV/GU/MV/NS/JB/SR/LC/SL/FS/AR	MS/SF/MP/MC/AM/BR/JD/BS	BR

Common Name	Scientific Name	Oneota	Woodland	Archaic
Purple Wartyback	*Cyclonaias tuberculata*	JB/LC	SF/DR/MP/MC/AM/JD	
Sheepnose	*Plethobasus cyphyus*	VV/GU/NS/LC/SR	MS/SF/DR/MP/MC/AM/JD	RR
Round Pigtoe	*Pleurobema coccineum*	PC//VV/GU/MV/NS/JB/LC/SR/FS/AR	MS/SF/MP/MC/JD/BS	
Elephant-ear	*Elliptio crassidens*		QR/SF/MP/MC/AM/JD/CR	
Spike	*Elliptio dilatata*	PC/GU/JB/AR	QR/VR/MS/PR/DR/MP/MC/AM/BR/JD/BS	BR/PR/RR/DR
Threehorn Wartyback	*Obliquaria reflexa*	PC/VV/MV/NS/SL/FS	SF/MP/MC/JD	
Mucket	*Actinonaias ligamentina*	PC/VV/MV/JB/SR/FS	QR/MS/SF/DR/MP/MC/AM/BR/JD/CR	RR/DR/BR
Butterfly	*Ellipsaria lineolata*	PC/VV/GU/MV/NS	SF/MP/MC/AM/JD/CR	
Hickory Nut	*Obovaria olivaria*	PC/VV/GU/MV/NS/LC/SR	MS/SF/MP/MC/AM/JD	
Deertoe	*Truncilla truncata*	VV/MV/NS/JB/LC	MP/MC/JD	
Fragile Papershell	*Leptodea fragilis*	PC/VV/GU/MV/NS		
Pink Heelsplitter	*Potamilus alatus*	PC/VV/GU/MV/SR/SL/FS/AR	QR/MS/PR/DR/BR/JD/BS	PR/DR/BR
Pink Papershell	*Potamilus ohiensis*	VV	MP	
Black Sandshell	*Ligumia recta*	PC/SL/AR	QR/MS/MP/MC/BR/JD/BS/CR	RR
Ellipse	*Venustaconcha ellipsiformis*		VR/BR	BR
Rainbow	*Villosa iris*			BR
Yellow Sandshell	*Lampsilis teres*	FS	MS/SF/MC/AM	
Fatmucket	*Lampsilis siliquoidea*	PC/VV/GU/MV/NS/SR/SL/AR	QR/VR/MS/SF/PR/DR/MP/BR/BS	PR/RR/BR

Common Name	Scientific Name	Oneota	Woodland	Archaic
Higgins Eye	*Lampsilis higginsi*	VV/LC	SF/MP/MC	
Plain Pocketbook	*Lampsilis cardium*	PC/VV/GU/MV/ SR	QR/MS/SF/PR/ DR/MP/MR/AM/ BR/JD/BS	PR/RR/ DR/BR

ple at the best location during the season most advantageous for taking desired plants and animals. By 7,000 years ago, Archaic peoples were harvesting deer during the fall and winter as a major food resource, along with many other animal species. The spring-summer resource base of Archaic people is not known.

During Woodland times, human groups were engaged in an annual fall-winter harvest of deer and elk as their primary sources of meat and skins for leather. Cool-season camps were generally positioned in the game-rich valleys of the dissected uplands, often many miles from larger river valleys. The largest number of deer seem to have been taken in the fall of the year, when these animals are in prime condition. Animal bones were broken open to extract the nutrient and fat-rich marrow. This marrow may have been mixed with dried meat and berries to produce a sausagelike food known in the early historic period as pemmican, which could be kept for a year or more and often served as a winter food resource.

During the summer months, many Woodland groups were concentrated along the margins of the larger waterways to harvest fish, mussels, turtles, waterfowl, and riparian mammals. At many locations, summer camps were positioned near beds of freshwater mussels and floodplain lakes seasonally restocked with fish. In mid to late summer as water levels dropped, nets were apparently used to harvest fish. In addition to netting in backwaters, fish appear to have been taken while spawning during the spring and early summer months.

It is not until the Late Woodland period at about A.D. 900–1000 that the peoples of the Upper Mississippi River Valley become involved in horticulture by tending small gardens planted in corn. The adoption of gardening did not occur until the seasonal round of wild food harvest became difficult under the stress of increasing human population density. This prevented effective cold-season movement, as the dissected uplands became occupied by some Woodland groups on a year-round basis.

At the end of prehistory we see development of the Oneota, who represent a distinct cultural tradition. The Oneota were the first to practice corn agriculture using field systems rather than the hypothesized garden plots. In addition to cultivated plants, the Oneota made extensive use of fish, mussels, waterfowl, and mammals during their summer residence at farming villages. During the cool season, most of the Oneota along the Upper Mississippi River are believed to have traveled west to hunt bison, deer, and elk, as well as to trade with neighboring peoples.

Dogs, the only domestic animal found in the pre-European period, were kept by Archaic, Woodland, and Oneota peoples of the Upper Mississippi River Valley. These animals served many functions in Native American societies, including carrying loads during annual movements and acting as alarm systems when intruders approached encampments. Dogs also ate animal and plant products that were not consumed by people. In times of special need or for certain ceremonies, dogs would be eaten. Dogs served as storage on the paw, to convert and store protein until needed by humans.

One of the more enigmatic aspects of the archaeological record is the artwork of past cultures. As in historic times, wood and bone were undoubtedly carved with artistic designs, fabrics were woven in decorative patterns, and hides were painted with symbols. Yet virtually none of that artwork has survived natural decay from the era before historic contact. What has been preserved is art rendered in pottery and stone. Ceramic designs have been described for more than a century and are generally used by archaeologists as chronological markers, though some efforts have been made to decipher design symbolism. For example, David Benn and others have correlated chevron motifs on Oneota pottery with hawk/thunderbird symbolism. Rock carvings and paintings, on the other hand, have long been reflected upon in the realm of art, in part because these forms are very difficult to date and interpret.

Rock art generally falls into three classes. Carvings on rock outcrops are called petroglyphs. Paintings are called pictographs. Both of these two classes are fixed in place, including walls of rockshelters used for habitation and ritual purposes. The third type of rock art found in the Upper Mississippi River Valley consists of small carved stones that are small enough to carry and trade. This portable rock art is sometimes found in datable camp and village deposits and in such cases it is therefore easier to determine the cultural affiliation and age of this class of rock art.

Petroglyphs and pictographs require exposed rock, and in the upper Midwest the Driftless Area provides thousands of suitable sandstone and limestone outcrops, including hundreds of shelters (fig. B.1). Because much of the remainder of the Midwest has been scraped and covered by glacial deposits, most of the known midwestern rock art is located within the unglaciated Driftless Area (fig. B.2). This area includes

B.1. An example of the thousands of sandstone and limestone rock outcrops in the Driftless Area.

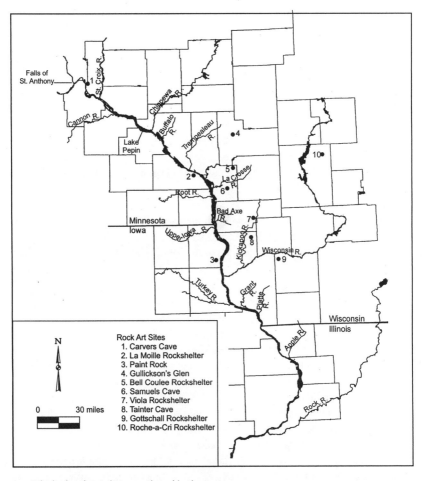

Falls of St. Anthony

St. Croix R.

Chippewa R.

Cannon R.

Buffalo R.

Trempealeau R.

Lake Pepin

● 4

10 ●

Root R.

5 ●
2 ●
La Crosse R.
6 ●

Minnesota
Iowa

Upper Iowa R.

Bad Axe R.

7 ●

Kickapoo R.

∞

Wisconsin R.

3 ●

● 9

Turkey R.

Grant R.

Platte R.

Wisconsin
Illinois

Apple R.

Rock R.

N

0   30 miles

Rock Art Sites
1. Carvers Cave
2. La Moille Rockshelter
3. Paint Rock
4. Gullickson's Glen
5. Bell Coulee Rockshelter
6. Samuels Cave
7. Viola Rockshelter
8. Tainter Cave
9. Gottschall Rockshelter
10. Roche-a-Cri Rockshelter

B.2. Principal rock art sites mentioned in the text.

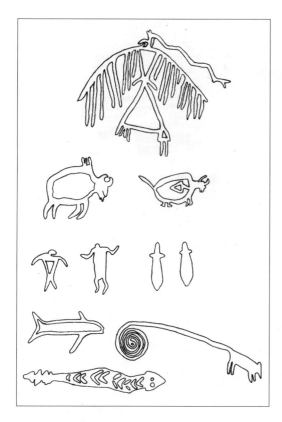

B.3. Facsimile of selected petroglyphs from the La Moille Rockshelter, including a thunderbird with speech line, buffalo (one with a heart line), humans, maces, a fish, a long-tailed mammal possibly representing an underworld spirit, and a rattlesnake.

the bluff lines along the Mississippi River trench, where some of the earliest reports of prehistoric rock art were made.

In 1766 Jonathan Carver described a cave along the Mississippi River below St. Paul, since named Carver's Cave, the walls of which were covered with hieroglyphs. In the early nineteenth century numerous explorers (including Zebulon Pike, Stephen Long, Henry Schoolcraft, and J. C. Beltrami) noted paintings on an outcrop near the mouth of the Yellow River in northeastern Iowa. To this day, this place is called Paint Rock. Unfortunately, the remaining Native art is only a shadow of what it was even in the early twentieth century when Ellison Orr documented its condition. Increase Lapham sketched a series of carvings on a bluff overlooking La Crosse in 1852, and in the 1880s Theodore Lewis traced a number of rock art sites along the Upper Mississippi River from northeastern Iowa to Trempealeau, including an elaborately carved shelter site near La Moille, Minnesota. These sites depicted buffalo, rattlesnakes, complete humans, human feet or heads, and thunderbirds, as well as abstract lines (fig. B.3). Many of these sites have since been destroyed by modern development, natural erosion, or neglect—including historic graffiti carved or painted over the original artwork.

One of the earliest scientific examinations of a rock art site was the 1879 rock art recordation and floor excavation of Samuels Cave, a short distance east of La Crosse.

B.4. Facsimile of selected petroglyphs at Samuels Cave, including a bird, buffalo, deer or elk, bow hunter, human with headdress (possibly a shaman), an abstract design, and a "turkey track."

When do short-horned buffalo "appear"

While the artifacts have been lost, the observed artwork was traced and published, and descriptions of the pottery were reported. Importantly, the accounts indicate the floor contained four stratified layers, and some pottery was tempered with crushed shell. We now recognize shell-tempered pottery as having been made by the Oneota Culture. Therefore, some or all of the artwork at Samuels Cave likely can be attributed to the Oneota complex at La Crosse, which dates from about A.D. 1300 to 1625. This interpretation is supported by the fact that the art at Samuels Cave includes several short-horned buffalo (fig. B.4), which was an important commodity for the Oneota but not for earlier Woodland and Archaic cultures in the Driftless Area.

During the first half of the twentieth century, Milwaukee Public Museum crews spent weekends searching out and photographing rock art sites in western Wisconsin but did little formal investigation. Ellison Orr and Charles Brown also recorded significant rock art sites in Iowa and Wisconsin, respectively, during this period, but it was not until the 1950s that a formal synthesis of Wisconsin rock art sites was undertaken by Robert Ritzenthaler of the Milwaukee Public Museum.

In 1958, in conjunction with his excavation of Driftless Area rockshelters, Warren Wittry excavated the Gullickson's Glen site in Jackson County. This site is situated within a dry wash canyon near the head of a tributary of the Black River. The walls were covered with many petroglyphs, ranging from deer/elk and buffalo to other mammals and birds to fish as well as humans (fig. B.5). Wittry's excavation found two major cultural deposits. Unfortunately, he did not prepare a report on this site, but the artifacts are curated at the State Historical Society of Wisconsin. Based on these collections, it is apparent that the upper cultural layer represents an Oneota occupa-

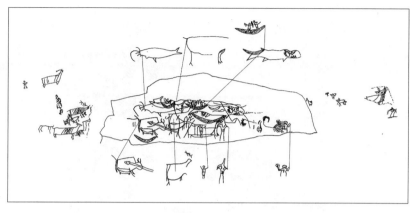

B.5. Facsimile of petroglyphs at Gullickson's Glen, including ribbed deer/elk to the left; the complex, interior central panel, with selected identifiable glyphs redrawn to the top and bottom; and various images to the right.

tion containing pottery typical of the Brice Prairie phase (ca. A.D. 1300–1400). The lower deposit contained Middle and Late Woodland pottery, dating from about A.D. 200 to 1000. Again, the rendering of short-horned buffalo at Gullickson's Glen suggests that at least some of the artwork was done by the Oneota visitors.

In the 1960s and 1970s Marshall McKusick, followed by R. Clark Mallam, reexamined rock art sites in northeastern Iowa. This work is being continued by Lori Stanley of Luther College in Decorah, Iowa. Dean Snow also published a Minnesota rock art synthesis in 1960, which was upgraded by Mark Dudzik of the Minnesota Office of the State Archaeologist in 1995.

Beginning around 1980, rock art research in the Driftless Area experienced a resurgence. Whereas in the late 1970s there were fewer than 50 rock art sites reported in this region, there are now nearly 200. Much of this work has derived from two organizations and a private individual. A major catalyst in this activity was Robert Salzer's recognition of exquisite Middle Mississippian–style paintings at the remote Gottschall Rockshelter. Salzer has devoted more than two decades to recording, interpreting, and excavating this site. David Lowe, a resident of the lower Wisconsin River Valley, has also devoted vast amounts of time to surveying and recording rock art sites along the southern margins of that valley.

The Western Wisconsin Regional Archaeology Program, operated by the Mississippi Valley Archaeology Center (MVAC) under the auspices of the State Historical Society of Wisconsin, also became involved in rock art research with the fortuitous discovery of previously unrecorded paintings at Samuels Cave in 1984 (fig. B.6) and at Roche-a-Cri State Park (fig. B.7) in early 1987. In addition, petroglyphs were found at the Viola and Agger Rockshelters during that period. These demonstrated that many rock art sites remained to be found. Cindi Stiles, then at the MVAC, initiated a formal program to relocate previously reported rock art sites and record their current conditions.

B.6. Charcoal pictographs discovered at Samuels Cave in 1984, including a buffalo (with a superimposed long-tailed petroglyph), a human form, and a possible bird.

B.7. Red pictographs at Roche-a-Cri State Park discovered in 1987, including a thunderbird connected to a human via a speech line.

In the 1990s the MVAC undertook a series of rock art studies that led to the discovery of numerous new sites, including the Bell Coulee Rockshelter and Tainter (formerly Arnold) Cave. Bell Coulee is a small shelter, the walls of which are carved with numerous abstract symbols and a series of distinct buffalo (fig. B.8). The Bell Coulee buffalo are different from other Driftless Area petroglyphs in that their entire bodies

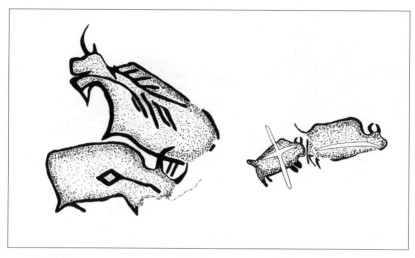

B.8. Selected buffalo petroglyphs from Bell Coulee Rockshelter, including at least one with a heart line and another that is superimposed with the Earth Maker cross symbol.

were ground away, forming intaglio impressions rather than the more common body outlines. One of these has a heart-line arrow running from the mouth into the chest area. This motif is found in late prehistoric and historic times from the Great Lakes to across the Plains and to the southwestern United States. The artwork at this site was formally recorded by photography and drawings. While no excavations have been undertaken, a few pottery sherds have been collected from rodent burrow piles. These indicate both Woodland and Oneota occupation, but the presence of buffalo images, particularly one with a heart line, suggests that this artwork may also be attributed to the Oneota. It is unlikely that buffalo ever roamed the remote interior valley where the Bell Coulee Rockshelter is located. Instead, Oneota artisans must have carved these figures based on memory from a seasonal hunt to the prairies of Iowa and Minnesota. Similarly, the large fish depicted at Gullickson's Glen could not have come from that dry wash bed but must have been based on memory.

Tainter Cave is a 250-foot-deep sandstone cavern located near the blufftops in the remote interior of the Driftless Area. The cave consists of three connected chambers, with natural light only penetrating the front of the first one. Although the cave has been marred by hundreds of historic names and dates, there are several distinct Native American–style petroglyphs near the entrance. In addition, there are nearly 100 charcoal drawings found on discrete panels in all three rooms. Many of these are beyond natural light, and charred birch bark torches litter the floor.

The drawings include deer, birds, humans, and abstract designs. One panel depicts a series of antlerless deer being shot by several bow hunters (fig. B.9). Several of the images are clearly meant to portray pregnant does, with fetal fawns drawn in their abdomens. Because does are impregnated during the fall rut and consistently deliver their fawns in May, the Tainter Cave drawings must represent a late winter–early

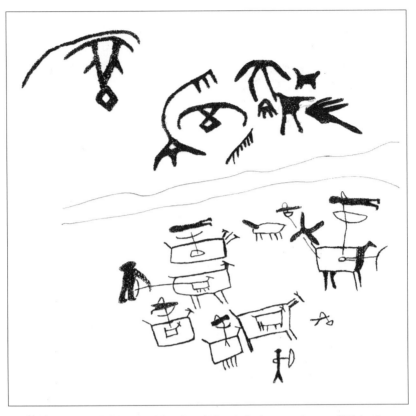

B.9. Charcoal drawings depicting sky and earth themes in the second room of Tainter Cave. Note the stylized birds above the natural horizontal fault and the bow hunters and pregnant deer below.

spring season. This coincides with the season of starvation, and the scene may recall a hunt of salvation or represent hope of future success.

Immediately above the hunting scene and separated by a natural horizontal fault is a panel that consists of abstract birds, wings, feathers, and bird feet. These are all sky symbols, and together this wall clearly depicts a common Native American worldview that segregates earth and sky.

There are indications for the age of the Tainter Cave drawings. The bow and arrow hunters indicate that the hunting panel was probably drawn after A.D. 500, when bow and arrow technology appears to have been adopted in this region. The cave is located in an area where numerous Late Woodland effigy mounds were constructed, and some of the drawn deer have features that resemble outlines of nearby effigy mounds mapped by Theodore Lewis a century ago. This portion of the Driftless Area lacks evidence of Oneota settlement, and therefore the art is probably not more recent than A.D. 1150, when Oneota replaced the Late Woodland cultures and the heart of the Driftless Area was abandoned. Three pottery sherds found in the cave are all in-

B.10. Charcoal drawing on the ceiling at the entrance to Tainter Cave depicting a bird and a possible cradleboard, with a facsimile of a cradleboard after Catlin.

dicative of Linn ware and the Millville phase, which dates from ca. A.D. 250 to 500. One of the images also is thought to depict an infant strapped in a cradleboard (fig. B.10). George Catlin, an early-nineteenth-century painter of American Indian life, and others document the use of cradleboards by many midwestern and Plains tribes in historic times. There is also archaeological evidence in the Driftless Area for the use of cradleboards well into prehistory. For example, the back sides of skulls from both the Rehbein and Raisbeck Mound Groups and at the Millville village site are flattened, a condition called cranial deformation, a common by-product of cradleboards. Raisbeck is primarily a Late Woodland Effigy Mound group, while Rehbein is a Millville phase and early Effigy Mound group. The Millville site is the type locale for the Millville phase. This circumstantial evidence suggests the art dates from ca. A.D. 200 to 1150. One of the drawings (a deer or elk) was directly dated via Accelerator Mass Spectrometry (AMS) dating, which produced an age of 1,300 years old.

One drawing at Tainter Cave may have even greater antiquity. While most of the drawings were done in sharp, crisp lines that form outlines, a drawing in the second room was done in broad lines and depicts a four-legged animal with long, straight horns (fig. B.11). It is not clear, but this could represent an earlier form of buffalo, such as *Bison occidentalis*, which became extinct nearly 10,000 years ago.

Portable rock art can also assist in recognizing styles from distinct cultures and time periods. Excavations at Oneota sites have recovered portable rock art ranging from catlinite tablets to etched pipes and sandstone slabs. These depict short-horned buffalo, turkey tracks, humans, maces, and abstract designs such as zigzag lines. Turkey tracks also occur on both Oneota and Late Woodland pottery and so are not temporally distinctive. Maces, on the other hand, are probably limited to late prehistoric Oneota times. Sheet-copper mace pendants have been found at Oneota sites in eastern and western Wisconsin, and a mace is depicted on the back side of a large catlinite tablet found at New Albin, Iowa (fig. B.12). Depictions of short-horned buffalo also seem to be restricted to Oneota artisans. A catlinite tablet recovered from quarry

B.11. Charcoal drawing of possible long-horned bison in the second room of Tainter Cave, perhaps representing a species that became extinct nearly 10,000 years ago.

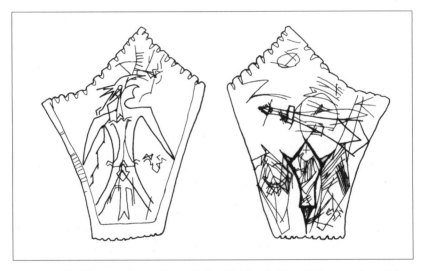

B.12. Facsimile of front and back of the catlinite tablet found at New Albin, Iowa. Front etching (left) is dominated by a birdman with a forked eye and an upside-down animal in the chest/abdomen. The complex back side (right) includes several mace forms, including one that is crossed by a bar and has an end that is comparable to the abstract design depicted in figure B.4 from Samuels Cave.

operations at the Midway Village site near La Crosse is etched with a bow hunter and a series of large animals, at least one of which is a buffalo with short horns (fig. B.13). The hump of this buffalo, as well as those of the other animals, is depicted as a series of parallel slashed lines, which is identical to the style used to paint the hump of a buffalo at Samuels Cave (see fig. B.6). Furthermore, each of the animals has a distinct flaring heart line that is crossed with a bar, in effect becoming a mace symbol. As`in-

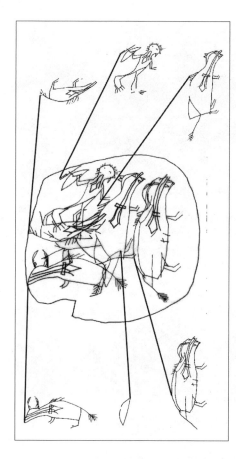

B.13. Tracing of the etched surface of a catlinite tablet from the Midway Village site that depicts a series of animals with macelike heart lines and a bow hunter. The individual animals have been redrawn along the outside, showing a clear buffalo and animals with a combination of buffalo and canine features.

dividual design elements, these crossed heart lines are identical to the mace on the New Albin tablet. As heart lines, they closely resemble one etched within a short-horned buffalo on a fragmented red tablet found along Riceford Creek in southeastern Minnesota, where early contact Oneota sites occur.

Finally, regional distribution studies can assist in estimating the age of rock art. For example, a number of rock art sites, such as at Roche-a-Cri State Park in central Wisconsin, are located on buttelike rock outcrops in the otherwise flat bed of abandoned Glacial Lake Wisconsin along the central portion of the Wisconsin River. These have not been dated, but intensive 1990s' survey and text excavations in that locale found extensive Late Woodland activity and virtually no late prehistoric utilization. Radiocarbon dating of the camp sites in that region verified that the Late Woodland occupation ended before A.D. 1150. Therefore, this area was also essentially abandoned during late prehistoric Oneota times. Consequently, most of the rock art at Roche-a-Cri and at other sites in former Glacial Lake Wisconsin probably dates to the Late Woodland period.

B.14. Historic graffiti surrounding the shaman petroglyph at Samuels Cave.

Similarly, distribution studies of various motifs along the Mississippi River seem to suggest that isolated human heads, feet, and hands correlate with locations of extensive Oneota activity. Conversely, these symbols do not seem to occur in the central Wisconsin River region, where the Late Woodland Effigy Mound people were the last major inhabitants.

Interpreting rock art, let alone understanding why it was created, is extremely difficult. Some images are recognizable as buffalo, snakes, fish, birds, or humans. Others are abstract symbols that occur in isolation or are repeated at many sites. Ethnographic comparisons to abstract designs on woven bags or to those painted on drums or faces offer one avenue for insight.

Rock art carvings, drawings, and paintings may have been created for any number of reasons, and the reasons may have changed through time. The rock art may represent historical stories of successful hunts or parts of rituals conducted in advance to ensure success. It may represent vision quests, where individuals fasted until contacted by a spirit. Rows of grooves may represent counts or simply be from sharpening bone awls or stone axes. We may never know why the carvings, drawings, and paintings were created or what they meant to the people who made them, but we continue to work toward understanding the images.

B.15. Saw marks around a charcoal drawing at the Gottschall Rockshelter created by a looter attempting to steal the art from the cave wall.

Preservation is another difficult aspect of rock art. These are rare and fragile aspects of the past. Through time they erode from wind, water, and freezing and thawing. Yet the vast majority of those lost in the twentieth century have been through neglect, ignorance, or sheer greed. It is almost impossible to find a pristine rock art site. Most, if not all, have been visited in historic times, and seeing modern names and dates is all too common. Within a year of discovery, Samuels Cave was being damaged by graffiti (fig. B.14). By the 1980s most of the prehistoric art at that site had been severely marred if not obliterated. Indeed, initial visits to the cave in the early 1980s found it being used for beer-drinking parties and saw nothing but modern graffiti on the walls. Most people who carve their names have no idea that they are carving over 500- or 1,000-year-old art. But once done, the damage is irreversible.

Then, there is greed represented by unscrupulous individuals who actually steal rock art to sell for profit. This has happened repeatedly in the American Southwest and impacted the Gottschall Rockshelter in the Driftless Area soon after the uniqueness and importance of the site were revealed to the public. In this case, someone trespassed onto the privately owned cave site and used a mason's saw to attempt to cut away one of the 1,000-year-old paintings (fig. B.15). The looter did not succeed, but the cut marks scarred the panel, including several cuts that sheered directly over a fabulous drawing of a raptor bird. Looting is infrequent, but it only takes one person to ruin this ancient art.

The Gottschall incident did have one positive outcome. Spurred by disgust at the attempted theft, the state of Wisconsin passed legislation, which was drafted by a task force created by the Wisconsin State Archaeologist Office, making it illegal to damage rock art intentionally.

Selected Archaeological Sites and Museums in the Upper Mississippi River Valley

Goodhue County Historical Society, Red Wing, Minnesota. Exhibit of local archaeology.

Winona County Historical Society, Winona, Minnesota. Replica of La Moille Rockshelter and petroglyph rock art.

Fountain City Area Historical Society, Fountain City. Exhibit of extensive local collection of prehistoric artifacts with identification key.

Perrot State Park near Trempealeau. Site of early historic Perrot(?)/Linctot post, conical and effigy mounds, and nature shelter exhibits on local archaeology (including replica of destroyed rock art panel).

Nicholls Mound and interpretive signs. Located 2.5 miles southeast of Trempealeau along the Great River Bike Trail.

Riverside Museum, La Crosse. Exhibits on prehistoric and historic lifeways along the Upper Mississippi River.

Myrick Park at La Crosse. Small effigy and conical mounds.

Riverside Cemetery, 1.5 miles north of Genoa. Nine remaining conical mounds from extensive group mapped by Increase Lapham in 1852, now with historic graves and headstones.

Battle at Bad Axe, 2 miles north of De Soto, and 1 mile south of Victory along Wisconsin's Great River Road (Highway 35). Signs along the highway facing Battle Bluff and Battle Hollow and markers near and in Black Hawk Recreation Area (county road BI [for Battle Island]).

Fish Farm Mounds, 4 miles south of New Albin, Iowa. Well-preserved Middle and Late Woodland conical mounds.

Effigy Mounds National Monument, located 3 miles north of Marquette, Iowa. Museum display of artifacts plus walking tours of effigy and conical mounds.

Villa Louis and Fort Crawford I, on "the island" at Prairie du Chien. Villa Louis is a mansion home established by fur trade magnate Hercules Dousman. The house rests upon a knoll that may have been an enormous American Indian mound and was initially used for the site of Fort Shelby (American) and Fort McKay (British) early in the War of 1812. The first Fort Crawford was constructed adjacent to the knoll following that war and was used until a Second Fort Crawford was constructed on the mainland beginning in 1829.

Wyalasing State Park located near Bagley, overlooking the confluence of the Wisconsin and Mississippi Rivers. Effigy mounds easily visible.

Nelson Dewey State Park above Cassville. Easily accessible and visible conical, linear, and chain mounds.

Selected Historic Sites in the Upper Mississippi River Valley

Perrot(?)/Linctot Post (1685–1686[?] and 1730–1731) in Perrot State Park near Trempealeau.

Fort St. Antione (1686–1698) wayside and historical marker along the Great River Road (Highway 35), east side of Lake Pepin in Pepin County.

Fort Folle Avoine Historic Park (1802–1803), a trading post near Webster.

1832 Black Hawk Trail (Crawford and Vernon Counties), culminating at the Bad Axe Battle Site near Victory. Signs and historical markers, including along the Great River Road (Highway 35).

Villa Louis and First Fort Crawford and Second Fort Crawford Hospital Museum (1814–ca. 1880), Prairie du Chien. State Historical Society of Wisconsin historic site and local museum.

Fort Snelling (nineteenth-century military garrison), St. Paul, Minnesota. Minnesota Historical Society Historic site.

Steamboat War Eagle (1870) artifact exhibit at the Riverside Museum, La Crosse.

Selected Sites in the Upper Midwest

Silver Mound site, located 2.5 miles northeast of Hixton, off Highway 95. This stone quarry site is the source of Hixton silicified sandstone.

Pipestone National Monument, Pipestone, Minnesota. The source area and quarry of catlinite.

Isle Royale National Park and the Keewenaw Peninsula of Upper Michigan. The source for most of the copper used for artifact manufacture in Wisconsin. An ancient quarry pit may be seen on Isle Royale.

Cahokia Mounds State Park, Collinsville, Illinois. A center of the Mississippian culture. Located at this site are an excellent museum and Monks Mound, the largest pre-Columbian earthen mound north of Mexico.

Aztalan State Park, near Lake Mills. Located on the Crawfish River, a branch of the Rock River, this is a Mississippian settlement from A.D. 1000 to 1100 from the Cahokia area positioned in the heart of effigy mound country.

Roche-a-Cri State Park, near Friendship. The only publically accessible and inter-preted rock art site in Wisconsin. Includes numerous petroglyphs and some red pictographs.

Natural Bridge State Park near Baraboo. The location of the Raddatz Rockshelter.

Devils Lake State Park, just south of Baraboo. Effigy mounds are located at both the north and south unit recreation area. The north unit, at the main park head-quarters, has more mounds, including panther, bear, and linears, although the south unit has a fine example of a bird mound.

Jeffers Petroglyphs State Preserve near the town of Jeffers in Cottonwood County, Minnesota. Well-preserved petroglyphs carved into Sioux quartzite may be viewed at this prairie locale. The atlatl hunters depicted here may be Archaic in age and may be some of the oldest rock art in the region.

Bascom Hill Effigy Mounds on the University of Wisconsin–Madison campus over-looking Lake Mendota. Nice example of bird effigy and other mounds.

Highway 60 wayside between Prairie du Chien and Wauzeka on the north side of the Wisconsin River. An easily accessible and fine example of small conicals and long linear mounds.

Ho-Chunk Bison Ranch along Highway 60 between Muscode and Gotham. Self-guided walking tour of a remnant group of conicals, linears, and an effigy mound overlooking the Wisconsin River. A lone bird effigy is also visible along the south side of Highway 60, a mile to the east.

Regional Museums with Archaeological Displays

Field Museum of Natural History, Chicago.

Dickson Mounds Museum, Lewistown, Illinois.

Putnam Museum of History and Science, Davenport, Iowa.

University of Iowa Museum, Iowa City.

Minnesota Historical Society Grand Mound and Interpretive Center, near International Falls.

Minnesota History Center, St. Paul.

Science Museum of Minnesota, St Paul.

State Historical Society of Wisconsin Museum, Madison.

Geology Museum, University of Wisconsin–Madison.

Milwaukee Public Museum.

Logan Museum of Anthropology, Beloit College, Beloit, Wisconsin.

Oshkosh Public Museum, Oshkosh, Wisconsin.

General Archaeology and Methods and Theory

Alex, Lynn M.
2000   *Iowa's Archaeological Past*. University of Iowa Press, Iowa City.

Ashmore, Wendy, and Robert J. Sharer
1996   *Discovering Our Past: A Brief Introduction to Archaeology*. Mayfield, Mountain View, California.

Birmingham, Robert A., Carol I. Mason, and James B. Stoltman (editors)
1997   *Wisconsin Archaeology*. Special issue of the *Wisconsin Archeologist* 78(1–2).

Fagan, Brian
1995   *Ancient North America: The Archaeology of a Continent*. Thames and Hudson, New York.

Renfrew, Colin, and Paul Bahn
2000   *Archaeology: Theories, Methods and Practice*. Thames and Hudson, New York.

Thomas, David Hurst
1998   *Archaeology*. Harcourt Brace College Publishers, Fort Worth, Texas.

Environment of the Upper Mississippi River

Becker, George C.
1983   *The Fishes of Wisconsin*. University of Wisconsin Press, Madison.

Curtis, John
1959   *The Vegetation of Wisconsin: An Ordination of Plant Communities.* University of Wisconsin Press, Madison.

Fagan, Brian
2000   *The Little Ice Age: How Climate Made History 1300–1850.* Basic Books, New York.

Hazard, Evan B.
1982   *The Mammals of Minnesota.* University of Minnesota Press, Minneapolis.

Hole, Francis D.
1976   *Soils of Wisconsin.* University of Wisconsin Press, Madison.

Jackson, Hartley H. T.
1961   *The Mammals of Wisconsin.* University of Wisconsin Press, Madison.

Martin, Lawrence
1965   *The Physical Geography of Wisconsin.* University of Wisconsin Press, Madison.

Mason, Ronald J.
1981   *Great Lakes Archaeology.* Academic Press, New York.

Ostergren, Robert C., and Thomas R. Vale (editors)
1997   *Wisconsin Land and Life.* University of Wisconsin Press, Madison.

Pielou, E. C.
1991   *After the Ice Age: The Return of Life to Glaciated North America.* University of Chicago Press, Chicago.

Prior, Jean C.
1991   *Landforms of Iowa.* University of Iowa Press, Iowa City.

Robbins, Samuel D.
1991   *Wisconsin Birdlife: Population and Distribution— Past and Present.* University of Wisconsin Press, Madison.

Theler, James L.
2000   Animal Remains from Native American Archaeological Sites in Western Wisconsin. *Transactions of the Wisconsin Academy of Sciences, Arts and Letters* 88:121–142.

The Wisconsin Cartographers' Guild
1998   *Wisconsin's Past and Present: A Historical Atlas.* University of Wisconsin Press, Madison.

The First Peoples and Their Setting

Kurten, Bjorn, and Elaine Anderson
1980   *Pleistocene Mammals of North America.* Columbia University Press, New York.

Lister, Adrian, and Paul Bahn
1994 *Mammoths*. MacMillan, New York.

Martin, Paul S., and Richard G. Klein (editors)
1984 *Quaternary Extinctions: A Prehistoric Revolution*. University of Arizona Press, Tucson.

Mason, Ronald J.
1997 The Paleo-Indian Tradition. *Wisconsin Archeologist* 78:78–110.

Palmer, Harris A., and James B. Stoltman
1976 The Boaz Mastodon: A Possible Association of Man and Mastodon in Wisconsin. *Midcontinental Journal of Archaeology* 1:163–177.

Thomas, David Hurst
2000 *Skull Wars: Kennewick Man, Archaeology, and the Battle for Native American Identity*. Basic Books, New York.

Wormington, H. M.
1957 *Ancient Man in North America*. Denver Museum of Natural History, Denver.

Archaic Tradition

Freeman, Joan E.
1966 Price Site III, RI 4, a Burial Ground in Richland County, Wisconsin. *Wisconsin Archeologist* 47:33–75.

Griffin, James B. (editor)
1961 *Lake Superior Copper and the Indians: Miscellaneous Studies of Great Lakes Prehistory*. Anthropological Papers No. 17. Museum of Anthropology, University of Michigan, Ann Arbor.

Martin, Susan R.
1999 *Wonderful Power: The Story of Ancient Copper Working in the Lake Superior Basin*. Wayne State University Press, Detroit.

Phillips, James L., and James A. Brown (editors)
1983 *Archaic Hunters and Gatherers in the American Midwest*. Academic Press, New York.

Pleger, Thomas C.
2000 Old Copper and Red Ocher Social Complexity. *Midcontinental Journal of Archaeology* 25:169–190.

Ritzenthaler, Robert E., and George I. Quimby
1962 The Red Ocher Culture of the Upper Great Lakes and Adjacent Areas. *Fieldiana Anthropology* 36:243–275.

Stoltman, James B.
1997 The Archaic Tradition. *Wisconsin Archeologist* 78:112–139.

Stoltman, James B., Jeffery A. Behm, and Harris A. Palmer
1984   The Bass Site: A Hardin Quarry/Workshop in Southwestern Wisconsin. In *Prehistoric Chert Exploitation — Studies from the Midcontinent*, edited by Brian M. Butler and Ernest E. May, 197–224. Occasional Paper No. 2. Center for American Archaeological Investigations, Southern Illinois University, Carbondale.

Wittry, Warren L.
1959a Archeological Studies of Four Wisconsin Rockshelters. *Wisconsin Archeologist* 40:137–267.
1959b The Raddatz Rockshelter, Sk5, Wisconsin. *Wisconsin Archeologist* 40:33–69.

Woodland Tradition

Arzigian, Constance M.
1987   The Emergence of Horticultural Economies in Southwestern Wisconsin. In *Emergent Horticultural Economies of the Eastern Woodland*, edited by William F. Keegan, 217–242. Occasional Paper No. 7. Center for American Archaeological Investigations, Southern Illinois University, Carbondale.
2000   Middle Woodland and Oneota Contexts for Wild Rice Exploitation in Southwestern Wisconsin. *Midcontinental Journal of Archaeology* 25:245–268.

Beaubien, Paul L.
1953   Cultural Variation within Two Woodland Mound Groups of Northeastern Iowa. *American Antiquity* 19:56–66.

Benn, David W.
1979   Some Trends and Traditions in Woodland Cultures of the Quad-State Region in the Upper Mississippi River Basin. *Wisconsin Archeologist* 60:47–82.
1980   *Hadfields Cave: A Perspective on Late Woodland Culture in Northeastern Iowa.* Report 13. Office of the State Archaeologist, University of Iowa, Iowa City.

Birmingham, Robert A., and Leslie E. Eisenberg
2000   *Indian Mounds of Wisconsin.* University of Wisconsin Press, Madison.

Boszhardt, Robert F., and Natalie Goetz
2000   An Apparent Late Woodland Boundary in Western Wisconsin. *Midcontinental Journal of Archaeology* 25:269–287.

Finney, Fred A., and James B. Stoltman
1991   The Fred Edwards Site: A Case of Stirling Phase Culture Contact in Southwestern Wisconsin. In *New Perspectives on Cahokia: Views from the Periphery*, edited by James B. Stoltman, 229–252. Monographs in World Archaeology No. 2. Prehistory Press, Madison, Wisconsin.

Freeman, Joan E.
1969   The Millville Site: A Middle Woodland Village in Grant County, Wisconsin. *Wisconsin Archeologist* 50:37–88.

Lapham, Increase A.
2000 [1855] *The Antiquities of Wisconsin as Surveyed and Described*. Smithsonian Contributions to Knowledge. Smithsonian Institution, Washington, D.C. Reprint, State Historical Society of Wisconsin, Madison.

Logan, Wilfred D.
1976 *Woodland Complexes in Northeastern Iowa*. Publications in Archeology 15. National Park Service, Washington, D.C.

Mallam, R. Clark
1976 *The Iowa Effigy Mound Manifestation: An Interpretive Model*. Report 9. Office of the State Archaeologist, University of Iowa, Iowa City.

McKern, W. C.
1931 A Wisconsin Variant of the Hopewell Culture. *Bulletin of the Public Museum of the City of Milwaukee* 10:185–328.

Mead, Barbara
1979 The Rehbein I Site (47-Ri-81): A Multicomponent Site in Southwestern Wisconsin. *Wisconsin Archeologist* 60:91–182.

Rowe, Chandler W.
1956 *The Effigy Mound Culture of Wisconsin*. Publications in Anthropology No. 3. Milwaukee Public Museum, Milwaukee.

Seeman, Mark F.
1979 *The Hopewell Interaction Sphere: The Evidence for Interregional Trade and Structural Complexity*. Prehistoric Research Series 5 No. 2. Indiana Historical Society, Indianapolis.

Silverberg, Robert
1968 *Mound Builders of Ancient America: The Archaeology of a Myth*. New York Graphic Society, Greenwich, Connecticut.

Stevenson, Katherine P., Robert F. Boszhardt, Charles R. Moffat, Philip H. Salkin, Thomas C. Pleger, James L. Theler, and Constance M. Arzigian
1997 The Woodland Tradition. *Wisconsin Archeologist* 78:140–201.

Stoltman, James B.
1979 Middle Woodland Stage Communities of Southwestern Wisconsin. In *Hopewell Archaeology: The Chillicothe Conference*, edited by David S. Brose and N'omi Greber, 122–139. Kent State University Press, Kent, Ohio.
1986 The Prairie Phase: An Early Woodland Manifestation in the Upper Mississippi Valley. In *Early Woodland Archeology*, edited by Kenneth B. Farnsworth and Thomas E. Emerson, 121–136. Kampsville Seminars in Archeology, vol. 2. Center for American Archeology Press, Kampsville, Illinois.
1990 The Woodland Tradition in the Prairie du Chien Locality. In *The Woodland Tradition in the Western Great Lakes: Papers Presented to Elden Johnson*, edited by Guy E. Gibbon, 239–259. Publications in Anthropology No. 4. University of Minnesota, Minneapolis.

Theler, James L.

1986   The Early Woodland Component at the Mill Pond Site, Wisconsin. In *Early Woodland Archeology*, edited by Kenneth B. Farnsworth and Thomas E. Emerson, 137–158. Kampville Seminars in Archeology, vol. 2. Center for American Archeology Press, Kampsville, Illinois.

1987   *Woodland Tradition Economic Strategies: Animal Resource Utilization in Southwestern Wisconsin and Northeastern Iowa*. Report 17. Office of the State Archaeologist, University of Iowa, Iowa City.

Theler, James L., and Robert F. Boszhardt

2000   The End of the Effigy Mound Culture: The Late Woodland to Oneota Transition in Southwestern Wisconsin. *Midcontinental Journal of Archaeology* 25:289–312.

Thomas, Cyrus

1894   *Report on Mound Explorations of the Bureau of Ethnology*. Twelfth Annual Report of the Bureau of American Ethnology, 1890–1891. Smithsonian Institution, Washington, D.C.

Tiffany, Joseph A.

1986   The Early Woodland Period in Iowa. In *Early Woodland Archeology*, edited by Kenneth B. Farnsworth and Thomas E. Emerson, 159–170. Kampsville Seminars in Archeology, vol. 2. Center for American Archeology Press, Kampsville, Illinois.

Cahokia and Aztalan

Barrett, S. A.

1933   Ancient Aztalan. *Bulletin of the Public Museum of the City of Milwaukee* 13.

Emerson, Thomas E.

1997   *Cahokia and the Archaeology of Power*. University of Alabama Press, Tuscaloosa.

Emerson, Thomas E., and R. Barry Lewis (editors)

1991   *Cahokia and the Hinterlands: Middle Mississippian Cultures of the Midwest*. University of Illinois Press, Urbana.

Freeman, Joan E.

1986   Aztalan: A Middle Mississippian Village. *Wisconsin Archeologist* 67:339–364.

Green, William, and Roland L. Rodell

1994   The Mississippian Presence and Cahokia Interaction at Trempealeau, Wisconsin. *American Antiquity* 59:334–359.

Milner, George R.

1998   *The Cahokia Chiefdom: The Archaeology of a Mississippian Society*. Smithsonian Institution Press, Washington, D.C.

Stoltman, James B. (editor)

1991 *New Perspectives on Cahokia: Views from the Periphery*. Monographs in World Archaeology No. 2. Prehistory Press, Madison, Wisconsin.

Oneota and Related Cultures

Anderson, Adrian, Allan Westover, Terrance J. Martin, Mathew L. Murray, Susan M. T. Myster, Barbara O'Connell, and L. Anthony Zalucha

1995 The State Road Coulee Site: 47Lc176. *Wisconsin Archeologist* 76:48–230.

Arzigian, Constance M., Robert F. Boszhardt, Holly P. Halverson, and James L. Theler

1994 The Gundersen Site: An Oneota Village and Cemetery in La Crosse, Wisconsin. *Journal of the Iowa Archeological Society* 41:3–75.

Arzigian, Constance M., Robert F. Boszhardt, James L. Theler, Roland L. Rodell, and Michael J. Scott

1989 Human Adaptation in the Upper Mississippi Valley: A Study of the Pammel Creek Oneota Site (47Lc61), La Crosse, Wisconsin. *Wisconsin Archeologist* 70(1–2).

Boszhardt, Robert F., Katherine Stevenson, L. Anthony Zalucha, James L. Theler, Michael J. Scott, and Charles R. Moffat

1994 La Crosse Area Oneota. *Wisconsin Archeologist* 75(3–4).

Boszhardt, Robert F., Thomas W. Baily, and James P. Gallagher

1985 Oneota Ridged Fields at the Sand Lake Site (47Lc44), La Crosse County, Wisconsin. *Wisconsin Archeologist* 66:47–67.

Gallagher, James P., Robert F. Boszhardt, Robert F. Sasso, and Katherine Stevenson

1985 Oneota Ridged Field Agriculture in Southwestern Wisconsin. *American Antiquity* 50 (3):605–612.

Green, William (editor)

1995 *Oneota Archaeology: Past, Present, and Future*. Report 20. Office of the State Archaeologist, University of Iowa, Iowa City.

Hollinger R. Eric, and David W. Benn (editors)

1998 Oneota Taxonomy: Papers from the Symposium on the 54th Anthropological Conference, 1996. *Wisconsin Archeologist* 79(2).

O'Gorman, Jody

1995 *The Tremaine Complex: Oneota Occupation in the La Crosse Locality, Wisconsin*. Museum Archaeology Program, Archaeology Research Series No. 3. State Historical Society of Wisconsin, Madison.

Tiffany, Joseph A.

1991 Models of Mississippian Culture History in the Western Prairie Peninsula: A Perspective from Iowa. In *Cahokia and the Hinterlands: Middle Mississippian*

Cultures of the Midwest, edited by Thomas E. Emerson and R. Barry Lewis, 183–192. University of Illinois Press, Urbana.

1998   Southeast Iowa Oneota: A Review. *Wisconsin Archeologist* 79:147–164.

Wedel, Mildred M.

1959   Oneota Sites on the Upper Iowa River. *Missouri Archaeologist* 21(2–4): 1–181.

Wilford, Lloyd A.

1941   A Tentative Classification of the Pre-Historic Cultures of Minnesota. *American Antiquity* 6:231–249.

1955   Revised Classification of the Prehistoric Cultures of Minnesota. *American Antiquity* 21:130–142.

Historic Period

Adams, Arthur

1961   *The Explorations of Pierre Esprit Radisson*. Ross and Haines, Minneapolis.

Blaine, Martha R.

1979   *The Ioway Indians*. University of Oklahoma Press, Norman.

Blair, Emma Hunt (editor)

1911   *The Indian Tribes of the Upper Mississippi Valley and the Region of the Great Lakes*. 2 vols. Arthur H. Clark, Cleveland.

Bray, E. C. (editor)

1970   *The Journals of Joseph N. Nicollet: A Scientist on the Mississippi Headwaters with Notes on Indian Life, 1836–37*. Translated by André Fertey. Minnesota Historical Society, St. Paul.

Bray, E. C., and M. C. Bray (editors)

1976   *Joseph N. Nicollet on the Plains and Prairies: The Expeditions of 1838–39 with Journals, Letters, and Notes on the Dakota Indians*. Minnesota Historical Society, St. Paul.

Catlin, George

1973   *Letters and Notes on the Manners, Customs, and Condition of the North American Indians*. 2 vols. Dover, New York.

Edmunds, R. David, and Joseph L. Peyser

1993   *The Fox Wars: The Mesquakie Challenge to New France*. University of Oklahoma Press, Norman.

Hickerson, Harold

1962   *The Southwestern Chippewas: An Ethnohistorical Study*. Memoirs of the American Anthropological Association No. 92. George Banta Company, Menasha, Wisconsin.

Hunt, George T.

1960   *The Wars of the Iroquois: A Study in Intertribal Trade Relations.* University of Wisconsin Press, Madison.

Jackson, Donald (editor)

1964   *Black Hawk: An Autobiography.* University of Illinois Press, Urbana.

Kellogg, Louise Phelps

1925   *The French Regime in Wisconsin and the Northwest.* Cooper Square, New York.

1935   *The British Regime in Wisconsin and the Northwest.* Da Capo Press, New York.

Long, Stephen H.

1978   *The Northern Expeditions of Stephen H. Long, the Journals of 1817 and 1823 and Related Documents,* edited by Lucile M. Kane, June D. Holmquist, and Carolyn Gilman. Minnesota Historical Society Press, St. Paul.

Nichols, Roger

1992   *Black Hawk and the Warrior's Path.* Harlan Davidson, Arlington Heights, Illinois.

Parker, John

1976   *The Journals of Jonathan Carver and Related Documents: 1766–1770.* Minnesota Historical Society Press, St. Paul.

Pike, Zebulon M.

1966   *Sources of the Mississippi and the Western Louisiana Territory.* University Microfilms, Ann Arbor, Michigan.

Radin, Paul

1990   [1923] *The Winnebago Tribe.* Bureau of American Ethnology, Thirty-seventh Annual Report, Smithsonian Institution, Washington, D.C. Reprint, University of Nebraska Press, Lincoln.

Schoolcraft, Henry R.

1966   [1821] *Travels through the Northwestern Regions of the United States.* March of America Facsimile Series, No. 66. University Microfilms, Ann Arbor, Mich.

1973   [1855] *Summary Narrative of an Exploratory Expedition to the Sources of the Mississippi River in 1820: Resumed and Completed by the Discovery of Its Origin in Itasca Lake in 1832.* Reprint, Kraus Reprint Company, Millwood, New York.

Thwaites, Reuben G. (editor)

1896–1901 *The Jesuit Relations and Allied Documents, Travels and Explorations of Jesuit Missionaries in New France 1610–1791.* 73 vols. Burrows Brothers, Cleveland.

Wedel, Mildred Mott

1939   The Relation of Historic Indian Tribes to Archaeological Manifestations in Iowa. *Iowa Journal of History and Politics* 23:353–362.

1986   Peering at the Ioway Indians through the Mist of Time: 1650–circa 1700. *Journal of the Iowa Archeological Society* 33:1–75.

Rock Art

Birmingham, Robert A., and William Green (editors)
1987   Wisconsin Rock Art. *Wisconsin Archeologist* 68(4).

Dudzik, Mark J.
1995   Visions in Stone: The Rock Art of Minnesota. *Minnesota Archaeologist* 54:99–108.

Lewis, Theodore H.
1890   Cave Drawings. *Appleton's Annual Cyclopaedia and Register of Important Events, 1889* 14:117–122.

Lothson, G. A.
1976   *The Jeffers Petroglyph Site: A Survey and Analysis of the Carvings.* Minnesota Prehistoric Archaeology Series No. 12. Minnesota Historical Society, St. Paul.

Lowe, David
1987   Rock Art Survey of Blue Mounds Creek and Mill Creek Drainages in Iowa and Dane Counties, Wisconsin. *Wisconsin Archeologist* 68:341–375.

McKusick, Marshall
1963   Ancient Iowa Lives On in Indian Rock Drawings. *Iowan.* 11:40–45.
1971   Art that Predates Columbus. *Iowan.* 19:8–13.

Orr, Ellison
1931   The Rockshelters of Allamakee County, Iowa, a Preliminary Survey. *Proceedings of the Iowa Academy of Sciences* 38:185–194.
1949a The Enlarged Crevices of Northeastern Iowa. *Minnesota Archaeologist* 15(1):5–8.
1949b The Enlarged Crevices Three and One-Half Miles South of Lansing, Iowa. *Minnesota Archaeologist* 15(1):9–23.

Ritzenthaler, Robert
1950   Wisconsin Petroglyphs and Pictographs. *Wisconsin Archeologist* 31:83–129.

Salzer, Robert J.
1987   Preliminary Report on the Gottschall Rockshelter (47IA80). *Wisconsin Archeologist* 68:419–472.

Snow, Dean R.
1962   Petroglyphs of Southern Minnesota. *The Minnesota Archaeologist* 24 (4):102–128.

Stanley, Lori
1993   Rock Art. In *Archaeological Investigations of the Bear Creek Locality Allamakee County, Iowa,* edited by David G. Stanley, p. 105–122. Reports of Investigations No. 155. Highland Cultural Research Center, Highlandville, Iowa.

Stiles-Hanson, Cindi

1987   Petroglyphs and Pictographs of the Coulee Region. *Wisconsin Archeologist*
        68:278–340.

Winchell, N. H.

1911   *The Aboriginies of Minnesota.* Minnesota Historical Society, St. Paul.

Sanford Archaeology District, 50, 165
Sasso, Robert, 51
Sauk County (Wisconsin), 45, 77, 82, 85, 204
Sauk tribe, 175, 182–186
Saukenuk, 183, 185
Schoolyard site, 165
Schuyler County (Illinois), 117
Schwert Mound Group, 47, 111
Scottsbluff points, 63, 71–72
seasonal/annual activities, 11, 16, 61, 69, 71–72, 80, 82–83, 86, 89, 93, 98, 101, 104–105, 107, 119, 125, 132–134, 137–139, 141, 143, 155, 167, 169–170, 181, 184, 189, 209, 212, 222
Shorewood Cord-Roughened, 111
shovel testing, 5
Shrake-Gillies site, 44, 165
silicified sandstone, 21, 65, 92; figures, 92, 116, 164–165; Hixton, 21–23, 59–60, 62, 65, 71–72, 91, 103–104, 132, 150
silver, 44, 107, 115; figure, 116
Silver Mound, 21–23, 60–62, 65, 71, 91, 175, 189
Silverberg, Robert, 107
Silvernale phase, 46, 154–155, 164–165
Silvernale site, 46
Sioux. See Dakota Sioux
Smithsonian Institution, 41
Sny-Magill Mound Group, 46, 91–92, 95, 100
social complexity: figure, 14
Sonota Culture, 119
Spring Valley Mound Group, 113
Squier Garden site, 147
Squier, George, 114, 147
Stanley, Lori, 49, 219
Starved Rock Collared, 146
State Road Coulee site, 50, 161, 170, 194, 206
Steed-Kisker site, 147
Steuben Expanded Stem points, 124, 127
Stevenson, Katherine, 50, 172
Stiles, Cindi, 219
Stirling phase, 146

Stoltman, James, 47–48, 64, 71, 149, 165; figure 48
Stonefield Village site, 45, 194
storage pits, 3, 89, 123–124, 143, 151, 165, 172, 179
Storck, Peter, 47
structures, 13, 46, 75, 114, 122–124, 145–146, 149–150, 164–165, 169, 172; figure, 150
subsistence, 12, 15–16, 32, 34, 57–59, 66–67, 69, 70, 81–83, 85, 101, 105–106, 119, 124, 131, 133, 138, 143, 157–158, 169, 179, 190, 193–213. See also deer, elk, bison, hunting, fishing

tablets, 159–160, 169–170, 223–225; figures, 224–225
Tainter Cave, 137, 155, 220–223; figures, 137, 191, 222–224
Taylor, Richard, 39
temper, 97–98, 121, 145–146, 149, 156–157
teosinte, 141
territories, 80, 89, 91, 95, 128, 131, 134, 138, 141, 154, 163, 183, 186
Thebes points, 71
Thomas, Cyrus, 41, 108, 114
Tillmont site, 48, 101, 113, 116–117
tobacco, 88, 89
tooth wear (human), 80, 87, 124, 127
trade. See exchange
Trane site, 161
Tremaine site, 162, 166, 169–170, 194, 207; figure, 161 (artifact)
Trempealeau Bluffs, 28, 46, 147, 176; figure, 147
Trempealeau County (Wisconsin), 22, 24, 43, 61
Trempealeau locality, 111, 153, 165, 183
Trempealeau Mountain, 12, 28; figure, 28
Trempealeau National Wildlife Refuge, 49
Trempealeau phase, 111, 113–114, 119, 127
tribes, 12, 128, 139, 191. See also specific tribes